poor queer studies

duke university press

durham & london 2020

MATT BRIM

poor queer studies

confronting elitism in the university

Printed in the United States of America on acid-free paper ∞
Designed by Aimee C. Harrison
Typeset in Warnock Pro and Antique Olive
by Westchester Publishing Services

Library of Congress Cataloging-in-Publication Data
Names: Brim, Matt, author.
Title: Poor queer studies : confronting elitism in the university /
Matt Brim.
Description: Durham : Duke University Press, [2020] | Includes
bibliographical references and index.
Identifiers: LCCN 2019035478 (print)
LCCN 2019035479 (ebook)
ISBN 9781478006824 (hardcover)
ISBN 9781478008200 (paperback)
ISBN 9781478009146 (ebook)
Subjects: LCSH: Gay and lesbian studies—United States. | Elite
(Social sciences)—Education—United States. | Queer theory—
United States. | Educational equalization—United States.
Classification: LCC HQ75.15 .B77 2020 (print) | LCC HQ75.15 (ebook) |
DDC 306.76010973—dc23
LC record available at https://lccn.loc.gov/2019035478
LC ebook record available at https://lccn.loc.gov/2019035479

Cover art: fStop Images—Emily Keegin, *Old, broken chairs in an
abandoned school*. Photograph. Courtesy of Getty Images.

For the students, faculty, and staff of
the College of Staten Island, City University of New York

and

For my first teacher, Ted

contents

acknowledgments

The underlying hope of this book—that Queer Studies might be reconceptualized as a cross-class, antiracist project that sparks collaboration among academic institutions with starkly different resources and reputations—would have been impossible without help from near and far.

First, I thank my students, who are the heart of this book, as well as my faculty and staff colleagues at the College of Staten Island, City University of New York. In so many ways, I have been helped by Jillian Báez, Alyson Bardsley, Maria Rice Bellamy, Sarah Benesch, Jean-Philippe Berteau, Jennifer Rubain Borrero, Carol Brower, Rosanne Carlo, Katie Cumiskey, Ashley Dawson, Rafael de la Dehesa, Jen Durando, William Fritz, Gloria Garcia, Patti Gross, Sharifa Hampton, Anne Hays, Jeremiah Jurkiewicz, Arnie Kantrowitz, Giancarlo Lombardi, Tara Mateik, Ed Miller, Gerry Milligan, Lee Papa, Sohom Ray, Simon Reader, Terry Rowden, Christine Flynn Saulnier, Linda Sharib, Ira Shor, Ilyssa Silfen, Francisco Soto, Judith Stelbaum, Nan Sussman, Sarolta Takács, Saadia Toor, and Nelly Tournaki.

Colleagues from across the CUNY system, which is a key institutional figure in this book, have been more than readers and interlocutors; they have been models of how to do queer work in an unconscionably underfunded public university. From CLAGS: Center for LGBTQ Studies, I thank Justin Brown, Yana Calou, Sarah Chinn, Benjamin Gillespie, Kevin Nadal, Jasmina Sinanovic, Kalle Westerling, Jim Wilson, and Martin Duberman, for giving faculty from poor schools a seat at the Queer Studies table. From the Faculty Fellowship Publication Program, thanks to Leslie Broder, Carrie Conners, András Kisery, Chris Schmidt, and Tshombe Walker, who were the first readers of the first incarnation of this book, and to Ria Banerjee, Megan Behrent, Alison Better, Sarah Hoiland, and María Julia Rossi for their inspiring feminist collaboration. Thank you to Dana-Ain Davis, director of the

Center for the Study of Women and Society at the Graduate Center, for inviting me to discuss my work in progress. Thanks to Jen Gaboury at Hunter College, Shereen Inayatulla at York College, Ken Norz and Lucinda Zoe at CUNY Central, Laura Westengard at City Tech, and Linda Villarosa at City College for collaborating around queer pedagogies. It has been an honor to work with the next generation of scholars at the Graduate Center, especially Rachel Corbman, Simone Kolysh, Melissa Maldonado-Salcedo, and Chris Morabito.

Looking further afield, I thank Warren Rosenberg and the members of 'Shout for hosting me for a talk at Wabash College, and Greg Mitchell and the students of Williams College for their warm welcome. My time in the Indiana University English Department and the Duke University Writing Program instilled in me not only a love of teaching but a love of pedagogy studies that inspires much of what follows, and I especially want to thank Susan Gubar, Christine Farris, Kathy Smith, John Schilb, and Joe Harris for their guidance. As I wrote this book, I enjoyed various kinds of help and collaboration from across the academy and beyond it, including from Peter Cramer, Cathy Davidson, Ramzi Fawaz, Rod Ferguson, Amin Ghaziani, Donald Hall, John Hawley, Stephanie Hsu, Jim Hubbard, E. Patrick Johnson, John Keene, David Kurnick, Heather Love, Dwight McBride, Maryann McKenzie, Koritha Mitchell, Ricardo Montez, Robert Reid-Pharr, Siobhan Somerville, Polly Thistlethwaite, Steven Thrasher, Valerie Traub, Ken Valente, and Robyn Wiegman. With their support and encouragement, Ken Wissoker, Josh Tranen, and Liz Smith at Duke University Press have made publishing this book one of the highlights of writing it. Two anonymous readers offered key insights and concrete suggestions that made revising the manuscript a reward rather than a chore.

It's strange to thank people for being themselves—funny, smart, loving, kind, tough, savvy, honest, and thoughtful—so I'll just say thanks for putting the life in work-life balance to Ava Chin, Cynthia Chris, Shelly Eversley, Maryann Feola, David Gerstner, and Sarah Schulman. Finally, thanks to Eric Hartman, for thinking it all through with me.

In addition to early support from CUNY's Faculty Fellowship Publication Program, as I wrote this book I was honored to receive a Distinguished CUNY Fellowship from the Advanced Research Collaborative at the CUNY Graduate School, a CUNY Academic Commons Open Educational Resource Faculty Fellowship, a CUNY Book Completion Award, PSC/CUNY Research Awards, and two Provost's Travel Fellowships from the College of Staten Island.

The introduction is derived in part from the article "Poor Queer Studies: Race, Class, and the Field," published in the *Journal of Homosexuality*, November 7, 2018. © Taylor & Francis, available online: doi.org/10.1080/0091 8369.2018.1534410.

The obituary for Larry Mitchell that opens chapter 1 was originally published in *The Gay and Lesbian Review / Worldwide* 20, no. 3 (2013): 11.

An earlier version of chapter 5, in a significantly different form, appeared in *Imagining Queer Methods*, edited by Amin Ghaziani and Matt Brim, published by New York University Press, 2019.

introduction

Queer Dinners

While access to college has become more egalitarian, *where* a student attends college and *what* she or he studies have become increasingly tied to social background and gender. —Ann Mullen, *Degrees of Inequality: Culture, Class, and Gender in American Higher Education*

What does [the] massive redistribution of wealth and widening of [the] class divide have to do with queer studies? It just happens to be the twenty-year moment when a gay rights movement and the field of queer studies have both emerged. There's no inherent reason why queer studies and gay politics would not reproduce the racialized class inequality and confusion that structure the larger society. But unfortunately, we can't enjoy the luxury of standing on the sidelines as innocent bystanders. We have been implicated. —Allan Bérubé, keynote address for "Constructing Queer Cultures," a conference sponsored by the Program in Lesbian, Bisexual, and Gay Studies at Cornell University, February 1995

People in forgotten places also act within the institutional and individualized constraints defined by racialization, gender hierarchy, and nationality, and the complex potential mix of these possibilities has produced its own academic specialties old and new.... *Constraints* does not mean "insurmountable barriers." However, it does suggest that people use what is available to make a place in the world. —Ruth Wilson Gilmore, "Forgotten Places and the Seeds of Grassroots Planning"

Bloomsbury Community College

"One cannot think well, love well, sleep well, if one has not dined well," writes Virginia Woolf in her touchstone 1929 study of gender, class, and genius, *A Room of One's Own*. The fictional context for Woolf's maxim about the intellect and the gut is a comparison of two meals, a lunch at a fantastically resource-rich men's college, "Oxbridge," and a dinner at "Fernham," a meagerly funded, upstart women's college. The stringy beef and watery prunes served to the young women of Fernham stand up poorly against the partridges in cream and the meringue-crested desserts served to the young men of Oxbridge, where mountains of gold and silver have for centuries been poured into lawns and libraries to produce the educated gentlemen of the empire. The men's food does not only look and taste better; the Oxbridge meal also lights a little fire in the spine (there is wine, I should mention), the glow of which travels anatomically upward toward its greater purpose: powering the famously, androgynously, incandescent mind. The food and wine, it turns out, are not sufficient in themselves to create genius, but they prepare the way. To the contrary, among the women at Fernham, with base hunger abated but the palate and mind dulled by those prunes, the evening conversation flags. A clear-eyed, unsatisfied guest, Woolf hesitates only a moment before writing of the women's college, "The dinner was not good."[1]

Another dinner scene ... a vending machine stands half empty, adding insult to dietary injury. Dinner waits behind glass, unspoilable. The new slot for credit cards blinks. It is nearing 6:30 p.m., and this is night school. Students enter my Black Queer Studies classroom, sit, unwrap their candy bars, and wrestle open their bags of chips. They've come from work or directly from another class that ended at 6:20 p.m. We will be in class until 9:50 p.m. We'll get hungry. During our ten-minute break at 8 p.m. the vending machine pushes more cookies, the occasional sticky bun, off its shelves. It's hard to smoke, call home, and get through the vending machine line all in ten minutes. Stragglers apologize. We turn back to Lorde or Baldwin, Nella Larsen or John Keene. One of the students is so pregnant she must periodically excuse herself to walk off her discomfort. In fact the evening's text is Barry Jenkins's Oscar-winning film *Moonlight*.[2] I turn on the projector. It doesn't work. The always-helpful tech person answers, comes quickly, fixes the problem, and leaves. The projector stops working again. One of my students stands up unasked: "I'll find another room." She returns and tells the class the number of the empty room. We pack up and file out, forty of us. We turn the corner and see another class entering our intended destination. Their projector was broken too, and they beat us to the new room. Eventually we watch *Moonlight* in a third classroom. The projector works, but the sound is screwed up, a mere whisper. We watch breathlessly, not daring to crinkle the candy wrappers, not daring to eat our dinner.[3] No time now for discussion. Class dismissed. This is the College of Staten Island (CSI) at the City University of New York (CUNY), a deeply underfunded urban university system committed to serving "the children of the whole people."[4] And this is perhaps the queerest school I know, the school at which I came to understand the need for Poor Queer Studies.[5]

In this book I take up the question of the relationship between Queer Studies and the material conditions under which Queer Studies is done in the contemporary academy, a question dramatized above in my reworking of Woolf's historical connection between thinking and dining in the university. How and where are meals turned into androgynously—I'll say queerly—incandescent minds in higher education today? If Queer Studies has over the past thirty years successfully argued, elbowed, and snuck its way into the academy so that its courses can be found in both likely and unlikely places—not only at our Oxbridges and Fernhams but at our Bloomsbury Community Colleges—we might shift attention, à la Woolf, to the question of the resources with and without which queer students and professors teach and learn and write across academic work sites. What does Queer Studies have to say about class sorting within the academy? What is the role of the field within the processes of stratification that can be said to divide the field from itself along the lines of class and institutional status? How might queer collaboration across peer and nonpeer institutions offer a model for the redistribution of intellectual and material resources, and how can that positively impact attendant racial disparities in higher education? How might Poor Queer Studies galvanize interclass, cross-institutional queer formations that do not rely on a unidirectional, aspirational model of progress? And most fundamentally, how can rethinking the work of Queer Studies in the context of students' relative material need and raced/gendered precarity, academics' professional liminality, and underclass institutional identity inform and potentially enrich the field, its pedagogies and theories, and the academy beyond it?

I begin by locating Queer Studies within the broader context of higher education, arguing that the field cannot be separated from the large-scale institutional production of racialized class stratification. As students are sorted on the basis of socioeconomic class by colleges that are themselves increasingly stratified by wealth-based rankings, Queer Studies also ruptures across its disparate sites of material production—that is, at schools high and low. I trace the ramifications of that overlooked queer self-difference and argue for a reorientation of the field away from its prestigious and well-known institutions and toward working-poor and working-class people, places, and pedagogies. I examine the ways Queer Studies has been a vector for upward professional mobility for faculty in the Rich Queer Studies pipeline, and I contrast such traditional, elitist mechanisms of academic advancement with a competing idea about queer professionalization: that, working against the grain of nearly all queer critiques of the neoliberal academy, Queer Studies professors might cultivate a vocational Queer Studies that trains students to become not only better queer theorists but better queer workers. For workers our students already are, if one teaches at all but a relative handful of selective colleges and universities. Centering Poor Queer Studies mothers, I connect academic life not only to work life but to students' home lives as well, exploring the ways that commuter students—who live at home with their parents, who are themselves mothers, who are first-generation immigrants, who are black and brown and ethnic white—become student teachers of Queer Studies within their homes and home communities (and thus create poor queer familial pedagogies very much in contrast to the bourgeois pedagogy of helicopter parenting that has been so loudly critiqued at high-status institutions). Taking John Keene's work of black queer experimental literature, *Counternarratives*, as my critical object, I telescope out from the Poor Queer Studies classroom to argue that within higher education there exists a widespread state of queer illiteracy that necessitates a reinvestment by Queer Studies in antielitist general education, a shift that might complement more privileged modes of queer-race interdisciplinary inquiry. Ultimately, I propose a model of queer ferrying between resource-rich and -poor institutions as a way of restructuring queer knowledge production in the academy. I begin, however, by naming the hyperstratified state of affairs that must, at present, define Queer Studies in the university.

Class Stratification in Higher Education

It is difficult to find an institution in the United States that sorts people by socioeconomic class as effectively as higher education, even as the university simultaneously proclaims and often fulfills its democratizing promise. In *Degrees of Inequality: Culture, Class, and Gender in American Higher Education*, Ann L. Mullen charts this bipolarity in higher ed: "At the same time that more young adults than ever before enter higher education, the college experience has become more disparate, ranging from living in plush campus dormitories and studying the liberal arts at prestigious universities to commuting from home to the local college to earn a preprofessional degree. While access to college has become more egalitarian, *where* a student attends college and *what* she or he studies have become increasingly tied to social background and gender."[6] Dissecting general democratizing trends in college attendance, Mullen argues that "because of the hierarchical nature of the U.S. higher educational system and the disparities in the rewards that it offers, it is no longer enough to simply look at who goes to college and who does not. To fully evaluate the promise expressed by the expansion of postsecondary education, one needs to examine the opportunities students of different backgrounds have to attend the various institutions within that system. In other words, we need to look not just at *who* goes to college, but at who goes *where* to college."[7] Of special importance for my project is the further point that where one goes to school overwhelmingly predicts both what one will study and whether one will continue that education. This pattern is borne out by Mullen's case study comparison of Yale University and Southern Connecticut State University. Students with high socioeconomic status tend to enroll at highly selective institutions like Yale, typically study fields in the liberal arts, and are more likely to continue on to PhD programs, while those with low socioeconomic status attend less selective institutions like Southern, choose preprofessional majors, and are less likely to enter graduate programs. On this last point, Mullen finds that "the differences are even more pronounced in relation to enrollment in PhD programs; nearly eight times as many liberal arts graduates enroll in PhD programs as do preprofessional graduates."[8]

As Mullen's work and a wealth of educational data have made clear, the tiered or ranked U.S. educational system does not merely reflect class disparities; it actively reproduces them by rewarding the most affluent students with admission to the most prestigious colleges and by channeling our poorest students and students of color into two-year and unranked four-year schools and, even more insidiously, into exploitative for-profit colleges.[9] Admission to two-year and lower-tier colleges, as opposed to higher-tier schools, dramatically reduces student graduation rates even as it increases student debt. Of course, most of our poorest high school students are excluded from higher education altogether: "In 2012, 82 percent of 18 to 24 year olds from the top family income quartile participated in college, compared with just 45 percent of those in the bottom quartile."[10] Young black men from low-income families are at particular risk of being excluded by systems of higher education.[11] Their relative absence from selective colleges starkly reveals for Kiese Laymon that "no matter how conscientious, radically curious, or politically active I encouraged [them] to be, teaching wealthy white boys ... [at Vassar] meant that I was being paid to really fortify [their] power."[12] Laymon makes operations of power visible, naming the ways demographic and institutional data ought to be translated as support of white supremacist, classist university culture.[13] The material conditions of racism—literally, the material absence of black male student bodies—shape the possibilities for what counts as the good work of education. Laymon now teaches at the University of Mississippi.

The failure of academia to increase enrollments of black students at the top one hundred colleges and universities has dramatic ripple effects.[14] Brittney Cooper traces the repercussions of institutional racism to the ranks of university faculty, where racist and sexist—and classist—hiring practices further disenfranchise people of color. Cooper writes,

> Today, when I travel to give lectures at universities across the country, it is not uncommon for Black faculty, particularly Black women faculty, to pull me aside and whisper that their working conditions feel unsafe, that their colleagues are passive-aggressive, that they are saddled with extra committee work, that they are called to mentor *all* the students of color who come through the department, and are subject to all manner of slights and indignities from colleagues and students alike. Meanwhile, on many occasions they note that there are today far less Black faculty on campus than there were in the 70s, 80s, and 90s. When I began my first academic job in 2009 ... at a flagship state university, I noted that I was the only Black person hired by the entire college of arts and sciences and one of only three Black faculty members that had been hired in the entire university that year.[15]

In the absence of blackness among her institutional cohort, Cooper looks back to *All the Women Are White, All the Blacks Are Men, but Some of Us Are Brave: Black Women's Studies*, for which she wrote the afterword to the volume's 2015 reissue and from which the above quote is drawn. As the academy produces the isolation of black faculty ("I was the only") and the overwork of black faculty ("saddled with extra committee work"), one response by black faculty has been "whispering," or creating fugitive, transitory communities in the midst of conditions hostile to sustained and generative in-person "blackademic" communities.[16] To the extent that the fugitive practices Cooper describes result from race-based exclusions from the top of the class-based, disproportionately white academic hierarchy—and precisely because *But Some of Us Are Brave* reminds us that black lesbian scholarship provided an early intersectional critique of the academy's race-class-gender-sexuality exclusions—I explicitly want to nominate Poor Queer Studies as simultaneously and necessarily a Poor Black Queer Studies knowledge project.

Returning to the case of undergraduate education, we see that the mechanisms of rich white fortification and poor and black exclusion are elaborate and the statistics staggering. One study puts this state of affairs succinctly in its title, "White Flight Goes to College": "The tracking of white students into the top-tier colleges perpetuates greater rates of white college completion, especially at elite colleges."[17] Prestigious schools actively cater to wealthy students and their families, ones who can pay for SAT preparation courses, tutors, tuition, and, so the logic goes, alumni donations. Legacy admissions provide a further boost, a form of affirmative action for the historically monied classes whom university administrators literally, if privately, line up to embrace. Admissions officers at top schools recruit from well-known feeder high schools, many of them private, expensive, and staffed with knowledgeable college counselors. The result, to cite only a few representative statistics, is that at the most selective institutions there are twenty-four times as many high-income students as low-income students.[18] The Ivy-Plus colleges enroll more students from the top 1 percent than from the bottom 50 percent of the income distribution.[19] While nearly 40 percent of college students receive Pell Grants (used by researchers as a proxy for low-income status, with 73 percent of all Pell Grant recipients coming from families making under $30,000 per year), at certain types of colleges only between 5 and 20 percent of students receive Pell Grants.[20] Not surprisingly, the most selective postsecondary institutions in the United States admit the fewest Pell Grant recipients. Though different studies use slightly different definitions of low-income students and selective colleges, there is widespread evidence that top-tier colleges amplify rather than redress the problem of class stratification.[21] As a general rule, in higher education, riches harm the poor.

One way to address this problem, at least in part, would be for resource-rich schools to admit more low-income students. Unfortunately, for all their smarts and money, these pillars of American education seem incapable of making such a change, despite years of mouthing their commitment to higher education equity.[22] A 2016 study by the Jack Kent Cooke Foundation finds that the "representation of low-income students at selective colleges and universities has not changed in ten years despite selective institutions' well-advertised, increased commitment to 'need-blind admissions' and 'no-loan financial aid' packages. All the while, the value of attending a selective college or university is clear, including higher graduation rates and higher pay for the individual, and greater productivity for the country."[23] That the most selective colleges cannot figure out how to admit smart, qualified, and interesting poor students in far greater numbers while they have proven themselves quite capable of figuring out how, legally, to perform tax wizardry by using offshore investments to achieve lucrative tax breaks on their enormous endowments, reflects not only ugly elitist values but also an ironic disconnect: schools like Harvard, Duke, Dartmouth, Stanford, Columbia, University of Southern California, and Johns Hopkins could use the riches earned in tax breaks to identify, inform, encourage, and admit the low-income students they refuse to see and to serve.[24] One study of the "hidden supply of high-achieving, low-income students" who do not apply to selective colleges argues that "the number of low-income high achievers is much greater than college admissions staff generally believe. Since admissions staff see only the students who apply, they very reasonably underestimate the number who exist."[25] To my mind, this underestimation is far from very reasonable, especially given the authors' estimate that "there are, in fact, only about 2 high-achieving, high-income students for every high-achieving, low-income student in the population."[26] Though very selective colleges (which are concentrated in metropolitan areas) look far and wide for alumni donations, they don't look far and wide for poor students: "In fact, we know from colleges' own published materials and communications with their authors that many colleges make great efforts to seek out low-income students from their metropolitan areas. These strategies, although probably successful, fall somewhat under the heading of 'searching under the lamppost.' That is, many colleges look for low-income students where the *college* is instead of looking for low-income students where the *students* are."[27] If the two authors of this study (from Stanford and Harvard) could find hidden high-achieving, low-income students and imagine ways to move them into selective colleges, why haven't the top one hundred schools been able to do the same? As recent reporting suggests, the most selective colleges and universities—those schools that own the top of the "Best Colleges" lists, those schools that "very reasonably" cannot see the "hidden" supply of high-achieving, low-income students—are motivated to reinforce rather than interrupt class inequality precisely by their commitment to maintaining their elite ranking.[28] Poor students are hidden by elitist educational institutions, not from them.

"We Have Been Implicated": Rich Queer Studies

The evidence is so overwhelming that we need not argue this case. We must baldly state it: class stratification is an intentional, defining, structural feature of the U.S. academy, one that overlaps with race sorting.[29] The solidity of that knowledge allows for other important interventions. I begin *Poor Queer Studies* with the fact of class stratification in order to give traction to the rather slippery connection that will be my primary focus here: the role of Queer Studies in the hierarchizing mission of higher education. Although it has long been associated with academic elitism—primarily with reference to its outsized interest in white gay male cultural production, the inaccessibility of its high queer theory, and its perceived postmodern, ivory tower anti-identitarianism that can discredit LGBTQ lived-identity experiences—Queer Studies has less often been understood as a mechanism for producing class inequity within higher education. Queer Studies has, in fact, consistently presented itself otherwise, as an antinormative, disruptive cog within the system rather than a producer of "palace discourses."[30] Queer Studies practitioners, such as myself, have pointed to our silo-busting interdisciplinarity, to our penchant for self-critique, to our embrace of the supposedly nonacademic as viable objects of study within the academy. To which I say, "Yes." We've told the story of our activist beginnings, twining together the birth of queer theory with the activism of Queer Nation, even as we've rewritten that popular but partial origin story by tracing Queer Studies back through earlier activisms and political commitments, including women of color feminism and, as I explore in chapter 3, our very ability to think "gay academic" as a position of leverage.[31] In doing so, Queer Studies has positioned itself as constitutionally against the grain, athwart the academy. Yes. When and where we find ourselves normal and normative, we level often careful and often cutting self-critique. Though higher education may present us with the neoliberal problem of queer radical possibility being incorporated and administered, we have, by making institutional management systems visible objects of critique, allowed ourselves to continue to imagine that a defining feature of the field of Queer Studies is its impulse to fuck up the academy. Admittedly ensconced, we can all the more dramatically position ourselves as subversives, thieves, vandals, committed to egalitarianism.[32] Again yes. But . . .

The problem with our story is that when Robin Hood stole he gave to the poor. And he didn't get paid to do it.

If the disruptive democratization of higher education has been Queer Studies' goal, dating back perhaps to the first conference of the Gay Academic Union in 1973, we have since failed. With notable exceptions, the field of Queer Studies as an academic formation has been and is still defined and propelled by the immense resources of precisely those institutions of higher education that most steadfastly refuse to serve representative numbers of poor students and to hire faculty without high-status academic pedigrees. Though my ultimate interest will be in dramatizing exceptions to this rule and in elaborating the relationship between exception and rule, I begin by more fully fleshing out the association of the field of Queer Studies with privileged sites of material production of queer knowledge. I will say here—and I will repeat this line throughout as a reminder to myself to follow the undervalued queer methodology of critical compromise—that we both are and are not our institutions. Critical compromise both isolates and dramatizes a problem and promotes a mode of relative questioning. To what extent does academic Queer Studies trade on the value—and therefore the values—of its wealthy institutions, thereby sustaining their commitment to structural inequality? Kristen A. Renn discerns a key tension created by the incorporation of queer methods in higher education research, namely, that "colleges and universities have evolved to tolerate the generation of queer theory from within but have stalwartly resisted the queering of higher education itself." "What is more nonqueer," she asks, "than traditional doctoral education or the tenure stream?"[33]

To compromise: as much as I agree with Renn's formulation, it is not always clear—at least to me—whether Queer Studies plays the protagonist or the antagonist in such a normalizing institutional narrative. We don't have Queer Studies PhD programs, after all, leaving Neville Hoad to wonder whether queer theory ever happened in the academy. "Anecdotally," Hoad notes in a 2007 essay reprinted in the 2011 volume *After Sex? On Writing since Queer Theory*, "there are now fewer rather than more jobs described using the keywords *sexuality, gender, queer*. Has there ever been a tenure-track position advertised and filled in 'queer theory,' despite a decade of training graduate students in the imagined subfield?"[34] The (apparent) absence of queer tenure-track positions is debilitating to the field, argues Hoad, for "the vitality of a set of intellectual questions cannot rely on the labor of faculty whose primary commitment and institutional responsibility is to something else." Like his fellow contributors, Hoad writes from the rhetorical position of "after sex." But his *when* is also very much a matter of *where*, a matter of having time in a place (University of Texas at Austin, a mega-rich "Public Ivy") that offers the "invigorating intransigence of continuing to work on a set of questions." In this light, the question of whether queer theory happened is interesting not because the field has been impossible to miss but because if queer theory happened it surely did so at precisely those happening locations from which Hoad and his fellow contributors launched their query, *After Sex?*—Austin, Chicago, Berkeley, Toronto, Tufts, Stanford, Santa Cruz, Davis, Emory, Harvard, Penn, NYU, Amherst, Columbia, Bryn Mawr, the CUNY Graduate Center, and Bates. If queer theory happened, it happened at the places that are most notable for having the resources to hyperinject intellectual vitality into faculty labor and that are, as a result, the only places where queer theory could have been noticed as having happened. And that class-based spectacularity makes all the difference. A Queer Studies tenure-track position at a no-name school—a job that I know to exist because I have that job—has little chance of being noticed, even in order to be criticized for being, in Renn's words, nonqueer. Queer or not, you'd never know it happened.

But a brief pause: Bates? Where is Bates? I had to ask. It's a small, liberal arts college in Lewiston, Maine. The 2017–18 fee for attending Bates is $66,720, so it's a fancy school—a Rich Queer Studies school, to use my nomenclature. At the same time, Bates does put a slight twist on things. It requires a compromise, for it reminds me to grapple with the question of how to think about even minor institutional exceptions to the rule in my exploration of class and Queer Studies.[35] I am therefore quite thankful to Erica Rand, the professor from Bates who positions her after-sex essay, titled "Queer Theory Here and There," uncomfortably among those of her fellow contributors precisely because of where she is writing from. Up in Maine, away, "there," Rand writes from outside the recognizable centers of Queer Studies, "away from the queer-theory action," as she puts it.[36] Rand knows where the action is. By locating queer theory in the usual places and locating Bates outside those places, Rand's contribution to the collection reminds us to look for queer theory elsewhere, which intersects with one important strand of my argument. At $66,720 per year, Bates remains an unexceptional example of the ways material resources buoy so much queer scholarship. But Rand at least marginally expands the story of queer theory to farther-flung locations than might be expected. We can go further.

A Queer-Class Fix

Class is barely indexed in most Queer Studies scholarship. I mean this literally; one only need look at the index of the books on the queer shelf. Yes, class can go by many indexical names, but surely "class" ought to be one of them, at least as long as it is de rigueur for queer theorists to include class nominally in our list of structures of experience and oppression: gender, sex, race, class, ability. You see that list everywhere, but class manages to slip away in the actual work of queer scholarship. Where class appears centrally, queer often does a disappearing act.

Queer Studies scholars have sometimes attended explicitly to queer-class intersections, with Lisa Henderson's *Love and Money: Queers, Class and*

Cultural Production and work in the areas of queer labor being notable examples.[37] Henderson helps me define class less rigidly than some of the social studies I cite above, since "class categories work in the vernacular and analytic ways to mark a cultural universe."[38] Class is, for Henderson, "the economic and cultural coproduction of social distinction and hierarchy."[39] My use of the term "poor," addressed more fully below, calls to mind not only an economic position or a cultural identity but, perhaps even more meaningfully, a sense of institutionalized disparity that is crucial to understanding my critique of the field of Queer Studies. Because "class" is a relational term, "poor" signifies not only that higher education is being defunded but that in relation to increasingly rich schools at the top of the hierarchy that hoard their money, poor schools are getting poorer.

When Queer Studies scholars have raised class issues around the concept of disparity, we have often situated those issues socioculturally rather than institutionally. In other words, we have conceptualized queer-class studies using an inside versus outside the academy model in important attempts to theorize our queer/raced/gendered (dis)connections. Certainly, organic queer-class work has emerged from university-affiliated thinkers whose class analyses are inseparable from their academic positions. Occasionally queer scholars have collaborated with experts outside academe to consider, as one early and exemplary book on the subject declares, "homo economics."[40] Or the academy has looked to community workers, activists, and artists such as Eli Clare, Samuel Delaney, and Leslie Feinberg to articulate the need for queers to recognize and address queer poverty and class stratification. Less often, queer scholars have navigated class issues methodologically by finding ways to subvert the researcher/researched divide through, for instance, participatory action research in which knowledge making becomes a shared, cross-class endeavor of coinvestigators from inside and outside institutions of higher ed.[41] Each of these approaches has contributed to the articulation of queer-class intersections, and much more bridge-building work needs to be done across the academy/community divide.

Poor Queer Studies differs from other queer-class scholarship, however, in that it frames its inquiry by considering class differences primarily within and oriented around the queer academy. Because higher education is one of the most hierarchical institutions in the U.S., and because Queer Studies has been incorporated—unevenly, to be sure—into curricula and research projects by teachers and scholars at every tier of academe, we have been remiss in failing to interrogate the relationship between Queer Studies done at colleges across class-based institutional tiers. Indeed, we could ask whether breaking down the borders of the academy/community divide has substituted for and deferred intra-academic interrogations of class structure among the queer professoriate. Institutionality thus threatens to abrogate one of the few reliable principles of queer perversity, tucked away in one of Freud's footnotes to his essay "The Sexual Aberrations": "The highest and the lowest are always closest to each other in the sphere of sexuality."[42] My hunch is that asymmetrical institutional statuses, the high and the low, can make for interesting, necessarily partial starting points for all involved. The situated lessons of *Poor Queer Studies* will, I hope, resonate with instructors and students at schools that have been left out of the story of Queer Studies, as well as with readers throughout queer academe who wish, in queer fashion, to see the field otherwise.

The absence of a Poor Queer Studies paradigm that might counterbalance current state-of-the-field work is particularly curious in light of the fact that concerns about academic elitism within Queer Studies are an undeniable part of the field's history. Perhaps we used to hear those charges rather more often than we do now. Notably, Jeffrey Escoffier in his 1990 essay "Inside the Ivory Closet: The Challenge Facing Lesbian and Gay Studies" posited a split between post-Stonewall scholars who increasingly enjoyed and industriously courted institutional status within the academy and pre-Stonewall writers and activists whose primary commitments were to their communities and to making scholarship accessible beyond the academy. This split was framed between the academy and the community, between accessibility and elitism, and between older and younger thinkers. Though she disagreed with the stark distinctions Escoffier's argument carved out, Lisa Duggan demonstrated an appreciation of Escoffier's critique of what he called "the younger group of scholars . . . , ambitious young teachers and bright graduate students who trained at elite universities and who occupy jobs at more prestigious institutions."[43] Narrating her own version of a Queer Studies split, Duggan initially charted the queer institutional divide along disciplinary lines, arguing that unlike their more employable queer peers in fiction-based English departments, "lesbian and gay *historians* are relatively isolated from two crucial sources of support—the material and institutional support of university history departments, and the intellectual engagement and support of other scholars in the field of lesbian and gay or queer studies. And for both academic and public intellectuals, isolation leads to material as well as to cultural impoverishment and decline. . . . Like any other field, lesbian and gay historians need material support and intellectual and political exchange. For us, isolation equals cultural and professional death."[44]

To what extent such discussions of disciplinary disenfranchisement among scholars at deep-pocketed institutions eclipsed attention to more stark structural disenfranchisements between poor and rich schools will be an ongoing point of interest in this study. In his 1996 review essay, "The Class Politics of Queer Theory," Donald Morton singles out for praise Nicola Field's *Over the Rainbow: Money, Class, and Homophobia* while criticizing a raft of scholars located in upper-class university settings (including Duggan) for "shadowboxing with a collapsing liberal state."[45] Morton approvingly quotes independent scholar Will Roscoe (from a Queer Studies listserv): "Much of queer theory seems radical only as long as we ignore the class-base of its production and dissemination."[46] Roscoe's voice reminds me that although I am primarily concerned with amplifying the work of Poor Queer Studies inside the academy, research into independent scholars' relationships to Queer Studies would surely open up interesting and varied sight lines onto the field, especially insofar as their work is sometimes adopted by Queer Studies (two examples being the seminal work of Jonathan Ned Katz and the genre-busting writing and editing of Alexis Pauline Gumbs). It is, in fact, an independent scholar without means with whom *Poor Queer Studies* most closely shares its vision.

Speaking in 1995 at Cornell University about the role of Queer Studies in the upward redistribution of wealth, working-class independent scholar Allan Bérubé enjoined his academy-based audience to act: "What does [the] massive redistribution of wealth and widening of [the] class divide have to do with queer studies? It just happens to be the twenty-year moment when a gay rights movement and the field of queer studies have both emerged. There's no inherent reason why queer studies and gay politics would not reproduce the racialized class inequality and confusion that structure the larger society. But unfortunately, we can't enjoy the luxury of standing on the sidelines as innocent bystanders. We have been implicated."[47] Queer Studies has been implicated, for it has indelible, field-defining, field-sustaining material and psychic associations with the most elite colleges and universities in the U.S., like the campus at which Bérubé delivered his talk.[48] Indeed, the early 1990s was a flashpoint for this critique, with high-class queer theory becoming largely synonymous with Queer Studies (I use the two somewhat interchangeably here, for instance). In 1994, Arlene Stein and Ken Plummer could already reference Diana Fuss's founding 1991 collection, *Inside/ Out: Lesbian Theories, Gay Theories*, to frame queer theory as "an academic movement—indeed, an elite academic movement centered at least initially in the most prestigious U.S. institutions.... Queer theory emerged in the late 1980s, publicized through a series of academic conferences held at Yale and other Ivy League universities, in which scholars, primarily from history and the humanities, presented their work on lesbian/gay subjects."[49] Stein and Plummer go on to suggest that queer theory, so invigorating and influential in the humanities, could more explicitly inform sociology as well, a field that had invented social constructionism in the first place. Their vision for expanding the disciplinary uses and places of queer theory also implicitly recodes its class locations as, potentially, someplace other than "Yale and other Ivy League universities."[50] That vision, unfortunately, didn't stand a chance. As I explore in chapter 2, disciplinary expansion could not help but secure professional elitism for queer theory, for one of the key functions of disciplinarity is to distinguish between the expert and the novice. Disciplinary expansion and crossover thus quickly subsumed class-based, anti-hierarchical crossover as the dynamic institutional queer move. We need to ask why the rise of interdisciplinarity, so critical of knowledge silos, did not de-stratify higher education in class terms, especially as the supposedly class-attuned framework of intersectionality has been the methodological byword for much interdisciplinary scholarship in the humanities and social sciences. And in the case of Queer Studies specifically, how is it that working across fields, sharing knowledge and knowledge practices, and pressing multiple analytic frameworks into service failed to impede the installation of rigid class taxonomies in the university? Why did queer interdisciplinarity not keep its own class-structured institutional houses more dis-ordered?

In fact, attempts at queer-class disordering of the academy often look like relatively enfranchised LGBTQ scholars studying disenfranchised queer people or cultural forms extrinsic to the academy but with whom and which we feel personal/political connections and intellectual attractions. In her study of interdisciplinary "object lessons," Robyn Wiegman wonders, "Given that subjects of knowledge are never fully commensurate with the objects they seek to authorize, what tactic is on offer from within identity knowledges to handle the contradictions between the educated elite and the subalterns we study and represent?"[51] Cathy Cohen, reflecting on the increasing institutionalization of Black Queer Studies in her foreword to *No Tea, No Shade: New Writings in Black Queer Studies*, edited by E. Patrick Johnson, appreciates that on the one hand the field "extends beyond the classroom into the streets [and] into movements . . . on behalf of and in partnership with black people who may never see the inside of our classrooms."[52] On the other hand, Cohen cautions that "as we descend deeper into the ivory tower we must ask ourselves at what cost. To what degree does incorporation challenge our relevance to the same communities who find themselves at the heart of our research?"[53]

Heather Love's body of work offers an important intervention into queer-class studies and so provides a touchstone for my thinking here. Like Cohen and Wiegman, Love is attentive to histories of working-class feminism and antielitist queer women of color, and she links those queer-class histories and knowledges to the ongoing ambivalences of Queer Studies toward class difference within its ranks.[54] This becomes clear in a recent discussion in which Love reiterates the value of examining queer-class connections from within Queer Studies as class-based scholars of the field, while noting that queer theoretical conversations about "materialism and crisis" are more likely to be centered around critiques of capital than around individual and collective class histories.[55] But problematically, for scholars for whom "queer studies was a route to upward mobility"—and I join Love in counting myself among this group—the fact of academic elitism in Queer Studies disorients at a level of lived experience that can make a class critique of the field less, rather than more, possible. When speaking about class, it is difficult not to get personal. Yet one doesn't want to pry. Bérubé, a master of dramatizing queer-class connections and to whom I turn more fully in chapter 3 for an exploration of "queer work," can thus ask, "Think about it—take any group of queer scholars—how much do you know about their sexual interests and desires, and how much do you know about their income, wealth, and class background? What's the major taboo operating here—economic or sexual?"[56] We mark ourselves in queer terms as we unmark ourselves in class terms, even as a function of our participation in the field. For this reason alone the collection *Resilience: Queer Professors from the Working Class* stands out among academic narratives.[57] In *Resilience*, queer professors turn back toward their lower-class roots, extending those histories into what for many is an ongoing sense of professional liminality and, though they are now members of the professoriate, economic precarity.[58] Rehistoricizing Queer Studies—and writing a new future for our field—depends on our willingness to tell such class stories not only from below but, overtly, from above and to be implicated in our current institutional positions. *Poor Queer Studies* tethers the cutting-edge, new-new queer ideas that inspire us to the material conditions of our work lives and not only to our most well-resourced, most noticeably fierce intellects.

Love, an English professor at an Ivy League school, turns to deviance studies in sociology to find a language and method by which Queer Studies might understand not only its deviant objects but also the material realities that quietly enable its constitutive claims to deviancy. Specifically, she reconsiders the uses of objectification, long decried by Queer Studies as normalizing, to perspectivize the institutional positions of self-described "subversive" practitioners of queer theory: "Queer theory was a revolt against scholarly expertise in the name of deviance, yet it resonated in many ways with academic norms. Queer academics might also be activist, organic intellectuals, radical experimenters in their personal, professional, and political lives, but they are also superordinates in the context of the university: professional knowledge workers, teachers, and administrators."[59] Asking, "Whose side are we on?," Love suggests that academicians are always university insiders, no matter what else we are. "Can we hold onto the critical and polemical energy of queer studies as well as its radical experiments in style and thought while acknowledging our implication in systems of power, management, and control?" Love asks. "Will a more explicit avowal of disciplinary affiliations and methods snuff out the utopian energies of a field that sees itself as a radical outsider in the university?"[60] Love's insights about the need to make our queer disciplinary affiliations explicit resonate with the project of *Poor Queer Studies* because they encourage a queer method of professional hair-splitting that might proceed, for example, with descriptive accounts of intra-academy differences among Queer Studies people and places. Or, to begin again, queer dinners. We know, having been told in any number of heartening and disheartening ways, the simple truth that all Queer Studies work is not equal. What we need to know better and reckon with is the structural truth that all Queer Studies working conditions are not equal. What if we connected our queer ideas and pedagogies to the material realities of their production (our research budgets and our college websites, our course loads and our commutes, our embodiments and our built environments, our leave time and our overwork, our library holdings and our bathroom gender policies, our raced work sites and our service work, our salaries and our second jobs) in order to understand those ideas and pedagogies as class- and status-based knowledges that cannot be universalized? What can telling the material histories of Queer Studies do to address the problem of class stratification in higher education? What if by engaging with such questions Queer Studies can fix the academy, not fuck it up?

Why "Poor" Queer Studies?

My argument is not that Queer Studies at rich schools isn't sometimes interesting and sometimes transformative and sometimes aware that its production is, first and foremost, a workplace issue. My argument is not that

Queer Studies happens only at rich schools. Indeed, my half-plagiarized question, What's poor about Queer Studies now?, comes from the opposite impulse: to take into consideration Queer Studies elsewhere and otherwise in the class-stratified academy. That work is being done, as demonstrated by internal university publications such as "'We Could Do That!' A Guide to Diversity Practices in California Community Colleges" and by studies published by academic presses such as the 2015 volume *Expanding the Circle: Creating an Inclusive Environment in Higher Education for LGBTQ Students and Studies*, edited by John C. Hawley.[61] These collections, the content of which cannot be separated from the institutional diversity of their contributors, serve as both counterevidence and evidence for my argument that while LGBTQ programs and curricula dot the educational landscape, the field of Queer Studies comes into view much more narrowly. "'We Could Do That!'" and *Expanding the Circle* mark a shift away from Rich Queer Studies even as they show the difficulty of such a shift. Expanding the circle that delimits the field names the work still to be done. I call that work Poor Queer Studies.

Laden with stigmatizing connotations, "poor" has fallen out of critical use, replaced by powerful analytics such as precarity and "asset-based" frameworks such as resilience.[62] "Poor" therefore seems an improper word to anchor a new Poor Queer Studies knowledge project. But I have several reasons for using the word. Far from flatly derogatory, my terminology, Poor Queer Studies, invokes a complex and contested set of meanings. Uncomfortably, it foregrounds a term associated with an outmoded figuration of socioeconomic hardship: "Of a person or people: having few, or no, material possessions; lacking the means to procure the comforts or necessities of life, or to live at a standard considered comfortable or normal in society; needy, necessitous, indigent, destitute. Sometimes: *spec.* so destitute as to be dependent upon gifts or allowances for subsistence. Opposed to *rich*."[63] Surely many of my students, in their pursuit of a degree that can (so the social mobility narrative goes) confer middle-class status, would reject this descriptor, which becomes sharper in tone as it proceeds until it ends in insulting negativity, "opposed to rich." The term "poor" tethers them too statically to the wrong end of an educational narrative premised on social mobility. I argue, however, that "poor" is far from a static term. Indeed, it accomplishes a good deal of descriptive and conceptual work, especially as it enables Poor Queer Studies to be positively opposed to Rich Queer Studies. As Poor Queer Studies foregrounds the lack of access to material resources that provides one of the most powerfully recurring threads in my queer classrooms, it also connotes other impoverishments—those holes in the field imaginary where Rich Queer Studies cannot see its own class- and status-based epistemologies. In other words, if we are not used to opposing Poor Queer Studies to Rich Queer Studies, this is because Rich Queer Studies has not conceptualized its poor queer blind spots concretely enough to be opposed to them. The fact that poor queer schools are getting poorer in relation to rich ones enlarges those blind spots, making cross-class relationships and ideas less visible. Actively opposing Rich Queer Studies is not only a way for Poor Queer Studies to be seen but a way to hold the field together in queer-class tension.

With the benefit of institutional distance from the places of Rich Queer Studies, Poor Queer Studies perceives the field's high-class deficits. Poor Queer Studies, in part, fills in those gaps and in the process renames a discipline typically imagined elsewhere that must be reimagined at unrecognizable and unfashionable schools such as the college where I work, the College of Staten Island. I'll begin to lay the groundwork for conceptualizing Poor Queer Studies by briefly sketching CSI's college portrait below. How are we queer, here? Chapter 1 expands that vision by tracing CSI's queer faculty genealogy and arguing for the value of historically based queer case studies of colleges that don't easily appear on the map of the field.

Finally, Poor Queer Studies locates the pedagogical convergence of Queer Studies with my students' socioeconomic as well as socioaffective "histories of arrival."[64] Contextualized by this larger trajectory, "poor" names a dimension of experience that, perhaps more than any other structure of difference *including sexuality,* forms the basis of my queer pedagogy at CSI. I cannot overstate this fundamental point. Though my pedagogical refrain (the explicit course topics, readings, vocabulary) is queerness, the bass notes for my Queer Studies pedagogy at CUNY are the racialized and gendered socioeconomic, material, and psychic realities through which reverberate that freighted meter of class status, "poor." Below, I want to play a few of those queer-class bass notes to set the tone for *Poor Queer Studies.*

Realizing Poor Queer Studies

Understanding the habitus of a Poor Queer Studies school from afar can be difficult. One can begin by looking at the statistics and the marketing that combine to create the college profile. While the broad context for *Poor Queer Studies* is the deeply class-stratified system of higher education in the U.S. within which the academic discipline of Queer Studies has struggled and grown, the more immediate site for my relocation of queer teaching and research is the deeply underfunded, open-admissions, public college where I work, CSI, as well as the larger university system of which CSI is a part, the working-poor CUNY. The College of Staten Island has a student population of 12,211 undergraduates and 1,036 graduate students, 343 full-time, tenure-track faculty, and 819 non-tenure-track faculty, 722 of whom are adjuncts. More than 70 percent of our first-time freshmen enter as associate degree students. Of the undergraduates, 43.6 percent are white, 26.5 percent Hispanic, 13.9 percent black, and 11.1 percent Asian.[65] More than half are "low-income students," and 15 percent have family incomes under $20,000.[66] Strikingly, CSI students have traditionally had the highest family incomes in the CUNY system due in large part to the particular demographics of the island's population. While CSI's student body overall is less racially diverse than CUNY schools in other boroughs, we have much higher rates of traditionally underserved white ethnic students, primarily Italian Americans, who are a protected class at CUNY.[67] Like their peers across the system, CSI students work, often full time. In one of my recent upper-level Queer Studies classes, students worked for money an average of thirty-two hours per week, in addition to taking care of children and/or parents, with whom most of them still live. Any number of recent headlines that claim to break the story that students are workers too read like old news to these student-workers.

And then there are the qualitative data captured in table I.1, "Realizing Poor Queer Studies." These daily observations and unremarkable interactions are where this project began, long before I poked my nose into the institutional research. Renny Christopher indexes the utility of such mixed methods of research into working-class pedagogy, writing that "to understand the situation of working-class students in higher education, scholars in working-class pedagogy have focused not only on empirical data but on qualitative information as well, both observational and biographical."[68] Mixing methods, my introduction also necessarily breaks form here, as these moments and impressions did not come to me in order or in a coherent research narrative. Working at an institution with a lot of poor and working-class students, you come to understand the incredible drama of class mobility. But, ironically, that drama often registers as boring, if not wholly unremarkable. The reality, the intersectional race-class-gender precarity, is often understood, pieced together, only later. It took me many years at CSI to realize I was teaching Poor Queer Studies.

Table I.1. Realizing Poor Queer Studies

It looks like	*When in reality*
Stasis, a Latina student in her seventh year of school.	She is terrified of graduating and remaining single without the excuse of college to defend her against her parents' heteronormative impatience.
Leaving a meeting with a student group and then bumping into a former student.	You remember that the white student you just bumped into was homeless when they took your course. This fact is brought to mind because one of the Latinx students in the meeting you just came from discussed being, currently, homeless.
A student bringing her four-year-old to class to avoid domestic violence.	The brown child's presence prompts a spontaneous pedagogical innovation. The queer studies students, in solidarity with their distressed peer, organically adapt to the changed classroom space by spelling out all the S-E-X words in our discussion.
Failure, an F paper written, judging by the punctuation, on a cell phone and pasted into Word.	He works two jobs and must use his phone to thumb in his essays during breaks between deliveries. He doesn't own a computer.
A general education class at an open-admissions, two-year and four-year institution.	Being unable to distinguish between students working toward their associate degree and those working toward their bachelor's degree. Being surprised at the frequent disconnect between a student's capabilities and her educational goals.
The Asian American gender-conforming student who never says anything.	They are transgender and need to leave home. But they never tell you, their queer studies professor, either of these things until years later, in an email from across the country.
Tiresome responsibility, a young single black mother.	She makes the decision to study abroad for a semester.
A mixed-race student who comes out as having a close relative who is HIV+.	Though he knows more than any of his peers about living with HIV/AIDS, he thinks Magic Johnson is no longer HIV+ because he is rich enough to afford the cure.
A moment of bonding after class between a white gay professor from the sticks and a white butch working-class lesbian student.	She asks, "Professor, are we going to read any books by white people?," revealing the moment to be one of shared white privilege forged through homosexual class identification.
A three-hour commute from the Bronx.	She is a young black lesbian who is closeted at home, who wanted to go away to school but couldn't afford it, and CSI is the furthest CUNY campus from her neighborhood. No one knows her at CSI.

Each of these examples marks a queer-class connection, intersections made busier by race and gender dynamics. They create the background and, now, the foreground for teaching Poor Queer Studies at my college. Plenty of other data inform these moments, including middle-class and even upper-class messages and meanings. This other data—the noise created nearer the top of the economic ladder that is almost always taken to represent higher education in general—can often drown out the poor queer data, which students and faculty are so incentivized to turn away from already. Even Poor Queer Studies offers such an incentive, if for no other reason than this: a Queer Studies professor inevitably models a direction, a high-status if not high-class queer career. My very presence links queerness to social mobility and superordinate status. Queerness, when it looks like a Queer Studies professor, looks like a way out, a way up, away from poor.

Relative success, judged by one's own lights, becomes a problem in this regard. How can I assert both that CSI is one of the queerest schools I know, a claim I pursue in chapter 1, and that it represents a site of queer marginalization and unknowability? How do I account for my annual salary, at age forty-seven and after thirteen years in this job, of $97,628? (Note: this statistic is public information because I am a public employee. Bringing the question of what that salary means—how it translates into class status in New York City, how it connotes failure or success to my students—is a terrific pedagogical prompt for my Poor Queer Studies classrooms. I wonder, if I taught at a private college, would I so readily disclose how much I make?) More generally, how does my analysis account for the inordinate successes of some of my colleagues, even as I insist on drawing readers' critical gaze back to the material and structural impoverishments of our work? Look at our recent history in the CSI English department alone. My colleague Tyehimba Jess won the 2017 Pulitzer Prize in Poetry and the 2017 Anisfield-Wolf Book Award for *Olio*. For her book of poetry, *Incendiary Art*, my colleague Patricia Smith won the 2018 Kingsley Tufts Poetry Award, the 2017 Los Angeles Times Book Prize, the 2018 NAACP Image Award, and was the runner-up for the 2018 Pulitzer Prize in Poetry. Faculty in our creative writing concentration alone include National Book Award finalists and have won three Guggenheims, multiple Fulbrights, two Whiting awards, multiple National Poetry Slam championships, the Library of Congress Rebekah Johnson Bobbitt National Prize, the American Academy of Poets Lenore Marshall Prize, multiple Pushcart Prizes, the Hurston/Wright Legacy Award, a Cullman Center Fellowship, multiple Publishing Triangle awards including the Bill Whitehead Award for Lifetime Achievement, the CLAGS Kessler lifetime achievement in LGBTQ Studies award, the MFK Fisher Book Award, the grand prize in documentary at the Nashville International Film Festival, and fellowships and residencies far too numerous to mention.[69] Beyond this faculty snapshot, CSI produced the second most Fulbright Scholars of any master's-level institution in the U.S. in 2016–17. Recently, CUNY was ranked sixth in the nation on CollegeNET's Social Mobility Index, meaning we are good at helping students who start poor rise through socioeconomic strata. And CSI was ranked number 504 on the 2017–18 Forbes list of "America's Top Colleges."[70] Beyond these and other measured successes lie the more persuasive daily experiences of students, faculty, and staff coming together to do good work for which we are proud of each other. I am painfully aware of being perceived by my CSI community as undermining that work by attaching it to "poor," though that would be a misinterpretation of my goals here. On the other hand, I have no worries about being perceived by my colleagues as undermining our work by attaching it to "queer."[71] That contrast helps to set the stakes of this study, for it implies a competing set of institutional attachments—poor versus queer—that I argue ought not compete, not at CSI and not in Queer Studies across the academy.

As this book turns toward an imbrication of queerness and class that schools and scholars turn away from, it wrestles with the question of queer-class research practices. Methodologically, this study confronts the "problem of impossible evidence" that attends queer scholarship, which is characteristically concerned with elucidating the "vagaries of embodied life."[72] Ruth Wilson Gilmore helps me to frame my encounter with the vagaries of queer-class institutional life when she writes that "people in forgotten places also act within the institutional and individualized constraints defined by racialization, gender hierarchy, and nationality, and the complex potential mix of these possibilities has produced its own academic specialties old and new: the various branches of the social sciences, area studies, ethnic studies, gender studies, cultural studies—the latter three dedicated to the study of disabling (in the sense of both debilitating and undoing; see Hart 2002b) constraints. *Constraints* does not mean 'insurmountable barriers.' However, it does suggest that people use what is available to make a place in the world."[73] With slippery issues of class and race and status at the heart of the matter, queer methodological constraints (or queer messes[74]) arise, particularly as I explore embodied pedagogical relations between teacher and student, professional distinctions between high-status and low-status Queer Studies professors, the relationship of scholar to institution, and the articulations of materiality to theory. Much of my queer-class research practice is grounded by anecdotal evidence and educated guesses about working in spaces of queer precarity in higher education, and I adapt the queer narrative case study model to represent and interpret that evidence. My approach values working people, both students and colleagues, as well as working with people. Student stories, which I typically reanimate here in composite form in order to anonymize them, galvanize the larger story about queer pedagogy and social class that I tell. Institutional spaces, including Queer Studies classrooms, offices, campuses, academic centers, and queer conferences, help to structure and inform those narratives of student and faculty access to and production of queer ideas.

My inquiry is therefore, at least in part, unavoidably parochial, arising from my queer professional positioning at CSI. It must be so, and this assertion opens out onto my larger argument about the ways that Queer Studies must encounter itself at institutions high and low and in between. A special issue of GLQ, "Queering the Middle: Race, Region, and a Queer Midwest," frames "the middle" as a new queer vantage, "a troubled, unstable perch buttressed by the dominance of the coasts and the 'South.'"[75] The middle references the Midwest and the idea of region, which become at once geographic locations and discursive formations. The authors position the middle as at once between urban and rural and also shot through by them. One result is that traditional queer mappings, such as urban migration narratives that tend to stabilize a country/city divide, are forced to incorporate a productive confusion of scale. Regionalism pulls extremes of urban and rural toward its powerful, indefinite optic, the middle. Attending to the regional enables dynamic interscalar perspectives at the level of the subnational and global to emerge as well.

Conceptually, the middle is stretchy, and so it can contribute to an analysis of Staten Island and the college named after it, even though Staten Island is certainly not Midwestern and though it is colloquially described as one of New York City's outer boroughs. As a forgotten object of a geographical imagination that privileges the urban/rural binary, Staten Island gestures toward a kind of epistemological middle space that concepts such as region help to elucidate. Region can "illustrate the unruliness of racial, class, and gender dynamics that transgress easy rural or urban organization and signal what escapes both metronormative locales and their alternative spaces."[76] Staten Island is urban in parts, but not compared to neighboring Manhattan or much of Brooklyn. It is located in the deep blue political culture of the East Coast, yet it voted overwhelmingly for President Trump. There are no lesbian or gay bars on this island of 500,000 residents, yet it is home to one of the queerest of CUNY's twenty-four campuses.

What I like about a theory of the middle is that it doesn't presuppose a perfect fit between critical lens and object of study but rather offers a flexible framework for thinking about place and queerness. Poor Queer Studies requires a similar kind of analytic, if for no other reason than that a study of any institution of higher education preconditionally excludes the study of most poor people because, systematically, most poor people are excluded from college education. In 2013, the nationwide college enrollment rate for "low-income students" (the bottom 20 percent of all family incomes) who had recently graduated high school was just 46 percent.[77] But only about 76 percent of children from poor families graduate high school in the first place.[78] So even if it were possible to define "poor" (as the bottom 20 percent, for instance), my focus on college students and the university spaces and protocols I am calling Poor Queer Studies would still construct a very partial object of analysis. But paradoxically, because "poor" cannot be precisely defined, I am able, within the limited context of the class-stratified academy, to use the term in a much more inclusive way than a strict definition permits. Neither CSI nor CUNY are uniformly or unambiguously poor. Nor are the students. Nor are the faculty. Yet impoverishment sets the conceptual baseline for much that happens here, even down to the finer points of heating and air conditioning as my college institutes cost-saving measures for the physical plant. When I take up concerns of the middle, of the working class, even at times of the upper classes and the rich, I hope to reveal the way that Poor Queer Studies can be more pertinent to those concerns than has been realized.

I propose that "poor," like "Midwest," operates as "both a material space and a discursive construct" within higher education.[79] "Poor" enables me to combine critical regionality with critical disciplinarity to conceptualize Poor Queer Studies through an analysis of queer pedagogy and scholarship at an outer-borough campus of the nation's largest, and by some measures poorest, public urban university. Of course, I also have to convince you that you should care, which is to say that I have to promise you that there will be a payoff for looking with me at and from my college. Siobhan Somerville, one of the coeditors of the "Queering the Middle" issue of GLQ, elsewhere provides a vital model of contextualized queer knowledge production within higher education. In "Locating Queer Culture in the Big Ten," Somerville describes her process of designing an undergraduate course around the question, "How . . . might we understand the role of Midwestern public universities like the [University of Illinois at Urbana-Champaign] in the production of queer culture?"[80] Creating an archive of queer University of Illinois artifacts such as Ann Bannon's lesbian novel *Odd Girl Out* (1957), which is set in a fictionalized "Champlain," helps to rewrite not only specific university histories that have hidden local queer cultural productions but also broad urban-centric histories of sexuality that have hidden suburban, rural, and regional queer data. Working from Somerville's model in chapter 1 especially, I use CSI as a case study for the production of queer knowledge in an overlooked place. My intention isn't to permanently center this particular work site or even to center the intellectual project of Poor Queer Studies to the exclusion of the heady archive of Rich Queer Studies, but to make the field stretchy enough to accommodate and respond to its many class locations.

My History of Arrival

I end this introduction with my history of arrival at CSI. How I came to CSI and how I came to this project are vital contexts for the knowledge produced in/as this book. In the winter of 2006, after three years on the job market in search of a tenure-track position, I received a job interview at the Modern Language Association annual convention (back when CSI could still afford to interview at the unconscionably expensive production that is the MLA) and, subsequently, an invitation for a campus visit for the position of assistant professor of Queer Studies in the English department. The story of my ultimate hire contains several quirky features of plot, setting, and character that I now recognize as fortuitous, for they have made it possible to imagine the narrative of this book. First, I had never heard of CSI, as perhaps the reader has not. I had lived on both coasts, in the Midwest, and in the South, but Staten Island was not on any of my maps. If it had been, I likely would have heard about its status as "the forgotten borough" or, as the title of a book by two of my colleagues has it, *Staten Island: Conservative Bastion in a Liberal City*.[81] But after living thirty-three-plus years in rural America, much of it surrounded by fields and farms and homophobia and racism, and, relatedly, having been closeted through nearly all of my twenties, I knew the most important fact of the job: it was in New York. Recent work in queer rural studies, had I had the benefit of it then, would not have made a dent in my single-minded queer career trajectory. It was gay New York or gay San Francisco or bust. So while I was delighted to be making my way to Staten Island for my campus interview that winter of 2007, I was initially also a bit dumbfounded to find that there was a Queer Studies job at a school I had never heard of. I had only heard about Queer Studies at places that I'd heard of—a meaningful tautology for this book.

Now, having received tenure and promotion at this job for which (quirky subplot) I came in runner-up, I am anything but surprised by the association of CSI with queer intellectual work. Now it is I who guarantees to disbelieving acquaintances and friends that professor of Queer Studies is a job and that it is a job at CSI, the sole public institution of higher education in the borough. Indeed, and I repeat, CSI is one of the queerest colleges I've known. This statement is perhaps the quirkiest one of all, for I attended Wabash College, an all-male, avowedly not gay undergraduate college, I earned a PhD in English at Indiana University, home to the famous Kinsey Institute (and the only graduate program to which I was accepted), and for the three years prior to beginning my tenure-track job at CSI, I held a Mellon Post-doctoral Fellowship in the University Writing Program at Duke University, the so-called birthplace of queer theory.[82] In an important way, the story of this book is the story of that career path, especially the first and last steps. The first step was from the farmland of Indiana to college at a place that would pay my way. I didn't fully understand that Wabash was a rich school; I just knew that I couldn't pay and that the college would offer me a substantial scholarship. By the time I took the most recent step, which brought me to CSI, I understood what a rich school was. I was coming from Duke, the Ivy of the South, its architecture Gothic revival, its lawns flat green, its gardens lush. I was going to CSI (no moving expenses, of course), which had settled into the partially renovated facilities of the notoriously abusive Willowbrook State School for children with intellectual disabilities (subject of Geraldo Rivera's 1972 exposé). My impression upon seeing CSI for the first time was that there were fewer trees than one might reasonably expect on a 204-acre campus. At this commuter school, parking lots trump landscaping.[83]

For my teaching talk during my CSI interview, I was asked to prepare a presentation called "What Happens in a Queer Studies Classroom?" My point for the moment is that my future colleagues were not actually asking what happens in a Queer Studies classroom. They were asking how I would teach Queer Studies here, to these students, at this school, in this system. Figuring out the answers to those questions, how to answer them, why they're important, has been my greatest challenge and joy for the past thirteen years. *Poor Queer Studies* tells the story of my reeducation in Queer Studies, here, in a place my field was not supposed, not imagined, to be.

chapter one

The College of Staten Island
A Poor Queer Studies Case Study

In Heat is a novel of rare purity, without a single fashionable line. —Boyd McDonald, *The Advocate*

When it doesn't work to change the conditions of exemplarity or explanation, something is deemed merely a case study, remanded to banal particularity. When it does, a personal or collective sensorium shifts. —Lauren Berlant, "On the Case"

We learn about worlds when they do not accommodate us. Not being accommodated can be pedagogy. —Sara Ahmed, "An Affinity of Hammers"

Larry Mitchell and the Unfashionable Line of Poor Queer Studies

In the spring of 2013, at the suggestion of my CSI colleague Sarah Schulman, I wrote the following obituary for Larry Mitchell in the *Gay and Lesbian Review*.

> Larry Mitchell helped clear the way for many of us, even if we didn't know it. When I met Larry in 2008 to interview him for this magazine, we discovered that we had grown up thirty miles apart in Indiana ("It was a nightmare!" he exclaimed, and I agreed). Only after I made my way to graduate school in Indiana, and then to New York, and then onto the faculty of the College of Staten Island, CUNY, did I learn that I'd been following Larry around my whole life.
>
> Thirty-five years apart, we had lived within a few blocks of each other in the St. George neighborhood of the forgotten borough. By the time I arrived, Larry had long since moved to the Lower East Side and retired

from the College, which was also home to his fellow queer luminaries Bertha Harris, Arnie Kantrowitz, Judith Stelboum, and Sarah Schulman. It was Sarah who introduced us, and I suddenly found myself sitting in Larry's living room, having finally caught up to him, and we became friends. From time to time after that, people would contact me about the GLR interview. These occasions gave me the chance to call Larry up and put new readers in touch. I treasure those phone calls—his resonant gay voice. Generous and pleased, he always said yes to those of us lucky enough to have followed.

Larry Mitchell, gay novelist and publisher, died of pancreatic cancer on December 26, 2012 in Ithaca, NY. With his lover Rick Morrison, Mitchell lived in New York City and Ithaca. He was 74.

Mitchell was best known for his unsentimental depictions of queer life in New York City's Lower East Side and East Village in the 1980s and '90s. His novels include *The Terminal Bar* (1982), *In Heat* (1986), *My Life as a Mole and Other Stories* (1988), which won a Lambda Literary Award, and *Acid Snow* (1993). His early *The Faggots and Their Friends between Revolutions* (1977), originally conceived as a children's book and illustrated by Ned Asta, secured Mitchell's reputation as a champion of radical queer life and politics. When neither straight nor gay presses would publish this book, Mitchell established his own press, Calamus Books, which specialized in gay male literature. *The Faggots and Their Friends* would be his most successful book, with three printings and 10,000 copies sold. He would go on to cofound the Gay Presses of New York. Mitchell's other notable publications include *Great Gay in the Morning: One Group's Approach to Communal Living and Sexual Politics* (1972) and the co-edited volume *Willard W. Waller on the Family, Education, and War* (1970).

Larry Mitchell was born in Muncie, Indiana on July 12, 1938. He matriculated at Colby College in Waterville, Maine in 1956 and moved to New York City in 1960 to attend graduate school at Columbia University, where he earned a doctorate in sociology. In 1969 Mitchell joined the faculty at Richmond College (later the College of Staten Island, CUNY) where he taught sociology, sexual liberation, and feminism for the next 25 years. As part of the "25 to 6 Baking and Trucking Society," a communal living and writing group in the St. George neighborhood of Staten Island, Mitchell found himself the subject of FBI surveillance: "For a year and a half they would steal our garbage. We had a lot of fun with them, because we weren't doing anything. It was wild."

At Columbia he had been a student of the ways power is exercised within culture, and this training would inform not only his thinking about gay liberation activism—he attended meetings of the Gay Liberation Front in the fall of 1969—but also his sociological approach to fiction. "I'm not a psychological writer," Mitchell claimed. "I don't really get into my characters' psychology. I'm interested in their behavior, in what they say, in what they do. And New York gay culture was very much like that: here we are, let's do it, what are we going to do?"

Ensconced on Second Avenue between Seventh and Eighth Street for much of the 1980s, Mitchell chronicled the behavior of the fellow gay revolutionaries, street kids, hourly laborers, addicts, and artists who made up his ever-shifting, ever-threatened community. His fiction defended against the dual threats of capitalism and assimilation, not only thematically but stylistically. Of *In Heat*, Boyd McDonald wrote, "it is a novel of rare purity, without a single fashionable line." As AIDS decimated both his neighborhood and his readership, and due to his increasing blindness, Mitchell stopped writing in 1993. A distinctive literary voice, Mitchell remains a treasured historian of marginalized gay cultures.[1]

I include this long remembrance, foremost, to honor Larry. The best way to do that, of course, is to read him, and that is my wish for you and for his work. But more than this, I suggest that Larry's novels, particularly *The Terminal Bar* (1982), in which one of the characters teaches part-time at the barely fictionalized College of Staten Island, help to make *Poor Queer Studies* imaginable. Poor Queer Studies exists at CSI because Larry—and the many others I name in this chapter—created the possibility for it to exist by bringing queer ideas and CSI into the same orbit and by leaving a record behind. But that record dissipates, fails to cohere. The trouble surrounding poor queer record keeping is a chief concern of this chapter. On the one hand, my colleagues' queer work is historical fact. Faculty at CSI have written important queer literature and scholarship here. Some of the earliest gay and lesbian studies classes in the U.S., as well as early women's studies and even men's studies classes, were taught here.[2] And in 2006 an indisputably queer line forward for the college was created when the English department advertised for the job of assistant professor of Queer Studies. There are still relatively few such expressly named academic positions. This is all in the record.

But for me, alongside the knowledge of that local queer history of writing, teaching, and learning at CSI has existed an uncanny feeling about that knowledge, a felt misconception. Counterintuitively, the more I learned about the college and my queer colleagues past and present, the stranger that knowledge became. I felt caught unaware, even as the facts of queer work at CSI piled up into what should have been a pattern. Nevertheless, the coordinates of this queer place weren't connecting in a way that made it recognizable as a Queer Studies place. In the introduction I wrote that it took me years to realize that I was teaching Poor Queer Studies, and that is true despite my formal job title providing a ready-made compass for that work and despite the evidence of historical queer referents. Despite my predecessors and my position, the way of this Poor Queer Studies professor was not clear. The queer history of CSI was certainly not hidden, but neither was it fully navigable. How was I to guide Queer Studies at CSI when following the line I had ended up on presented such a problem?

Writing Larry's obituary helped, for as I read his novels, his short stories, and his brilliant queer manifesto *The Faggots and Their Friends between Revolutions*, illustrated by Ned Asta, I began to link the inscrutability of Queer Studies at CSI to the institution's equally inscrutable underclass institutional identity.[3] Boyd McDonald's keen observation that Larry's second novel, *In Heat*, "is a novel of rare purity, without a single fashionable line," began to resonate more generally as I considered the place Larry worked. The College of Staten Island is not fashionable. Queer Studies here is not fashionable. In this chapter I explore Queer Studies done unfashionably at CSI and pursue the implications of that queer-class idea, especially insofar as to be unfashionable in Queer Studies is to be unrecognizable in the larger field. I continue to be struck by how difficult the work of imagining Poor Queer Studies has been, even in the face of substantial evidence of its presence. In relation to its overarching discipline, one known in no small part for its critical cachet, can Poor Queer Studies be known and valued without being pursued in the same fashion? How can the work of following, out of fashion and behind the class curve, register as a viable method for doing Queer Studies? On the map of Queer Studies, a discipline with a vanguard complex, how does one follow an unfashionable line?[4]

To begin to make the unfashionable recognizable, I shift the perspective from which the dominant stories of Queer Studies have been told. Though it would be impossible and undesirable to turn one's back on the rich and compelling field constructions that go most generally by the name of Queer Studies, I pause early in this book to forge an association between the discipline and the relatively unknown, deeply underfunded, historically working-class institution that hired me in this line, the College of Staten

Island, CUNY. A class-conscious reorientation of Queer Studies responds to the question, What does the work of Queer Studies look like from the point of view of regional or mid/lower tier or unranked schools that occupy the margins of—or don't figure at all in—influential Queer Studies narratives and field assessments?[5] To answer that question requires queering the act of institutional historicization by writing a narrative that describes and evokes the "queer here" of schools such as CSI.

To historicize and conceptualize Poor Queer Studies at the College of Staten Island, in this chapter I construct a queer CSI archive that showcases the college's queer faculty, though always keeping staff and students closely in mind. It turns out that there is quite a lot to say about queer teaching and writing at CSI. Despite being a relatively young institution, with its earliest incarnation as Staten Island Community College appearing in 1955, CSI has a storied queer history. Before presenting that queer record, I want to highlight one of its key features, namely, that it exists. The force of this statement relies on the fact that the poor queer institutional record's very existence is surprising. It is unexpected or, to put it differently, the Queer Studies imagination casts about without landing at CSI. But why? That imaginative failure occurs at the intersection of class-based education, quirky location, and the proximate elsewhere of recognizable models of more cosmopolitan and well-resourced Queer Studies. Poor Queer Studies names a socioeconomic, geographical, and imaginative field relation. The goal of queerly historicizing CSI is not only to paint a detailed portrait of the place and its people, though that is a goal. The more important conceptual work of the chapter, work that I hope can be adapted to other contexts, is to defamiliarize Queer Studies along class lines and to suggest that class-inflected unrecognizability can offer a primary enabling heuristic. What does it mean for the trope and tool of class-based unrecognizability to serve as one's field guide?

Making Poor Queer Studies imaginable can be thought of as a methodological intervention, an effort to articulate the background logic for why and how one can and cannot write a book about Queer Studies from poor and working-class two-year and nonselective four-year institutions. To put that conceptual approach into practice, I adapt two interdisciplinary research methods, the queer narrative case study and queer archival practice. Eric Hartman identifies the queer utility of the narrative case study as a research method in clinical social work, arguing that "the capacity of the narrative case study to capture stories and allow for the unfolding of situated meanings, including the discontinuities between sexual and class identities ... , makes it an ideal method for queer inquiry."[6] In reconnecting sexuality and class, Hartman draws on the work of Yvette Taylor and Karen Krahulik, both of whom demonstrate the potential of case studies to produce fine-tuned disruptions of the ordinariness of what Taylor terms "stratifying homosexualities" or "(middle)class subjects [who] can speak in voices that are heard, achieving mobility, subject-hood and even 'ordinariness' which may not be all that queer."[7] Unlike Hartman, and like Taylor and Krahulik, I do not work in the clinical environment, but I find value in Hartman's idea that "the queer narrative case study [can] ... describe the non-normative phenomena of the case, provide analysis of the impact of normative cultural pressures on the queer subject, and show how meaning [is] made out of the liminal aspects of the case."[8] Reframing these thinkers for my own purposes, I turn from the individual to the institutional case, asking what meaning can be made by studying a place at the margins of Queer Studies.

By telling the story of CSI in granular detail, and by constructing a formal (if inevitably partial) record of queer work at the college, I hope to make good on the introduction's extravagant claim that CSI "is the queerest school I know," not simply by proving how queer CSI is but by explaining how knowing how queer CSI is has required new forms of queer knowledge production. In other words, the queer narrative case study doesn't simply illuminate a given or recognizable form of queerness that has yet to be recorded, but, rather, it provides a method for making queer-class knowledge recognizable even though that situation resists narrativization and recognition because of the specifics of the queer-class relations imminent there. A key lesson of this chapter is that the material hurdles that must be negotiated when doing the work of creating Poor Queer Studies transform into the epistemological hurdle of recognizing that creation as queer-class knowledge. The College of Staten Island is a case study in recognizing what Poor Queer Studies knows, and that it knows.

The first thing to know about CSI is that we do everything on a shoestring budget, or no budget at all, starved as we are by the CUNY system, the City of New York, and, primarily, the State of New York, as the CUNY budget is controlled by the governor's office and state officials in Albany, New York. In comparison to the rest of the colleges in the system, CSI is underfunded by about one-third, according to former English department chair Ashley Dawson.[9] A higher education budget is a thing, it seems, to be cut, and cut, and cut by governor after governor after governor. A budget sets a boundary, not only balancing dollars and cents but circumscribing the possibilities of achieving goals and visions that, in themselves, are not bounded by money. When the distance between the vision and the budget becomes too great, the vision falters while the slashed budget remains. If a vision is outlandish, it will falter in the face of a reasonable budget. But CSI's admirable visions are not outlandish. The problem is that our budget is not reasonable, though with repetition (cut, cut, cut) the unreasonable masquerades as the reasonable. Austerity names the normalization of this process. In this way, expectations shrink or, as often happens at CSI, visions begin to sound like empty rhetoric. Or, perversely, our hard-earned achievements are used as evidence to make the case that we can succeed without resources. Our achievements are, stupidly, taken as proof that education can be built on air. That is not what our achievements prove.

Throughout this book, I connect the evidence of being a woefully underfunded, even poor school to the curricular and disciplinary work of Queer Studies done on a shoestring. Our queer work happens among our other work, within a context of deprivation. At the CSI English department's 2018 commencement ceremony, the student speaker offered a clear and compelling thesis. His big idea, the first and most important point he wanted to make in the spotlight of his parting address, was this: CSI needs to fix the heating and air conditioning. Freezing and sweating through years of classes seems to have left a strong impression on him about how to improve higher education. When a smart student from a poor college connects learning to the physical environment in these terms, he reveals the shortsightedness of debates in higher education about consumer students or pampered students or sensitive students—a favorite preoccupation of Rich Queer Studies. He draws us back to the reality of the vending machine dinner, not the new recreation center or fancy dorms or the question of doing queer work "in the community," all of which speak not only to the ways the built environment of rich schools structures thought at those schools but also to the ways that those thoughts get transposed from provincial hieroglyph to the lingua franca of Queer Studies.

The City University of New York is broke, and this fact is more important to Queer Studies as a field than the creation of a Queer Studies professorship at either CSI or at Columbia. Students at CUNY's Brooklyn (a.k.a. "Brokelyn") College and Queens College, two of the system's most prized institutions, document their deteriorating campuses on social media (@cuny_brokelyn_college and @cunyqueensneedschange). I strongly encourage readers to view these Instagram accounts immediately, as the conditions they expose beggar description. They not only show how defunding looks but also suggest how it smells. These documentary efforts have gained the attention of the press, yet budgets stagnate under Governor Andrew Cuomo and his hand-picked

CUNY board of trustees.[10] One of the largest university systems in the U.S. and, by virtue of its geography, home to an unparalleled queer density in higher education, CUNY is falling apart. But Queer Studies seems not to know how important this fact is. To put this differently, Queer Studies seems not to appreciate how queer ideas dissipate—how they are sweated and shivered away—at precisely the places where queer experience saturates education and should robustly inform the production of the field. One goal of this book is to piece together the story of why that queer lesson, though it isn't new, hasn't taken root and flowered as a broad queer disciplinary concern.

To Not Be Choosy

I began this chapter with Larry Mitchell because of my extraordinary personal discovery of having followed him from rural Indiana to Poor Queer Studies at CSI. But the work of methodically following Queer Studies out of fashion requires a broader historical view and, as I explore further, an archival practice. A special place in that archive belongs to two CSI English professors, Arnie Kantrowitz and Judith P. Stelboum, who were longtime colleagues and who characterized themselves as family in their coauthored chapter, "A Date with Judith," published in *Sister and Brother: Lesbians and Gay Men Write about Their Lives Together*. In 1973, Kantrowitz offered a course titled Homosexuals and Literature at Staten Island Community College (which would merge in 1976 with CUNY's short-lived experimental upper-division Richmond College to form CSI). Kantrowitz, who retired from the college after forty-one years of teaching (1965–2006) and whose office I now occupy, published an analysis of his Homosexuals and Literature class in *College English* in 1974.[11] He wrote, "Calling an English elective 'Homosexuals and Literature' was calculated to arch a few eyebrows at Staten Island Community College. . . . The main result of the course title was that we were a small but hardy group, and a totally gay one. The one professed heterosexual who appeared the first day never returned in spite of an almost effusive effort to make her feel welcome."[12] This "totally gay" community college class was one of the first gay studies courses offered anywhere.[13]

When my deeply supportive and proactive colleague Maryann Feola arranged a dinner with her dear friend Arnie (who cofounded the Gay and Lesbian Alliance Against Defamation, or GLAAD, and served as vice president of the Gay Activists Alliance, or GAA) and his partner, Larry Mass (who cofounded the Gay Men's Health Crisis), I learned that Arnie was not alone teaching queer-themed literature in the English department. His longtime colleague and friend Judith P. Stelboum, who for years edited the *Harrington Park Lesbian Fiction Quarterly*, taught courses in lesbian literature at Staten Island Community College during the same period and, crucially, designed and taught the first "woman's course" at the college in the spring of 1971 or 1972. These courses were offered in the years immediately following the Stonewall riots and the formation of visible gay activist groups including the Gay Liberation Front and GAA. They also came on the heels of CUNY's implementation of an open admissions policy and a (brief) period of free tuition for all, changes demanded and won through protests led by black and Puerto Rican students in the late 1960s. The Search for Education, Elevation, and Knowledge (SEEK) Program, the nation's first "opportunity program," had been founded at CUNY in 1966, and Audre Lorde was helping to found Black Studies from a lesbian feminist perspective at CUNY's John Jay College. In these queer, raced, and gendered contexts, Kantrowitz and Stelboum offered Staten Island Community College's white working-class students—and white working-class queers—courses in women's studies and gay and lesbian studies, fields that were just finding their names.

An antielitist, class-conscious, liberation vision of education grounded the early feminist and queer classes at Staten Island Community College. Kantrowitz argues forcefully that "seen in an academic context, the relationship of such seemingly disparate forces as gay liberation and education becomes clear. Educators, like homosexuals and other groups, have begun to define education according to what it is we do rather than by acting out the traditionally prescribed professorial role. It is a shift from the prescription of frustratingly unreachable ideals and confining stereotypes to the description of working realities."[14] Stelboum reflects on that first woman's studies course in her 1972 essay, "Woman's Studies at a Community College: A Personal View," writing, "My experience as student and a teacher leads me to believe that to encourage competition, to support intellectual elitism, is antithetical to everything that one wants to achieve in a successful woman's course.... To continue such an elitism based on class and intellect is to destroy the sense of solidarity that is necessary for the women's movement if it is to succeed in changing our society, in a personal and social sense, for women and inevitably for men too."[15] Accept all, serve all. For a few years in the early 1970s, this was the CUNY mission put into practice, imperfectly, to be sure, but in ways that democratized the student body in terms of class, race, ethnicity, gender, and, crucially, sexuality. Professors, and perhaps especially community college professors, were able to attend to those students once they were in the classroom by engaging them in what we might, from today's perspective, call anti-neoliberal pedagogies: teaching and learning in the context of activist social movements, public funding for all, and non-individualistic approaches to knowledge production.[16]

Stelboum's rejection of intellectual competition and Kantrowitz's openness to teaching all students in his gay studies classes reflect a broader, historical, justice-oriented, queer ethos of many CSI educators. In a nutshell, elitist education is bad education. That sounds too simple, so I'll put it differently. When we're choosy about whom we teach, we limit learning. Once more: class segregation in the university limits the sphere of influence of thinkers from lower classes, even as it expands the sphere of influence of thinkers from upper classes, whose thinking masquerades as all there is to learn in the academy. That's bad education. An ethos of expanded thinking and learning—open admissions—has roots in CUNY history but also, at CSI, in the college's unique physical and psychic geographies. The sole public institution of higher education in the borough, CSI must offer both two-year and four-year undergraduate degrees by state decree. Such institutions used to be called comprehensive colleges. Now CSI is identified by CUNY as one of the senior colleges in the system, a nominal shift about which many in the campus community are skeptical, as the new designation attempts to more explicitly differentiate four-year institutions from the community colleges. But we educate all comers at CSI. Because CUNY's two-year colleges must have an open admissions policy, and because CSI offers two-year degrees, CSI has by default a 100 percent acceptance rate even for students seeking admission for the bachelor's degree, provided the applicant has either graduated high school or will have earned a high school equivalency diploma before matriculation at CSI. With a 100 percent admission rate, we can't be choosy at CSI, which gives us the chance to see the dramatic benefits of not being choosy.

From today's Queer Studies perspective, the pedagogies that were exploding at CUNY in the early 1970s may seem radical rather than unfashionable. But to the extent that Queer Studies makes its way within and through places of institutional elitism, Kantrowitz's and Stelboum's antielitist principles and, more to the point, their actual workerly intellectual practices run directly counter to Queer Studies at its bought-and-paid-for best. Though Rich Queer Studies often claims radicality, the choosiness of selective colleges in fact limits the radical potential of elite education to enact class and race equality. Perhaps Rich Queer Studies can be both radical and elitist. We might, at the least, insist that claims to the former do not cancel out the latter.

I heard a version of the following anecdote three times as I wrote this book (all three instances were unprompted by me). A professor from a Rich

Queer Studies school is busy sorting through applications by students petitioning to join the professor's Queer Studies class. These are not applications to the highly selective/elite colleges at which the professors teach, but rather they are applications to a class. These students have already made the cut and matriculated, against the long odds of their schools' much-touted low acceptance rates or thanks to legacy admissions. I don't have more information about how the three professors made their selections, and I am not arguing that their choices were unfair. They might have selected the poorest of the bunch (and knowing two of them, I wouldn't be surprised to learn of their thoughtful, class-conscious decision making). Rather, at issue is the fact that they were choosing at all. More than mere administrative busywork, the extra labor of sorting out potential Queer Studies students from each other suggests the presence of a regime of unending evaluation at gatekeeper colleges. Competition, hoop-jumping, ass-kissing, and proof of belonging comingle to create a barrier to Queer Studies knowledge—even for the students who, once again, make the cut. In this environment, strategically working one's way into a professor's presence (i.e., glomming on) becomes a tactic of being a good student, of progressing, of being on the inside of Queer Studies. Of being quite literally in the room. Being chosen and rewarded may well prove damaging to the students unlucky enough to be caught up in such systems of constant competition. Nevertheless, the learned protocols of endless proving constitute a kind of knowledge practice, one inculcated and ingrained precisely as academic protocol at sites of intellectual competition and among already winnowed (disproportionately wealthy) students. In this way the voice of what we might, at our most judicious, call "academic wherewithal" ventriloquizes the voice of class and status distinction, altering it just enough to render bald-faced elitism as savvy professionalism. We might venture that the field of Queer Studies is not foreign to its initiates primarily due to its language being overly technical or its concepts too theoretical. Students learn completely foreign languages all the time. Perhaps Queer Studies is foreign to some because, as a professional qualification, the field insists that its students, like its most well-placed practitioners, speak in its terms of distinction.[17] Students educated outside of privileged systems of education do not learn to compete-speak in these ways. Faculty who are educating students outside of privileged systems of education understand, thanks to their students and their faculty forerunners, how terribly fashionable those competition-driven protocols are.

Unfortunately, the trend within undergraduate education at CUNY, a system of eleven senior colleges and seven community colleges, mirrors larger shifts in higher education. The year 1999 marked a dark return, a renewed commitment by the university to a new version of its pre-1971 racial elitism. In the last two decades, CUNY leadership's decisions about resources, admissions, and publicity reflect the prioritization of a small handful of CUNY schools (Brooklyn, Queens, City, Hunter, and sometimes Baruch) over the majority, including all of the community colleges. The system has become in that time more internally divided along race and class lines. A controversial 2015 article in *The Atlantic*, which the authors revised after blowback from CUNY, tracks the data:

> Since it went through an aggressive, system-wide overhaul that began in 2000, the City University of New York's top five colleges—Baruch, Hunter, Brooklyn, Queens, and City—have been raising admission standards and enrolling fewer freshmen from New York City high schools. Among the results has been the emergence of a progressively starker two-tier system: CUNY's most prestigious colleges now increasingly favor Asian and white freshmen, while the system's black and Latino students end up more and more in its overcrowded two-year community colleges.... This race disparity within the CUNY system widened most noticeably after the 2008 recession, when CUNY's bargain tuition rates began drawing more middle-class families. Applications surged. That same year, CUNY increased its math SAT admission requirement 20 to 30 points for the five highly selective colleges. Department of Education records show that by 2012, the number of black public high school students enrolled as freshmen into the system's top five colleges had decreased by 42 percent. Latinos dropped by 26 percent.[18]

Meanwhile, enrollment of black and Hispanic students at the open-admissions two- and four-year CSI has been on the rise. Since 2008, undergraduate black student enrollment has increased from 11.9 to 13.9 percent of total enrollment and Hispanic enrollment has increased from 14.6 to 26.5 percent of total enrollment. The percentage of Asian/Pacific Islanders has risen from 10.5 to 11.1, while the enrollment of white students in relation to total enrollment has fallen from 62.5 to 43.6 percent.[19] Demographic changes on Staten Island, in part the result of people of color being gentrified out of Brooklyn, have driven some of these shifts at CSI. But one relatively hidden contributing factor is much more practical. In 2008, CSI began direct shuttle bus service from the Staten Island Ferry Terminal to the college, streamlining the commute from other boroughs to the campus. This has allowed students from people-of-color-majority boroughs to make their way to an open-admissions college that had previously been much less accessible by public transportation—and much whiter. An open-admissions policy combined with improved access has enabled CSI to buck the trend of race and class elitism at some other senior CUNY colleges. My point is that the pattern of choosy schools undermining democratic education can be identified at different scales across higher education, including within CUNY. As I argue in chapter 2, this trend is driven from the top.

The Interruptive Archive of Poor Queer Studies

Meeting Poor Queer Studies on its unfashionable, open-access, lower-tier terms requires patience and sustained attention. Recognition takes time. Poor Queer Studies' apparent incoherence looks, ironically, like a failure to do Queer Studies right. It looks like an effortful approximation of Queer Studies, a rough translation of the class-unencumbered field "Queer Studies." The incoherence of Poor Queer Studies at CSI forces us, in turn, to ask coherence-producing questions, ones that make sense of the fact that we're asking queer questions here. The question is not, How is queer theory best taught? The question is certainly not, Are these (kinds of) students capable of learning queer theory? Rather, Poor Queer Studies asks, How do we teach queer theory to our students, who work for money full-time and take night class? That's a great question. Every teacher should ask their version of this class-conscious question.

Unfortunately, Rich Queer Studies professors, who have been given the responsibility and the privilege of defining the field, often do not frame their work in this way. Rich Queer Studies is at a disadvantage here. Because its ideas and practices are easiest to see, they are also easiest to criticize for this sleight of hand, this will to generality. A random example is Kyla Wazana Tompkins's excellent pedagogy essay, "We Aren't Here to Learn What We Already Know," which appeared in *Avidly*, an "independent channel of the *Los Angeles Review of Books*."[20] Under the heading Some Notes on How to Ask a Good Question about Theory That Will Provoke Conversation and Further Discussion from Your Colleagues, Tompkins offers a list of recommendations. I find this list to be incredibly thoughtful, and I distribute it in my classes. But I've learned to make one seemingly minor, hand-written amendment. The section heading should read, Some Notes on How to Ask a Good Question about Theory That Will Provoke Conversation and Further Discussion from Your *Elite* Colleagues. A small edit, but if I spell out the meaning of that revision we can see a miniature example of the larger problem Queer Studies has created for itself. Tompkins's contribution is aimed most directly, though unmarkedly, at students and professors who, like her, are aligned with rich colleges where students don't have to work for money or take care of children or parents. The price of tuition, fees, and room and board at Pomona College, where Tompkins works, was $69,496 for the 2018–19 school year. Her advice for teaching theory grows from her experience of teaching in that place over an extended time period. Three of the first six bullet points of pedagogical advice presume that students generally possess that most important of intellectual gifts, surplus time. "Read theory three times," the student is told. Bullet point three advises, "Take a break." Bullet point five instructs student to "linger over passages." And who could argue with these prompts and pointers? I invite you to attend a class at CSI when I read these bullet points out loud. You will hear silence, the sound of disconnection. Or you will hear laughter, the sound of class solidarity. These instructions are the tools of Rich Queer Studies, but they are published as general advice. Because Tompkins offers so much good advice, it may not occur to us (or it may seem small of us) to sort out the class dynamics of the piece.

Chapter 2 takes up a handful of other examples of the ways generalizing from the top of the academic hierarchy imposes a false logic of upward mobility onto Queer Studies. Divorced from its privileged contexts, unmarked Queer Studies becomes something we can all, supposedly, do. This logic demotes what Poor Queer Studies professors and students are actually doing to something other than Queer Studies, a translation of the original, a poor man's copy. But how to not be a bad copy—a classic queer question remade as a queer-class question. A poor queer institutional archive offers a formal, unfashionable solution to the problem of copying, which is the problem of the incoherence of poverty. The Poor Queer Studies archive of this chapter not only collects data but also arranges it in provincial, even plodding ways that slow down rather than speed up the field and in doing so interrupt the misrecognizing imperative of Rich Queer Studies. What follows is the interruptive queer archive of CSI.

The College of Staten Island has the second-oldest women's studies major program in the country and one of the oldest women's centers, named after Professor Bertha Harris, author of the noted experimental lesbian novel *Lover* (1976). Marlene Springer, though she was judicious in her decisions about how and where to be out professionally, was president of CSI from 1994 to 2007, a period that saw the college increase its academic standards while remaining open-admissions and initiate the transition from a five-year to a seven-year tenure clock. In the thirteen years that I have been at the college (since 2007), two of our three provosts have been out gay men, the previous one for the first time in his professional life. As he publicly remarked during his keynote at the college's 2017 Lavender Graduation ceremony, his decision to be out and visible at work was based largely on CSI opening that possibility up to him in a viable way. In that same time period, four deans of the humanities and social sciences, a position that oversees more than half of the college faculty, have been queer (two gay men, two lesbians). Other top administrators are openly gay and lesbian. At CSI, putting all of this in writing, here, is not a punishable offense. It is my job.

It gets better. CSI has out staff members in offices throughout campus, many of whom work in primarily student-facing jobs and in leadership roles. In fact, our queer staff members are some of the most active LGBTQ advocates on campus. Though the college has lost valuable LGBTQ staff to retirement, we have or recently had an out Arab American lesbian director of academic support, an out lesbian director of the Office of Student Life, an out lesbian staff member in Veterans Support Services, an out Latina lesbian director of the SEEK Program, out queer librarians and library staff members, out queer staff members in Student and Enrollment Services as well as in College Testing, in the Counseling Center, and as part of individual departmental staff. Finally, we have a truly incredible out gay coordinator of the LGBTQ Resource Center, Jeremiah Jurkiewicz. The ever-growing Resource Center occupies dedicated space thanks to the institutional savvy and determination of many, foremost out lesbian Dr. Christine Flynn Saulnier.

From year to year, CSI has approximately thirty faculty on our "out list," compiled and publicized so that students can find discipline-specific academic support.[21] Of course, many queer faculty do not make it onto this opt-in list, and not all queer faculty are out. In a 2016 Campus Climate Survey conducted by Rankin and Associates Consulting, 41 faculty out of a total of 308 faculty respondents indicated that they identified as LGBQ, Asexual, or (non-Heterosexual) Other.[22] My own estimate, having invested a significant amount of time in reaching out to the campus community in my formal role as the Queer Studies professor and for two years in the role of director of the Women's, Gender, and Sexuality Studies program, is that approximately 10 percent of CSI's 360 tenure-track faculty are out as queer at work. By any of the above measures, CSI would seem to have more out queer faculty members than other CUNY campuses. Knowing, to a reasonable degree, the number of out faculty and staff allows CSI and CUNY to do a certain kind work. Visibility helps students find us, and it promotes an easy queer collegiality. It's nice relating by way of queerness with other members of the campus community, backward or boring as that may sound. Queer visibility at CSI, with the support of the administration, has also enabled CSI to initiate and sustain broader LGBTQ organizing, as when our campus founded the CUNY-wide Queer Faculty and Staff Working Group in 2012, thanks largely to the vision of my colleague, queer theory and cinema scholar David Gerstner. With the backing of the broad Working Group network, individual members have very effectively engaged with CUNY administrators to implement policies that improve the lives of LGBTQ students, faculty, and staff across the system. Visibility, grassroots organizing, and faculty and staff out lists provide invaluable empirical evidence of queerness at CSI and CUNY. Nevertheless, while quantification can give us a queer measure of a campus, it doesn't always tell what that measure means.

One thing visibility means for queer faculty and staff is that we are not merely seen but are looked to—by each other, by students, by the administration—and asked to engage. Many of us therefore understand part of our jobs to be contributing to the queer life of the college in extracurricular ways. While some staff members' job descriptions explicitly include campus diversity work, many do not. Yet queer staff consistently participate in LGBTQ programming, including semesterly coming out panels, queer student orientation or Pride Kamp, and Lavender Graduation. Like all faculty, queer faculty are required to perform service work at the departmental and campus-wide level, and we do. But queer faculty at CSI, like women and faculty of color at the college, tend to do extra service work, a pattern that holds across higher education. The roster of recent queer events and programs that faculty have organized, participated in, raised funds for, taken classes to, publicized, sponsored, and volunteered for would take more words than I can devote here to that record. I want to recognize, however, that in 2019 CSI celebrated its third annual lecture in Black Queer Studies, and that each year the event has been standing room only.[23] At times, queer campus service work takes more hours per week than teaching, though service work ebbs and flows while coursework remains fairly consistent. Problematically, at a commuter school, queer-related service work and the product of that work are easily overlooked. Students and faculty alike have little opportunity to happen upon events randomly, as our commutes are precisely timed. Many events are held at night or during twice-weekly club hours, when multiple activities and meetings compete for community members' time, crowding each other out. Yet together, faculty, staff, and students have worked to sustain extracurricular opportunities for queer learning and engagement. An important larger meaning emerges: at CSI our queer work has adapted to the class-based temporalities of coming and going. As chapters 3 and 4 explore further, that adaptation takes on important meaning for student workers, who rush between their jobs and school, and for students who live with their parents and siblings and who bring their queer educations back into their family homes.

I have argued that public lists of out queer administrators, staff, and faculty and the extracurricular programming on campus contribute to the queer energies that sustain the LGBTQ community at CSI. We might understand that data as part of a living queer archive, a collection of events and interactions that can be caught up in the historical record but that were most meaningful in the moment. A living queer archive has local purpose and local value, and while such a record falls rather flat on the page, it is nevertheless important as the basis for reconstructing its lived meanings, even if only for those CSI community members who lived or followed that history.

But a Queer *Studies* archive will inevitably privilege scholarship, creative work, and teaching, the prongs of higher education identified with knowledge production, aesthetic inquiry, and their pedagogical relays. Though it is unlike the more ephemeral, on-the-ground queer archive of campus programming and service, a Queer Studies archive nevertheless reflects the conditions of its production. Specifically, the intellectual and creative work of CSI faculty, as well as the kinds of explorations our campus pedagogies enact, become meaningful as a class-based Queer Studies archive that is easily overlooked or misrecognized.

Creating a recognizable Poor Queer Studies archive raises questions about formatting. In scholarly books, lists and detailed data sets are often partitioned off in appendixes. Changed to endnotes, footnotes become separated from the context of the prose that they are meant to illuminate. Acknowledgments float thin in the frontmatter as bibliographies sit heavy in the backmatter. The body of a book contains its argument and examples that together create its narrative, which citation should only judiciously interrupt. Given these standard, formal protocols, a problem arises in the present chapter. I want to foreground Queer Studies scholarship at CSI, yet bibliographies are backgrounded as a matter of formatting. If it is to be seen and conceptualized, a Poor Queer Studies reference list cannot be normatively located but rather needs to be produced within and as the text of my argument. The formal interruption is fundamental to the argument it appears to interrupt. More problematic still, bibliographies—including the one at the end of this book—have a way of hiding the names we don't look for, don't know to look for, and don't recognize. The bibliographic trip from *A* to *Z* not only draws our attention to landmark scholars but requires us to reproduce those landmarks as signs that we've learned the scholarly terrain. The bibliography below, even in its abridged form, is meant to interrupt the practice by which Poor Queer Studies dissipates when collected and coded as alphabetized, landmarked backmatter. The works I cite now, in advance of the traditional bibliography, do not interrupt our ability to learn the story of Poor Queer Studies. Rather, they are the listy evidence of the existence of such a story. By including a queer CSI bibliography here, I hope to break both form and the scholarly habit of mis/underrecognizing Poor Queer Studies authors and texts. Here is what we've been up to at CSI:[24]

Jillian Báez, Assistant Professor of Media Culture

"Structurelessness 2.0." *WSQ: Women's Studies Quarterly* 41, no. 3 (December 6, 2013): 253–56. https://doi.org/10.1353/wsq.2013.0082.

"Towards a Latinidad Feminista: The Multiplicities of Latinidad and Feminism in Contemporary Cinema." *Popular Communication* 5, no. 2 (June 2007): 109–28. https://doi.org/10.1080/15405700701294079.

Matt Brim, Associate Professor of Queer Studies

"After Queer Baldwin." In *After Queer Studies: Literature, Theory and Sexuality in the 21st Century*, edited by Tyler Bradway and E. L. McCallum, 87–101. New York: Cambridge University Press, 2019.

"*Counternarratives*: A Black Queer Reader." In *Imagining Queer Methods*. New York: New York University Press, 2019.

With Amin Ghaziani, eds. *Imagining Queer Methods*. New York: New York University Press, 2019.

"Poor Queer Studies: Class, Race, and the Field." *Journal of Homosexuality* (November 7, 2018): 1–19. https://doi.org/10.1080/00918369.2018.1534410.

With Melissa Maldanado-Salcedo. Review of *LGBTQ Politics: A Critical Reader*, edited by Marla Brettschneider, Susan Burgess, and Christine Keating. *Teachers College Record*, 2018.

With Cynthia Chris. "Editors' Notes." *WSQ: Women's Studies Quarterly* 42, nos. 3–4 through 45, nos. 1–2 (fall/winter 2014 through spring/summer 2017).

With Amin Ghaziani, eds. "Queer Methods." Special issue, *WSQ: Women's Studies Quarterly* 44, nos. 3–4 (fall/winter 2016).

James Baldwin and the Queer Imagination. Ann Arbor: University of Michigan Press, 2014.

"Larry Mitchell: Novelist of New York Gay Life." Obituary. *Gay and Lesbian Review Worldwide* 20, no. 3 (2013): 11.

"Queer Pedagogical Desire: A Study Guide." *WSQ: Women's Studies Quarterly* 41, nos. 3–4 (fall/winter 2013): 173–89.

"*United in Anger: A History of ACT UP Study Guide*." Online educational resource (55 manuscript pages). *United in Anger* [documentary film]. Dir. Jim Hubbard. March 2013. http://www.unitedinanger.com/?page_id=808.

"Edmund White and Rakesh Satyal Headline First Kessler Conversation of the Year." *CLAGS (Center for Lesbian and Gay Studies) Newsletter*, spring 2012, 6.

"James Baldwin's Queer Utility." *ANQ: A Journal of Short Articles, Notes, and Reviews* 24, no. 4 (2011): 209–16.

With Amin Ghaziani. "The Problems with 'Post-gay.'" *Sexual Behavior, Politics, and Communities Division Newsletter of the Society for the Study of Social Problems*, fall 2011, 2–3, 8–9.

"Larry Mitchell, Novelist of the Dispossessed." Interview. *Gay and Lesbian Review Worldwide* 16, no. 4 (2009): 34–35.

"Teaching the Touching Text; or, How to Lay 'Hands' on Your Students." In *The Hand of the Interpreter: Essays on Meaning after Theory*, edited by G. F. Mitrano and Eric Jarosinski, 135–50. Cultural Interactions: Studies in the Relationships between the Arts, ser. 3. New York: Peter Lang, 2009.

"The LGBTQ Short Story." In *LGBTQ America Today*, edited by John Hawley, 1131–37. Westport, CT: Greenwood, 2008.

"Papas' Baby: Impossible Paternity in *Going to Meet the Man*." *Journal of Modern Literature* 30, no. 1 (2006): 173–98.

Cynthia Chris, Professor of Media Culture

With Matt Brim. "Editors' Notes." *WSQ: Women's Studies Quarterly* 42, nos. 3–4 through 45, nos. 1–2 (fall/winter 2014 through spring/summer 2017).

With David A. Gerstner, eds. "Engage!" Special issue, *WSQ: Women's Studies Quarterly* 41, nos. 3–4 (winter 2013). https://doi.org/10.1353/wsq.2013.0073.

ACT UP/NY Women and AIDS Book Group. *Women, AIDS, and Activism*. Boston: South End, 1999.

Kathleen M. Cumiskey

"Marriage Equality." In *Encyclopedia of Critical Psychology*, edited by Thomas Teo. New York: Springer-Verlag, 2014.

Rafael de la Dehesa, Associate Professor of Sociology/Anthropology

"NGOs, Governmentality, and the Brazilian Response to AIDS: A Multistranded Genealogy of the Current Crisis." *Feminist Studies* 43, no. 2 (2017): 262–90.

With Ananya Mukherjea. "Building Capacities and Producing Citizens: The
Biopolitics of HIV Prevention in Brazil." *Contemporary Politics* 18, no. 2
(2012): 186–99.

*Queering the Public Sphere in Mexico and Brazil: Sexual Rights Movements in
Emerging Democracies*. Durham, NC: Duke University Press, 2010.

David Gerstner, Professor of Cinema Studies

Queer Screens. Series editor. Wayne State University Press.

"Strange Days: Christophe Honoré's Multimedia Trilogy." *Cinéaste* 44, no. 2 (spring
2019): Web Exclusive.

"Queer Film." In *The Palgrave Handbook of the Philosophy of Film and Motion
Pictures*, edited by Noël Carroll, Laura Teresa Di Summa-Knoop, and Shawn
Loht. New York: Palgrave Macmillan, 2018.

"The Boys in the City: Disintegration, Transformation, and Cinematic Texture in
William Friedkin's New York City Films (1970–1980)." In *The Boys in the Band*,
edited by Matt Bell, 163–89. Detroit: Wayne State University Press, 2016.

With Julien Nahmias. *Christophe Honoré: A Critical Introduction.* Contemporary
Approaches to Film and Media Series. Detroit: Wayne State University Press,
2015.

"Choreographing Homosexual Desire in Philippe Vallois's *Johan.*" *Camera Obscura:
Feminism, Culture, and Media Studies* 28, no. 3 (84) (2013): 125–57.

With Cynthia Chris, eds. "Engage!" Special issue, *WSQ: Women's Studies Quarterly*
41, no. 3 (2013). https://doi.org/10.1353/wsq.2013.0073.

Queer Pollen: White Seduction, Black Male Homosexuality, and the Cinematic. New
Black Studies Series. Urbana: University of Illinois Press, 2011.

"Christophe Honoré's *Les chansons d'amour* and the Musical's Queer-abilities."
In *The Sound of Musicals*, edited by Steven Cohan, 188–99. London: BFI/
Macmillan-Palgrave, 2010.

"Queer Modernism: The Cinematic Aesthetic of Vincente Minnelli." Revised and
reprinted in *Vincente Minnelli: The Art of Entertainment*, edited by Joe
McElhaney, 252–74. Detroit: Wayne State University Press, 2009.

"Turned Inside/Out: Violent Inversions of Heterosexuality in Vincente Minnelli's
Home from the Hill." In *Hetero*, edited by Sean Griffin, 111–28. Albany: State
University of New York Press, 2009.

"De Profundis: A Love Letter from the Inside Man." In *The Spike Lee Reader*, edited
by Paula J. Massood, 243–53. Philadelphia: Temple University Press, 2008.

"Queer Internationale: Pedagogy and Modes of Cultural Production in the Twenty-
First Century." In *21st-Century Gay Culture*, edited by David Powell, 85–94.
Newcastle, UK: Cambridge Scholars, 2008.

"Can't Take My Eyes Off of You: Andy Warhol Records/Is New York." In *City That Never Sleeps*, edited by Murray Pomerance, 90–101. New Brunswick, NJ: Rutgers University Press, 2007.

"Queer Turns: The Cinematic Friendship of Marcel Duchamp and Charles Demuth." In *Marcel Duchamp and Eroticism*, edited by Marc Décimo, 105–15. Newcastle, UK: Cambridge Scholars, 2007.

"Ricordi! Peter Wells, Memories of a Queer Land." In *New Zealand Filmmakers*, edited by Ian Conrich and Stuart Murray, 121–33. Detroit: Wayne State University Press, 2007.

Manly Arts: Masculinity and Nation in Early American Cinema. Durham, NC: Duke University Press, 2006.

Ed. *The Routledge International Encyclopedia of Queer Culture*. London: Routledge, 2006.

"Dancer from the Dance: Gene Kelly, Television, and the Beauty of Movement." *Velvet Light Trap*, 2002, 48–67.

"Unsinkable Masculinity: The Artist and the Work of Art in James Cameron's 'Titanic.'" *Cultural Critique*, no. 50 (2002): 1–22.

"Queer Modernism: The Cinematic Aesthetic of Vincente Minnelli." *Modernity* 2 (2000). http://castle.eiu.edu/~modernity/modernity-1999.html.

"'Other and Different Scenes': Oscar Micheaux's Bodies and the Cinematic Cut." *Wide Angle* 21, no. 4 (October 1999 [2004]): 6–19.

"Queer Angels of History Take It and Leave It from Behind." *Stanford Humanities Review* 7, no. 2 (autumn 1999): 150–65.

"The Production and Display of the Closet: Making Minnelli's *Tea and Sympathy*." *Film Quarterly (ARCHIVE)* 50, no. 3 (1997): 13.

Jean Halley, Professor of Sociology

Horse Crazy: Girls and the Lives of Horses. Athens: University of Georgia Press, 2019.

With Amy Eshleman. *Seeing Straight: An Introduction to Gender and Sexual Privilege*. Lanham, MD: Rowman and Littlefield, 2017.

Boundaries of Touch: Parenting and Adult-Child Intimacy. Champaign: University of Illinois Press, 2007.

Anne Hays, Assistant Professor and Instruction Librarian

"A Question of Space: Surveying Student Usage of LGBTQ Resources in the LGBTQ Student Center Library and the Campus Library." *New Review of Academic Librarianship*, January 10, 2019, 1–14. https://doi.org/10.1080/13614533.2018.1564336.

"Reading the Margins: Embedded Narratives in Feminist Personal Zines." *Journal of Popular Culture* 50, no. 1 (2017): 86–108.

Darryl Hill, Professor of Psychology

"Sexual Admissions: An Intersectional Analysis of Certifications and Residency at Willowbrook State School (1950–1985)." *Sexuality and Disability* 34, no. 2 (June 2016): 103–29. https://doi.org/10.1007/s11195-016-9434-z.

Trans Toronto: An Oral History. New York: William Rodney, 2012.

With Edgardo Menvielle, Kristin M. Sica, and Alisa Johnson. "An Affirmative Intervention for Families with Gender Variant Children: Parental Ratings of Child Mental Health and Gender." *Journal of Sex and Marital Therapy* 36, no. 1 (2010): 6–23.

"A Method for the Margins: A Trans Feminist Oral History." In *Handbook of Research with Lesbian, Gay, Bisexual and Transgender Populations*, edited by William Meezan and James I. Martin. New York: Routledge, 2009.

With Edgardo Menvielle. "'You Have to Give Them a Place Where They Feel Protected and Safe and Loved': The Views of Parents Who Have Gender-Variant Children and Adolescents." *Journal of LGBT Youth* 6, nos. 2–3 (2009): 243–71.

"Dear Doctor Benjamin: Letters from Transsexual Youth (1963–1976)." *International Journal of Transgenderism* 10, nos. 3–4 (2008): 149–70.

"Differences and Similarities in Men's and Women's Sexual Self-Schemas." *Journal of Sex Research* 44, no. 2 (2007): 135–44.

"'Feminine' Heterosexual Men: Subverting Heteropatriarchal Sexual Scripts?" *Journal of Men's Studies* 14, no. 2 (2007): 145–59.

"Gender Identity Disorders in Childhood and Adolescence: A Critical Inquiry." *International Journal of Sexual Health* 19, no. 1 (2007): 57–75.

"Gender Identity Disorders in Childhood and Adolescence: A Critical Inquiry." *Journal of Psychology and Human Sexuality* 17, nos. 3–4 (2006): 7–34.

"On the Origins of Gender." In *Trans/Forming Feminisms: Trans-Feminist Voices Speak Out*, edited by Krista Scott-Dixon, 39–45. Toronto: Sumach Press, 2006.

With Brian L. B. Willoughby. "The Development and Validation of the Genderism and Transphobia Scale." *Sex Roles* 53, no. 7 (October 1, 2005): 531–44. https://doi.org/10.1007/s11199-005-7140-x.

"Coming to Terms: Using Technology to Know Identity." *Sexuality and Culture* 9, no. 3 (2005): 24–52.

"Sexuality and Gender in Hirschfeld's *Die Transvestiten*: A Case of the 'Elusive Evidence of the Ordinary.'" *Journal of the History of Sexuality* 14, no. 3 (2005): 316–32.

"Trans/Gender/Sexuality: A Research Agenda." *Journal of Gay and Lesbian Social Services* 18, no. 2 (2005): 101–9.

"Female Masculinity." Book Review. *Journal of Men's Studies* 10, no. 2 (winter 2002): 237.

"Genderism, Transphobia, and Gender Bashing: A Framework for Interpreting Anti-transgender Violence." *Understanding and Dealing with Violence: A Multicultural Approach* 4 (2002): 113–37.

Tara Mateik, Associate Professor of Media Culture

SOLO EXHIBITIONS, PERFORMANCES, AND SCREENINGS

Heavy Lifting, Starting from Scratch. Handwerker Gallery, Ithaca College, Ithaca, NY (2015).

Valley of the Dolls Ladies' Wardrobe ScreenTest (Judy Garland). Morbid Anatomy Museum Brooklyn, NY (2015).

Army of Revolt, Strange Bedfellows: Collaborative Practice in Queer Art. Ithaca College, Ithaca, NY (2014).

Friends of Dorothy. Segal Theater, Center for the Humanities, Graduate Center, CUNY, New York (2013).

Putting the Balls Away, performance. Film and Electronic Arts Program, Bard College, Annandale-on-Hudson, NY (2012).

Unauthorized Interview (*Live from Studio 54*, 1977–82). Extended Remix, 2012, 30 min. On Location Participant Inc., New York (2012).

SELECTED EXHIBITIONS, PERFORMANCES, AND SCREENINGS

Toilet Training. List Projects: Civil Disobedience. MIT List Visual Arts Center, Cambridge, MA (2017).

Making It Easier on Yourself (installation) and *Making It Harder on Yourself* (installation). Starting from Scratch, Handwerker Gallery, Ithaca College, Ithaca, NY (2016).

Operation Invert, "Transforming Provocations." Flaherty NYC, Anthology Film Archives, New York (2016).

Putting the Balls Away, ConteSting/ConteXting SPORT, with nGbK at Kunstraum Kreuzberg/Bethanien. Berlin, Germany (2016).

Love Hangover featuring the Tin Man. Sun Screening Vol. II, Videology Brooklyn, NY (2015).

Predatory Formations, My First 3D. Microscope Gallery, Brooklyn, NY (2013).

PYT, Immortal Kombat. The Vault, SPACES, Cleveland School of the Arts, Cleveland (2013).

Strange Bedfellows: Collaborative Practice in Queer Art. Handwerker Gallery, Ithaca College, Ithaca, NY, and A+D Gallery, Columbia College, Chicago (2013).

Kicked in the Nuts (2012). One Minute Film Festival, MASS MOCA, North Adams, MA (2013).

Zurück an Absender. Raw & Rare, Leslie Lohman Queer Caucus for Art, Lesbian, Gay, Bisexual, Transgender Caucus for Art, Artists & Historians, College Art Association (juried) New York (2013).

Seahorse. Herstory Inventory: 100 Feminist Drawings by 100 Artists, Raw/Cooked: Ulrike Müller, Brooklyn Museum, Brooklyn, NY (2012).

Case 133 and *Countess V., the Dearest Friend of the Empress Eugénie.* Noise Carousel, Newhouse Center for Contemporary Art, Snug Harbor Cultural Center, Staten Island, NY (2011).

Toast, A Gay Bar Called Everywhere (With Costumes and No Practice) by Emily Roysdon, The Kitchen, New York (2011).

Putting the Balls Away. MOMA PS1 Greater New York Cinema, PS1, Long Island City, NY (2010).

Men with Missing Parts: Queer Visitors from the Marvelous Land of Oz, Hot Festival, Dixon Place, New York, NY; *Operation Invert,* Slippery Mess, Brattle Theatre, Boston, MA (2010).

Operation Invert, She Devil 4 edition. Studio Stefania Miscetti, Rome, Italy (2010).

Society of Biological Insurgents, Operation Invert, Toilet Training, Suggestions of a Life Being Lived. SF CameraWork, San Francisco (2010).

Endless Love and PYT. Shapeshifter, Issue Project Room, Brooklyn, NY (2009).

Case 133. Psychosexual Metamorphosis, The Left Hand of Darkness, The Project, New York (2008).

Society of Biological Insurgents. Tingle Tangle Club, as part of Absolutely Venomous Accurately Fallacious (Naturally Delicious), Deitch Studios, Queens, NY (2008).

The Tin Woodsman Does Love Songs by Diana Ross. The Stone, New York (2008).

Intersecticide. New York Underground Film Festival, Anthology Film Archives, New York (2006).

Dykes Can Dance (DCD). Dance Dance Revolution, Neiman Gallery, Columbia University, New York (2004).

Edward Miller, Professor of Media Culture

"Clean Feet and Dirty Dancing: The Erotic Pas de Deux and Boys in the Sand." In *Pornographic Art and the Aesthetics of Pornography,* edited by Hans Maes, 205–20. New York: Palgrave Macmillan, 2013.

Tomboys, Pretty Boys, and Outspoken Women: The Media Revolution of 1973.
University of Michigan Press, 2011.

Gerry Milligan, Associate Professor of Italian

"Aesthetics, Dress, and Militant Masculinity in Castiglione's *Courtier.*" In *Sex,
Gender and Sexuality in Renaissance Italy,* edited by Jacqueline Murray and
Nicholas Terpstra, 141–59. New York: Routledge, 2019. https://doi.org/10
.4324/9781351008723.

Moral Combat: Women, Gender, and War. Toronto: University of Toronto Press, 2018.

"Behaving like a Man: Performed Masculinities in Gl'ingannati." *Forum Italicum* 41,
no. 1 (2007): 23–42.

"Masculinity and Machiavelli: How a Prince Should Avoid Effeminacy, Perform
Manliness, and Be Wary of the Author." In *Seeking Real Truths: Multidisci-
plinary Perspectives on Machiavelli,* edited by Patricia Vilches and Gerald E.
Seaman, 149–72. Leiden: Brill, 2007.

Ananya Mukherjea, Associate Professor of Sociology

With Raphael de la Dehesa. "Building Capacities and Producing Citizens: The
Biopolitics of HIV Prevention in Brazil." *Contemporary Politics* 18, no. 2
(2012): 186–99.

Sohomjit Ray, Assistant Professor of English

"Legibility, Erasure, and the Neoliberal Assimilation of Same-Sex Desire in
Dostana." *South Asian Review* 34, no. 3 (2013): 159–74.

Simon Reader, Assistant Professor of English

"Wilde at Oxford: A Truce with Facts." In *Philosophy and Oscar Wilde,* edited by
Michael Bennett. London: Palgrave, 2016.

"Social Notes: Oscar Wilde, Francis Bacon, and the Medium of Aphorism." *Journal
of Victorian Culture* 18, no. 4 (December 2013).

Terry Rowden, Associate Professor of English

"The 'Top' of the Heap: Race, Manhood, and Legitimation in My Life in Porn: The
Bobby Blake Story." *Black Camera: An International Film Journal,* April 2011.

With Elizabeth Ezra. "Postcolonial Transplants: Cinema, Diaspora, and the Body
Politic." In *Comparing Postcolonial Diasporas,* edited by Michele Keown, David
Murphy, and James Proctor, 211–27. New York: Palgrave Macmillan, 2009.

"A Play of Abstractions: Race, Sexuality, and Community in James Baldwin's
Another Country." *Southern Review* 29, no. 1 (1993): 41–50.

Christine Flynn Saulnier, Professor of Social Work

"Deciding Who to See: Lesbians Discuss Their Preferences in Health and Mental Health Care Providers." *Social Work* 47, no. 4 (2002): 355–65.

With Elizabeth Wheeler. "Social Action Research: Influencing Providers and Recipients of Health and Mental Health Care for Lesbians." *Affilia* 15, no. 3 (2000): 409–33.

Sarah Schulman, Distinguished Professor of the Humanities

NOVELS

Maggie Terry: A Novel. New York: Feminist Press, 2018.

The Cosmopolitans. New York: Feminist Press, 2015.

The Mere Future. Vancouver: Arsenal, 2010.

The Child. New York: Avalon, 2007.

Shimmer. New York: Avon, 1998.

Rat Bohemia. New York: Dutton, 1995.

Empathy. New York: Dutton, 1992.

People in Trouble. New York: Dutton, 1990.

After Delores. New York: Dutton, 1988.

Girls, Visions and Everything. Seattle: Seal, 1986.

The Sophie Horowitz Story. Tallahassee, FL: Naiad, 1984.

NONFICTION

Conflict Is Not Abuse: Overstating Harm, Community Responsibility, and the Duty of Repair. Vancouver: Arsenal Pulp, 2016.

The Gentrification of the Mind: Witness to a Lost Imagination. Berkeley: University of California Press, 2012.

Israel/Palestine and the Queer International. Durham, NC: Duke University Press, 2012.

Ties That Bind: Familial Homophobia and Its Consequences. New York: New Press, 2010.

Stagestruck: Theater, AIDS, and the Marketing of Gay America. Durham, NC: Duke University Press, 1998.

My American History: Lesbian and Gay Life during the Reagan/Bush Years. New York: Routledge, 1994.

PLAYS (PUBLISHED)

Mercy. In *Robert Gluck and Sarah Schulman.* Brooklyn: Belladonna, 2009.

Carson McCullers. New York: Playscripts, 2006.

PLAYS (PRODUCED)

Enemies, a Love Story—adapted from I. B. Singer. Wilma Theater, Philadelphia, 2007.

Manic Flight Reaction. Playwrights Horizons, New York, 2005.

Carson McCullers. Playwrights Horizons, New York, 2002.

FILMS

Jason and Shirley and Me, directed by Stephen Winter, written by Stephen Winter, Jack Waters, and Sarah Schulman, 2015.

Mommy Is Coming, directed by Cheryl Dunye, cowritten by Sarah Schulman and Cheryl Dunye. Berlin Film Festival selection, 2012.

United in Anger: A History of ACT UP, directed by Jim Hubbard, produced by Jim Hubbard and Sarah Schulman. New York premiere: Museum of Modern Art. International premiere: Ramallah, West Bank, 2012.

The Owls, directed by Cheryl Dunye, cowritten by Sarah Schulman and Cheryl Dunye. Berlin Film Festival selection, 2010.

Francisco Soto, Professor of Spanish

"Havana Noir." *Review: Literature and Arts of the Americas* 42, no. 1 (May 1, 2009): 141–43. https://doi.org/10.1080/08905760902816410.

"'The Dream of Paradise': Homosexuality and Lesbianism in Contemporary Cuban-American Literature." In *Cuba: Idea of a Nation Displaced,* edited by Andrea O'Reilly Herrera, 285–300. Albany: State University of New York Press, 2007.

"Queer Parody and Intertextuality: A Postmodern Reading of Reinaldo Arenas's 'El cometa Halley.'" In *Desde aceras opuestas: Literatura-cultura gay y lesbiana en Latinoamérica,* edited by Dieter Ingenschay, 245–54. Madrid: Iberoamericana, 2006.

Review of *Before Night Falls,* by Julian Schnabel. *Chasqui* 30, no. 1 (2001): 172–76. https://doi.org/10.2307/29741661.

"Adolfina's Song: Parodic Echoings in Reinaldo Arenas's 'El Palacio de Las Blanquísimas Mofetas.'" *Confluencia* 16, no. 1 (2000): 71–81.

Reinaldo Arenas. Woodbridge, CT: Twayne, 1998.

Reinaldo Arenas: The Pentagonia. Gainesville: University Press of Florida, 1994.

Conversacion con Reinaldo Arenas. Madrid: Editorial Betania, 1990.

Reinaldo Arenas: Tradition and Singularity. New York: New York University Press, 1987.

Saadia Toor, Professor of Sociology

With Shefali Chandra, eds. "Solidarity." Special issue, *Women's Studies Quarterly*
42, nos. 3–4 (winter 2014).

An interruptive Poor Queer Studies bibliography draws the reader's slowed-down attention to a collection of scholarship and creative work that otherwise would not register as a place-based body of work. It therefore provides one tactic for reforming our habit of failing to recognize Poor Queer Studies and failing, therefore, to let queer scholarly density accrue in the places of Poor Queer Studies. Extended internal chapter acknowledgments offer another such tactic. This whole chapter, in fact, is an acknowledgment. I delight in naming and thanking my colleagues, whom I have followed and with whom I presently work at CSI. It is important to note that the colleagues I list above situate their work in various ways and that not all of us use "Queer Studies" as the disciplinary frame or clarifying lens for that work. Further, coming from departments across institutional divisions and schools, we don't always have a sense of what we are all up to in our LGBTQ-oriented or -inflected scholarship. We don't all teach in the Women's, Gender, and Sexuality Studies program, though many of us do. At CSI there is no Queer Studies concentration within the WGS program, and no distinct Queer Studies academic formation or faculty reading group. There is no Queer Studies Archive within the College Archives and Special Collections, though we've had some initial discussions. I present the evidence of Poor Queer Studies, then, not knowing precisely how it adds up. What does it mean that sometimes I don't know about the Queer Studies work happening across my own campus? As I discuss below, not knowing how queer knowledge adds up and fits together in my small institutional context produces a red flag and a reminder to dwell in but also revise and resist dominant Queer Studies narratives that, impossibly, produce the field as coherent.

Mis-fitting Knowledge

In "An Affinity of Hammers," Sara Ahmed sees power and possibility in that which does not fit. She writes that "we learn about worlds when they do not accommodate us. Not being accommodated can be pedagogy. We generate ideas through the struggles we have to be in the world; we come to question worlds when we are in question."[25] Ahmed's article appears in the "Trans/Feminisms" special issue of *TSQ: Transgender Studies Quarterly* and contains a vision of an affinity of trans/feminist hammers chipping away at boundaries that police "women," a category within which all women experience the hammering of not being accommodated. Ahmed also references her earlier work on the broad category of diversity, where she employs a similar analysis of failed accommodation within institutions: "In *On Being Included: Racism and Diversity in Institutional Life* (2012), I discuss diversity work in two senses: the work we do when we aim to transform an institution (often by opening it up to those who have been historically excluded), and the work we do when we do not quite inhabit the norms of an institution. These two senses often meet in a body: those who do not quite inhabit the norms of an institution are often those who are given the task of transforming those norms."[26] Ahmed perceives opportunities for producing knowledge from the position of the unaccommodated, those who don't fit into institutional norms. To not fit neatly within a structure, a relationship, a field can be both a struggle and also a chance to know something else or some way else. From being questioned, one can question.

If, as I have suggested, Queer Studies is in question at CSI and Poor Queer Studies institutions, Ahmed alerts us to the possibility that our odd disciplinary positioning can also enable questioning. Things—people, subjects, trajectories—that don't quite fit raise questions. Following Ahmed but, even more so, following my colleagues past and present at CSI, I recognize that we are Queer Studies misfits, and I learn how to mis-fit Queer Studies. Not fitting, mis-fitting, one learns mis-fitting methods. Those methods proceed unfashionably, by not being choosy, by interrupting the flow, even by sustaining the misrecognition of one's job so as not to fit it in with high-class models of Queer Studies. I follow Ahmed's thinking here, and I simultaneously follow my colleagues as Queer Studies outliers. In the misfit between CSI and the more recognizable class knowledges of Queer Studies (including Ahmed's), the details of Poor Queer Studies become recognizable as valuable queer data, even as they are also pressure points that make one aware of a lack of accommodation. Those pressure points where one is chipped away at and that are often experienced as racialized and gendered vulnerabilities leave one open to doubt, but that doubt also enables queer-class inquiry. The two questions I've been asked most frequently over the past decade when I tell people what I do are, "What is Queer Studies?" and "Why do you teach at the College of Staten Island instead of Columbia or NYU?" The first question has been an accommodating one because it has allowed me to chart the pleasurable distance of my queer-class intellectual trajectory. The second question was for a long time an embarrassing one because it forced me to accommodate the unpleasant fact that I have not been accommodated within more recognizable institutional places. At some point, I started taking these questions seriously. That is, I started turning them around, turning them to face each other to see if they could become useful.

In her study of queer steel mill workers in and around Gary, Indiana, Anne Balay describes the value for her narrators of sharing their experiences with her and the reader, despite their anonymity. Balay finds that "crafting and sharing a story is one way to gain control over the contradictions of being working-class and queer, and possibly a member of another minority as well, and many of my narrators weave powerful stories born of necessity and alienation."[27] It seems to me that telling the story of Poor Queer Studies similarly requires grappling with potentially alienating queer-class contradictions, though in my study those contradictions emerge between the upper-class positioning of the discipline and the poor and working-class realities of the institution. My study is not an ethnography like Balay's, nor an autoethnography. But because a Queer Studies professor is attached both to their discipline and their institution by questions of accommodation such as I asked above, the queer-class contradiction is mediated in no small part by their individual class history. Poor Queer Studies professors can even embody that contradiction—or, perhaps I should say that class-inflected contradictions of field-knowledge and workplace can feel embodied: internalized, materialized, borne. Each story of the dissonances of Poor Queer Studies is therefore a narrative told from particular class locations within the field, within higher education, and within personal history.

What social class do I come from? My background is rural Indiana middle class: an hour's ride on the school bus to a small public school, enough food, a cold house in the winter, no models of LGBTQ living, looming fundamentalist Christianity, implicit and explicit racism, the glorification of work. Like the rest of my family, I grew up working jobs associated with teenage rural life: detasseling corn, factory work, fast food, delivery boy, an office job working for the county. My grandparents were a mechanic, a bartender, a farmer/factory worker, and a country barber. My dad was drafted and sent to Vietnam, and so he was able to attend college and then to become a certified public accountant, businessman, and, for a number of years, a country preacher. Only recently has he stopped working two full-time jobs at once. My mother, a high school graduate, was his secretary until their divorce. For years afterward she worked at flea markets, then as a "chip girl" in a casino, and now at age seventy she packs denim jeans into boxes in a factory. Although in the past twenty-five years I have sometimes worked two jobs at once, I have worked on neither farm nor factory since leaving Indiana. Unlike the rest of my family, I am gay. As is typical of many middle-class queer young people, I was made to understand (in my case, through my mother's relentless homophobia) that gay difference was shameful, disgusting, and sinful. Academic achievement became a way out, though my world remained small. It didn't occur to me to apply to a college outside of Indiana, for example, and I remained closeted until my late twenties. When I told my mother, she said if she had known she would have sent me away to be "fixed." My path through the academy, as outlined in this book's introduction, eventually opened out onto a broader world, one where the terms of my existence—being a white gay man and being educated and being increasingly part of an urban middle class (which is very different from the rural middle class)—often transparently buttress and imply each other. When I am asked, "What is Queer Studies," I am able to accommodate that question because it reflects my own experience of gay academic re-subjectification, a remaking of one's queer identity through schooling that is dependent on the past but, primarily, distinct from it.[28] Paradoxically, for nearly these exact reasons, I am able to accommodate the question, "Why do you teach at the College of Staten Island instead of Columbia or NYU?" That question prioritizes not my present Queer Studies position but the hidden injuries of my rural queer-class subjectification that make moving on and moving up a source of ambivalence and insecurity. In other words, that question is precisely my own.

Perhaps nothing has made me more aware of my queer-class contradictions than being an HIV+ Poor Queer Studies professor in the CUNY system. The multiple statuses designated by that personal and professional phrase, "HIV+ Poor Queer Studies professor," reflect the ways that the field operates as a site of class ambivalence for me. For ten of the thirteen years I have been employed by CUNY, I have been HIV+. Because I am a well-educated, gay, white, gender-normative professional person, one might expect me to have relatively uncomplicated access to HIV medications. One might expect, given that I work for the City University of New York—the largest public urban university in the U.S. and, given its location as well as its size, perhaps the U.S. university system with the most HIV+ students, faculty, and staff— that I would have health insurance with a workable prescription drug benefit. One might expect that being a professor in the university named after the city that has witnessed 100,000-and-counting deaths from AIDS would afford peace of mind via affordable access to life-saving HIV medication. But my employee prescription drug benefit is structured in such a way as to shift the bulk of the cost of my HIV medication to me after the first $10,000. Medications for HIV cost over $30,000 per year. I am told by people who are trying to help me that if my Welfare Fund (which provides supplemental health benefits, including prescription drug coverage, to enrollees in CUNY's basic health insurance package) had to absorb the cost of HIV medications, the fund would go broke and then none of my comrades would have prescription drug coverage either.

And so I do the Poor Queer Studies professor HIV hustle. I join clinical trials to try to get free meds. I plead with the drug maker Gilead, but I am told I make too much money to receive their assistance (unless I lie or forge tax documents). I switch insurance plans, and then spend weeks per year on the phone trying to get my new HMO to reimburse for supposedly covered services. I watch my new insurance plan's premiums shoot through the roof. I switch insurance plans again, though never with a guarantee that the medications or services I need will be covered. You can't find that out, naturally, until you've joined the new plan. I add my partner to my plan. I drop my partner from my plan. If I make the wrong choice, I have to wait a year to choose again. Sometimes I yell at my Welfare Fund colleagues. Sometimes they yell at me. Sometimes I just pay up, hoping for something good to happen later. Amazingly, through all of this I have had perhaps the best HIV/AIDS doctor in New York City, a man who told me when he walked into the examining room at the clinic at Bellevue Hospital in 2009 that one day I was going to die of something but that it wouldn't be AIDS. And so far he's been right. So far I have found ways to put a couple pills—now one pill—per day in my mouth and swallow. If it tells me nothing else, eating that pill every day tells me about the particular ways class is scaffolded in my life—around employment, around sex, around race, around geography, around luck, around both privilege and precarity. It reminds me that this Poor Queer Studies professor's HIV hustle is still working, even as it frequently reminds me that nothing is forever—certainly not reliable and stress-free drug coverage. It reminds me that if I'd contracted HIV thirty years ago, I'd be dead; that if I were a transwoman and/or a woman of color, or a black gay man, especially in the American South, I might still die from AIDS racism; that if I were HIV negative I would be in another class of employed person, someone for whom "basic" healthcare is intended. Ultimately, the pill I manage to take teaches me one undeniable Poor Queer Studies lesson: if you aren't rich and you need life-saving or life-sustaining or life-long healthcare, you are *fucked*. How fucked is a question of intersectionality. As an HIV+ Poor Queer Studies professor, that is my personal, professional opinion.

The question Ahmed helps us ask, "Why do you fit here rather than there?," is one I now not only ask my students but share with them. Why are we here, in this Poor Queer Studies course at this school? I teach a lot of general education courses, and most of my students are surprised to find themselves in a Queer Studies course at all. With one exception, the twelve different CSI courses I have taught—all of them Queer Studies courses— aren't coded in the college catalog in a way that makes them recognizably Queer Studies classes. They are often designated as pluralism and diversity courses, however, so they fulfill a graduation requirement, and that is a weighty detail. Why are you here, I ask? Bureaucracy, many answer. The class fulfills a requirement. My all-time favorite quote from a student came on the first day of one semester when I introduced our "U.S. Literature: Multicultural Perspectives" course as a Queer Studies course. A student in the back of the room responded loudly, but not to me, "I only needed two credits to graduate, and now I'm in a Queer Studies class?" Turns out she was an incredible student, but not an exceptional one. I see students like her all the time.

Paying attention to the ways students at working-poor and working-class colleges fit into a Queer Studies class produces knowledge about unrecognized relations to the field. In the above example—"I only needed two credits to graduate, and now I'm in a Queer Studies class?"—Queer Studies poses a bureaucratic risk. Its obscurity within the larger curriculum operates as a red flag, a warning that one has diverged from an academic path that may already be only dimly lit for students at underfunded schools, for first-generation students, for students seeking courses that translate directly into work skills. Queer Studies always represents a political risk, whether at a rich or poor school. But at poor schools, the political risk sits alongside the risk of walking the tightrope of class, where a misstep can have enormous consequences in the struggle to earn a degree.[29] Poor Queer Studies pedagogy navigates the entwined political and the bureaucratic risks to students as it queers the path to graduation.

The Poor Queer Studies project of queering the upward mobility that comes with earning a college degree requires attention not just to the bureaucratic stress experienced by our students but, as is the case everywhere, the dissemination of queer knowledge. Ideally, the queer knowledge disseminated in the Poor Queer Studies classroom will offer a number of critical handholds that can be useful in conceptualizing how normative bureaucratic systems work, such that queering the path to graduation can become a way of clearing the path to graduation. But while queer knowledge is helpfully distributed in this scenario, I want to be clear to distinguish between a redistribution of queer knowledge and a redistribution of material resources. Queer Studies can mistake the two, and the field in fact seems to depend on the notion that creating queer knowledge produces a redistributive socioeconomic effect. The best queer evidence I know to support such a hope is the evidence by which Queer Studies helps poor and working-class students to graduate and become modestly upwardly mobile. This is to say that the evidence for laying claim to any form of class consciousness within the field imaginary comes precisely from those places in the queer academy from which the field has not been imagined.

The downward distribution of queer knowledge (from top tiers of knowledge production to lower tiers of knowledge dissemination) counters the upward redistribution of wealth in some ways. Poor Queer Studies students get college credits for taking Queer Studies courses that teach Rich Queer Studies content, and they therefore advance toward a college degree, and a college degree increases lifetime earning potential. Queer scholarship translates into courses and coursework and passing a course and graduating. And graduating is, at CSI and schools like it, a constant question. Many students don't fit in, drop out. Being in question around Queer Studies reflects a state of precarity for students at poor and working-class schools: how will this unknown class, this questionable topic operate in connection to the unknown and questionable process of earning a college degree? And because so many students at poor schools don't graduate, Poor Queer Studies is also potentially more attuned to its relationship to the nonacademic tomorrow that many of our students, having dropped out, will face.

In her introduction to "On the Case," a special issue of *Critical Inquiry*, Lauren Berlant writes, "When it doesn't work to change the conditions of exemplarity or explanation, something is deemed merely a case study, remanded to banal particularity. When it does, a personal or collective sensorium shifts."[30] This chapter has been an investigation of how and why my personal sensorium has shifted as a professor of Queer Studies at CSI. That shift required grappling with the class-based barriers to reconceptualizing Queer Studies as Poor Queer Studies, from institutional unfashionability to broken toilets to rates of student persistence. A key barrier was my own educational background; not having attended or taught at a school like CSI, I was unable to recognize its class-structured possibilities for contributing to the field. A crucial change in my thinking happened only once I understood that "the conditions of exemplarity" within the general(izing) field of Queer Studies require that queer work at schools such as mine be diminished, adding up to "merely a case study." Yet queer work exists here. This misfitting between a theory of exemplarity and the queer here of csi, though it can (thinking back to Ahmed) be experienced as a hammering, can also produce a wider sensorium, a queer-class understanding. Of course, it may not produce a collective sensorium in the sense of a queer cross-class understanding, especially for those at an institutional and perhaps intellectual remove from the potentially "banal particularity" of this queer-class case. The next chapter, then, is written with an eye toward shifting the collective sensorium precisely by indexing not only the queer theoretical expanses but also the provincialisms, the sometimes banal particularities, of Rich Queer Studies.

chapter two

"You Can Write Your Way Out of Anywhere"
The Upward Mobility Myth of Rich Queer Studies

Like many professors I naively believed that the more I moved up the academic ladder the more freedom I would gain, only to find that greater academic success carried with it even more pressure to conform, to ally oneself with institutional goals and values rather than with intellectual work. I felt enormously lucky that I was able to succeed in the academic world as a radical, dissident thinker. —bell hooks, *Teaching Community*

Judith Butler and a community college professor walk into a bar ... *ba dum bum*. —humorous

A monumental determinant of what jobs which candidates will be offered is pedigree.... Select job candidates garner coveted posts not so much through individual merit as through the prestige of their associations. —Lynn Arner, "Working-Class Women at the MLA Interview"

You can write your way out of anywhere. —attributed to Eve Sedgwick

Rich Queer Studies

In the introduction I argued that although Queer Studies, like many disciplines, can and does ignore class stratification in the academy by locating the problem somewhere beyond its field, we ought to characterize the exclusion of low-income students, who are disproportionately students of color, and working-class faculty from the most recognizable places of Queer Studies as nothing less than a field-defining, field-constituting problem. That is, we should define the field of Queer Studies at all times through consideration of the material conditions that structure its ideational problems, its affects, its pedagogies, its troubles. In this chapter, I pause to further consider certain Queer Studies workplaces—Rich Queer Studies schools—paying special attention to the ways that status both propels and divides the field.

As this last sentence suggests, to think about status is to think about academic mobility and stasis. This chapter therefore asks how professors move around the places of Queer Studies, how some rise, how some don't. It's a chapter about the way individual and institutional statuses intertwine to make and move Queer Studies and its practitioners, or not, and about the way professors' often slippery class identifications mediate our institutional statuses in complex—and indeed, moving—ways. And it's a chapter about, or rather a chapter that enacts, the emotional, class-based vicissitudes of writing about Queer Studies people, including friends, colleagues, and stars, in order to write about the field. My use of "we" in this chapter sometimes indicates my identification with everyone in our field. Elsewhere, "we" reflects my status-based affiliation with low-down Queer Studies places and with people who feel like class outsiders in the field.[1] I try to use my whiteness to put pressure on class quietude and to consider certain queer-race contradictions that a study of class stratification raises.

Moving among academic locations reveals the surprisingly unqueer, sovereign role of status in the field of Queer Studies. Some institutional sites, the ones where sovereign status accrues, both provide pinpoint coordinates and spread across the field. These are the places of Queer Studies that, quasi-imperially, have the ability to inhabit all Queer Studies classrooms across all tiers of the academy. Yale offers a more than serviceable example of such a sovereign site, for a tour of the field of Queer Studies almost inevitably runs through—and often begins with—that status-laden university. Judith Butler going to Yale to be a lesbian. Eve Sedgwick going to Yale and not being a lesbian. The Center for LGBTQ Studies (CLAGS) almost going to Yale before being sabotaged by New Haven's young white gay star, John Boswell.[2] What are the effects in the present of taking the unavoidable Queer Studies tour through places such as Yale, or through schools with different statuses that are also on the familiar Queer Studies itinerary, such as the University of California at Santa Cruz or New York University or the University of North Carolina at Chapel Hill or the CUNY Graduate Center or, more recently, Harvard University and Columbia University (more complete lists of Queer

Studies tourist destinations will follow)?[3] And what are the risks of such a tour, of queer exemplarity, of turning to individual places and thinkers as examples of Rich Queer Studies? How do we deal with the fact that some of the most well-trodden of queer routes also run through institutional sites that are indisputably, chronically antagonistic to many forms of queer/race/gender/class difference? How does status enable and sustain that contradiction?

I will argue for the Poor Queer Studies approach of bringing status, often implicitly coded as institutional background, into the foreground. Rich Queer Studies encodes status in its texts by failing to rigorously link queer knowledge production to its well-resourced production sites. To stick with the exemplary Yale for a moment, we see Butler (who earned her PhD at Yale) writing in her 1991 essay "Imitation and Gender Insubordination" that "the professionalization of gayness requires a certain performance and production of a 'self' which is the *constituted effect* of a discourse that nevertheless claims to 'represent' that self as a prior truth. When I spoke at the conference on homosexuality in 1989, I found myself telling my friends beforehand that I was off to Yale to be a lesbian, which of course didn't mean that I wasn't one before, but that somehow then, as I spoke in that context, I *was* one in some more thorough and totalizing way, at least for the time being."[4] Butler mentions Yale one more time in passing later in that same paragraph, a paragraph that begins with a connection between professionalization and gay selfhood but that ultimately ends, having circled around, unwound, and destabilized the lesbian "I" as Butler so remarkably does, in no place. In this essay Butler explores the incoherence of "lesbian," not the incoherence of "Yale." In fact, Yale not only lends a "totalizing" coherence to the discursive work of constructing the "lesbian," which is the ostensible crux of Butler's jokey anecdote above; Yale also lends coherence to the work of deconstructing the lesbian "I," which is the crux of Butler's critical project in the remainder of the piece and across her early work. But this second function of Yale, its grounding of the act of destabilizing identity, disappears from view. I would argue that Yale becomes background so that the lesbian "I" can be performatively undone between those hardworking quotation marks. Context is everything in humor, but gender insubordination turns out to be no laughing matter. To move past the humorous anecdote ("I was off to Yale to be a lesbian"), we must move past the context of the joke. We must get serious, but not about Yale. We must seriously forget that Yale provides the material conditions for the production of knowledge about sexuality, a realm of experience that Butler elsewhere argues cannot be consigned to the "merely cultural" but, rather, must be understood within the framework of political economy.[5] Butler's minor joke that she was "off to Yale to be a lesbian" thus places and necessarily dis-places the vibrant critical work ahead. In response, Poor Queer Studies decodes what has been encoded: the high-class, high-status context of Yale that grounds Butler's effort to shift the ontological ground upon which she speaks as a problematically funny lesbian.

Let me put this more simply. When I teach "Imitation and Gender Insubordination" to my poor and working-class students at CSI, it's not the word "lesbian" that we have the real trouble with. It's the word "Yale." The joke is on us because the joke is not for us. The inside joke is for Butler's friends. For us, a funny joke might be the epigraph I invented for this chapter: "Judith Butler and a community college professor walk into a bar . . . *ba dum bum.*" That joke occurs on our class terms, and it's funny in part because it remakes Butler as the outsider—but not because she's a lesbian, a word we are prepared to trouble with Butler's idiosyncratic if not exactly funny help. Our joke estranges Butler because she goes to Yale, the site of her professionalization in Rich Queer Studies and the meaning of which Butler leaves us to parse out on our own. But no one in my classes, Poor Queer Studies professor included, has ever been to Yale. Is it funnier to say that one is "off to Yale to be a lesbian" than that one is "off to the College of Staten Island to be a lesbian"? Surely it is, but why? What does Yale bring to the joke of lesbianism that CSI does not? If jokes and gender alike get their sizzle from insubordination, then the funny thing—not funny ha ha but funny odd— about professionalizing as a questionable lesbian at Yale is the fact that that joke is acted out precisely at a place of ordination, a place of "ordering, arranging, or placing in ranks of order."[6] When a lesbian goes to Yale, her identity can become insubordinate, disordered, destabilized. Yale, it turns out, is exactly the right, rich, stable place to go off to in order to effect a particular kind of gender—but not class—insubordination. The material conditions of knowledge production, which enable the backgrounding of class, make this very specific and even provincial lesbian idea go.

But of course my students and I do know Yale. How could we not? What do we know? We know its name and its status . . . from the outside. We have class-based knowledge. And that means that we have, at least, the beginning of a question about how sexual knowledge is, probably, traded upon differently there than here. We have a hunch *that* sexual knowledge is traded upon differently there. We have a Poor Queer Studies orientation, a critical viewpoint, if not a full view. We know what's funny and what's not. Queer CSI students often tell me that the college is the only place they can be queer or that it is the most liberating space in their lesbian, gay, bi, trans, queer, asexual lives. From a Poor Queer Studies perspective, I am more familiar with lesbians who go to our college so that they can be lesbians (and here, too, there are failures), not so that they, theoretically, can't be. Of course Butler's "lesbian" lives in the past, fittingly beyond the always-suspect act of imitation. Still, in our difference, Butler reaches us, compels us, even unsettles us. Starting where we are, we can therefore enjoy a reciprocal pedagogical relationship with Butler, learning from her and teaching back to her by editing her queer-class ideas to reflect our own queer-class knowledge. By the end of the lesson, my students learn how to pay Butler the compliment, one she has in all seriousness earned, of laughing along with her joke.

It is interesting and perhaps instructive to return to another scene of queer theory's emergence, as told by Professor Henry Abelove. In attempting the difficult work of understanding his affluent queer students, Abelove nearly orients the relatively young field of Queer Studies toward a critique of its unmarked, high-class institutional affiliations. Ultimately, however, he declines to address the implications and risks of wedding Queer Studies to elite education. In "The Queering of Lesbian/Gay History," published in *Radical History Review* in 1995, Abelove reflects on his experience teaching lesbian and gay history to his undergraduates at Wesleyan, a school at which, "because of a series of happy accidents, [he] ha[d] been placed for nearly the whole of [his] teaching career."[7] Abelove, who dedicates his essay to his students, not only notes the institutional setting as Wesleyan but also qualifies his findings with explicit reference to the particular student population whom he had, it is clear, the privilege to teach and learn from. He writes, "My conclusions are based on a very limited sample of queers—all of them students and at only one university. They may or may not be typical of queers elsewhere."[8] Here, Abelove explains his research methods by noting the bounds of his study, a reasonable and standard scholarly practice. At the same time, however, he seems not quite to know those bounds. Are his students, for whom "marginalization isn't their preferred trope," typical of queers elsewhere or not?[9] If one has only, ever, been surrounded by affluent young LGBTQ students, what can one say about queer pedagogy generally? Such questions seem to fall away in Rich Queer Studies. Abelove's real concern in this essay is his students' shifting identifications over the years from lesbian and gay to queer, a shift he perceives not only in nomenclature but in how his students respond to the lesbian and gay histories that constitute his classroom texts. The change is that, unlike their predecessors, more recent crops of "queer" students do not experience kinship with or ownership of gay and lesbian histories or historical texts in which gay and lesbian people exist as "persons with deep subjectivity and a capacity for original and decisive action."[10] This last phrase of Abelove's is so important to him as a gay man teaching lesbian and gay history that he repeats it, with humor and sadness, four times in the course of his short essay. Why do his newly queer students not own the history that their gay male professor so clearly thinks is theirs?

My guess, though not Abelove's, is because they can afford not to—by which I mean not simply that money can buy queer possibility but that one of the queer-class affordances of attending Wesleyan is the option to refuse gay and lesbian subjectivity. An affordance, in my adaptation of that word from perceptual psychology, is what the class-encoded environment offers or offers up as a possible action to the class-encoded individual.[11] While Abelove considers the explanatory power of social class—"Our university is expensive, and these queer students tend to be mostly well-off and bourgeois"—that explanation won't do. He continues, "I doubt that these students' queerness is a class-determined phenomenon. . . . What I do think likely is that their class position may help them to be confident in the expression of their queerness in the classroom."[12] Just a page later Abelove notes of his queer students that "virtually all of them have read at least a little in Foucault," who becomes an emblem of a certain knowingness, "a body of assumptions, opinions, and dicta shared widely in, and absorbed readily from, the university world around them."[13] At the heart of his students' knowingness lies a postmodern sensibility linked to "the university world around them" yet somehow unlinked to social class, except as class provides for the confident expression of their views—but expressly not a foundation for them. Abelove can therefore dissociate the class-based affordances of the persons and place and pedagogy that have surrounded him "for nearly the whole of [his] teaching career" from his students' reactions and, I would add, from his own reading of those reactions.

My students at CSI certainly do not have the confidence of expression that Abelove associates with "well-off" Wesleyan students. Yet like Abelove's mid-1990s queer students, my students make little effort to tell me what they think I want to hear, and that's another kind of confidence of expression created by the very differently classed university world around them. Of course, at a commuter school, the veil between the university world and the rest of the world is so porous as to be invisible, and a certain Staten Island/Brooklyn brand of no bullshit explicitly informs classroom work at the college. Perhaps postmodern queerness no longer holds the same sway among the elite Cardinals of today's Wesleyan University. Certainly it does not hold sway with my students, the diverse Dolphins of CSI. They're avowedly gay, lesbian, bisexual, transgender, gender-nonconforming, asexual, and queer. Mostly, in this Poor Queer Studies professor's classes, they're avowedly straight. Further, they nearly all seem to like gay and lesbian history, and they admire, learn from, and sometimes even model themselves after "persons with deep subjectivity and a capacity for original and decisive action," ironic as that may sounds to queers.[14] Of my LGBTQ students, some are out, some are not, but coming out is not passé. It is often still risky to come out when one lives at home, as most of them do, on Staten Island, in the Bronx, in Queens, in Brooklyn. It seems to me that my students constantly think sexuality through class, even if that thinking comes in the form of inarticulate negotiations of their sexual liberation—for coming out is still that to them—amid the material resources that constrain them.

In dismissing the possibility that his students' queerness is class based—despite the high-class evidence of their subject formation—gay and lesbian studies professor Abelove points up, by failing to fully predict, the no doubt slippery queer-class connections within the then-burgeoning field of Queer Studies. Steven Seidman, writing from within the academy but looking beyond it, asks in a 2011 essay about queerness and social class, "Class matters . . . but how much?" He claims that gay and lesbian culture from the 1970s to the 1990s became more class mixed, gender mixed, and race mixed, and offers these shifts as explanations for why class has not been foundational for social analyses of queer life in the contemporary U.S. as it has in the U.K. Framing queer theory as a "thoroughly post-Marxist discourse . . . one that pivots on the critique of institutionalized or compulsory heterosexuality and gender binary rather than political economy and social class," Seidman argues that "there is virtually no effort [within critical sexuality studies] to ground class analysis in a critique of political economy."[15] Asking whether "class should be at the center of critical sexuality studies," Seidman writes, "Here too we need to be clear. At issue is not whether lesbian, gay, and queer life is class structured or whether class is a dimension of inequality within queer life, but *whether it's a central axis of difference and hierarchy*. In other words, *are queer lives and cultures class based?*"[16] What he seems to mean with this question is, essentially, "Are queers segregated by class?" as, he claims, they were before Stonewall. In response to his question, "*Are queer lives and cultures class based?*," Seidman responds, "I will argue the negative case."[17]

Poor Queer Studies attempts to explain that class already sits at the center of Queer Studies once higher education is understood to be part of other socioeconomic processes that shape queer society. This is to say that from a Poor Queer Studies perspective, which offers a bottom-up vision of queer intellectual life and culture in the class-stratified context of higher education, the answer to Seidman's question can only be, Yes, queer educational lives are class based or class segregated. I would even argue that this field offers an object lesson in what it means for queer lives and cultures to be class and race sorted, for higher education might be more closely aligned with class relations and racial capitalism (including the political economies of slavery) than with democracy (its governing political logic). Indeed, compared to democratic ideals, white supremacist race-class alignment better reflects American higher education's longest history, a history in which campuses were "seedbeds for racial thought" and in which "slave-generated wealth ... establish[ed] and endow[ed] some of the nation's most revered institutions."[18] With these revelations in mind, we might ask what about American life, including eroticism and desire, is *not* based in that same race-class history?

And what if we broaden the definition of "class based" beyond "class segregated"? What if the class basis for queer life included the ways queers understand their sexual selves as emerging from their class identity, or being defined by (or against) their surrounding race-class practices, or arising out of a class-based view of the world? Rich Queer Studies, to return to Abelove's generous pedagogy essay, demonstrates the extent to which queers always already know—including know themselves—through class. Not only do we know through class as early and as thoroughly as we know through sexuality, but class-stratified education sets the formal stage for acquiring new ideas about queerness, or not. What, other than class access to knowledge that transforms into self-knowledge, could explain the coincidence that "virtually all of [Abelove's affluent students had] read at least a little in Foucault"? Precocious as queer kids both rich and poor may be, would they all have found Foucault? Through class distinction comes the knowledge that gives truth-meaning to "queer" at Wesleyan, as remarkably demonstrated by Abelove's students. Class doesn't merely structure queer life; it is an important base determinant of ways, including educational ways, that we come to know our sexual selves. Thanks to Black Queer Studies and Latinx Queer Studies, we are much better at tracing queerness through the deep, intimate, even determinative meanings of race than of class.

With academe as its model of the larger social structure, Poor Queer Studies can see that it is only by setting aside the fact that much of life is grounded in and committed to class hierarchy—which does not always preclude class mixing—that we can disarticulate queer life from the economic processes that shape it, including into class arrangements. Indeed, other than by privileging highly rigid models of separatism, how can one distinguish the "dimension of inequality" from the "central axis of difference" in a poor queer life or a rich queer life?[19] In his memoir, *Returning to Reims*, Didier Eribon identifies education as a key battleground for contesting his class and sexual identities. He writes that in his "miraculous" trajectory from familial poverty through university education, "the project of remaking myself ... came to apply both in the domain of sexuality and in the domain of class, but in contradictory ways. In the former domain, it was a case of appropriating and claiming my insulted sexual being. But in the latter it was a case of uprooting myself from my origins. I could put it this way: in one case I needed to become what I was, but in the other I needed to reject what I was supposed to have been. *Yet for me these two activities went hand in hand*."[20] "Why," Eribon asks, "should we be obliged to choose between different struggles being fought against different kinds of domination? If it is the nature of our being that we are situated at the intersection of several collective determinations, and therefore of several 'identities,' of several forms of subjection, why should it be necessary to set up one of them rather than another as the central focus of political preoccupation—even if we are aware that any movement will have a tendency to posit the principal division of the social world specific to it as the one that must take priority?"[21] Seidman's broad distinction between the work of queer theory and the critique of political economy may still hold water, but this suggests a failure of queer theory's class projects rather than a definitive pronouncement about the potential for such projects. In other words, only by first setting aside the class-based organization of education—only by setting aside the deeply engrained and entwined institutional bases of life as we know it in the world around us—can Seidman's queer/class disarticulation work. Seidman's view, oddly enough, reinforces the normalization of de-classed (Rich) Queer Studies. Against that status quo, I am arguing that Poor Queer Studies—and all Queer Studies—cannot be understood except through its class-based institutional life. Eribon's book offers just such an understanding.

If this claim does not seem obvious, that is because social class operates as an especially slippery and unrecognized source of difference for queer life. Yes, sometimes precocious lower-class youth find and read Foucault. And certainly familial homophobia, as a defining feature of queer experience, cuts across all class lines.[22] Yet if, to gain critical traction, we follow Seidman by considering the narrower case of Queer Studies, there can be no doubt that social class must be a central axis of the field. It must be so as long as higher education not only sorts queers by class but also constructs class-based thresholds of queer intelligibility—that is, as long as education offers different ways to those sorted by class to understand their queerness in relation to their stratified place in (or not) the university world, which is to say, their world. Abelove's students think they're queer (not gay and lesbian) not simply because they're affluent but because Wesleyan, as a class-based institution, presents queer affluence as a threshold of and for self-knowledge. The poor student, having found and read Foucault and having found Wesleyan, might well find herself needing to switch her class affiliation (to "betray" her class roots) in order to know herself as queer at a Rich Queer Studies school. Hers is no less a class-based queerness than is the queerness of her rich peers. She may not only hide her lower-class background as part of the performativity of queerness; she may, having earned a Wesleyan degree, one day actually change classes. Does her "class fluidity," or her ability to engage in queer-class mixing, prove that her queer life and culture is not class based? My suggestion is that we might view things from quite the other direction: the deep histories of class and the power of class to shape sexual knowledge might well be the bases for the student's queer fluidity. Class mixing is not dispositive of class-based queerness; rather, it invites an investigation of how class-based queers mix and, crucially, of the ways queer-class mixing in the academy puts class beyond the scope of queer investigation. At the very least, I suggest that we cannot rule out the possibility that queer lives and cultures can be class based, even if they are not experienced as such.

Queer Status Agents

Queer Studies did not just happen at the places of Rich Queer Studies. These sites are not, merely, the institutional hosts for this or that conference where big Queer Studies news is made and where, occasionally and theatrically, big Queer Studies fights are fought. Rather, rich places play key roles in the most widely known (and often contradictory) origin stories of Queer Studies. Indeed, Queer Studies gained field status thanks to its not-incidental affiliations with sites that hold and hoard valuable institutional status. Status itself, I will argue, represents a constitutive ingredient of the field of Queer Studies, which became hypermobile very quickly thanks to the sovereign institutional statuses of the schools it chose to define itself in and from and through and also, as Butler's example imagines but does not demonstrate, against.

Practically speaking, how did Queer Studies happen at rich schools? Because Queer Studies departments are few, individual Queer Studies scholars and institutionally affiliated clusters of scholars have played an outsized role in the construction of the field's status. I call these scholars "Queer Studies status agents" or simply "queer status agents." I find this shift to the individual or the cluster (which often coheres under the banner of interdisciplinarity and as a subset of women's and gender studies) to be a fascinating and underexplored aspect of the material production of Queer Studies. Queer status agents, often disciplinary outliers within traditional departments yet luminaries in our field, have thus had to do a special kind of work in and for the field. At the same time, in that some status bearers have become not just agents but Queer Studies stars, they have assumed a special relationship both to the field and to the status-bearing institutions they move Queer Studies within and toward and through. The shift to the individual queer status bearer no doubt occurs within racialized and heteronormative university financial logics that, while they mostly fail to fund deep queer structural changes such as Queer Studies departments or large-cohort, multiyear queer-of-color postdoctoral fellowships, will sometimes invest in individuals on whom they will bestow status in order to have their status (read: diversity cred) increased in return. These status agents shoulder much of the work of field definition, even though the privilege of being a queer status agent seems to align with neither individual scholars' antihierarchical queer impulses nor the content of their intellectual projects. At the intersection of individual creativity and institutional authority lies this paradox of queer status.

Navigating my way through a class- and status-based Queer Studies critique means, at times, overlaying personal and institutional registers. The Queer Studies status agent indicates my attempt to position Queer Studies practitioners as members of a professional class who, in meaningful ways, figure the field. And though my intention is to draw out relationships between the Queer Studies status agents and the status of their institutions, my formulation risks making people symbols of those institutions. The phrase "status agent" attempts to foreground our complicated individual/institutional agencies.

Those without the institutional material resources that enable us to be "in the Queer Studies mix" are told (from near the top of the ivory tower) that professional death awaits.[23] Included in the field of Queer Studies rhetorically but excluded materially, the unresourced professor becomes, supposedly, a professional zombie, a member of the scholarly walking dead. In contrast, material support can animate research activity. Isolation is kept at bay by the workplace affordances, such as guaranteed and adequate travel funds, that enable intellectual sociality. "Queer Studies status agent" thus also names the personal/professional join where material support for one's scholarship quickens into what we recognize as a professional life. No zombie. Of course, professional queer lives cannot always be sustained at the famous places of Queer Studies, and sometimes they are sustained at Poor Queer Studies schools that have found a way to pool resources. Nevertheless, the notion of the Queer Studies status agent at least partially explains the dramatic correlation between the liveliness of the field and the academic sites (which are sometimes microsites) that materially nurture and sustain professional queer lives.

A Hierarchy We Can Believe In

We are *of* our institutions, even as we are often deeply at odds with them. With this notion in mind, we can consider with nuance the extent to which and the means by which we take on and reproduce the statuses of our institutions, as well as the ways that doing so informs our work and our other professional relationships. Writing for the collection *Presumed Incompetent: The Intersections of Race and Class for Women in Academia*, Ruth Gordon discovers "community in the midst of hierarchy" when she is welcomed into the Northeast Corridor Collective of Black Women Law Professors. "It was a nurturing community," Gordon recalls, "and you only needed to be a female and black to be a member; hierarchy was imperceptible within this cocoon."[24] While it may be personally rewarding and professionally beneficial, however, forging community can easily leave structural concerns unaddressed. Gordon sees hierarchy operating alive and well in her field of legal teaching, dividing tenure-track and non-tenure-track professors and schools with high rankings from the rest. From her perspective teaching at a law school, Gordon notes the irony that

> many of us spend our professional lives contesting hierarchy and exclusion—whether on the basis of race, gender, or class—but when it comes to academia . . . we appear to have finally found *a hierarchy we can believe in*. It not only goes unquestioned but is often at the core of our complaint. Thus, [one] excellent study focuses on access by white women and people of color of both genders to the sixteen most prestigious law schools. But most of us, regardless of gender, race, or class, do not teach

at those schools, nor do most of the law students in this country attend them. . . . It is fitting to contest racism and sexism and attempt to neutralize class barriers, but this battle is at the margins, and it is somewhat puzzling to me why the system as a whole remains unchallenged. Surely we can listen to each other even more at conferences and workshops, read each other's work without the blinders of institutional affiliation, and try to open ourselves to each other. We can chip away at hierarchy within our ranks.[25]

Here, Gordon sees a troubling dynamic between minority law professors' explicit commitments to inclusion and their implicit commitments to stratification by institutional rank, "a hierarchy we can believe in." A symptom of that problem, "exclusion" is measured only by considering access denied at the top of the academic hierarchy. But what is the relationship between access to those rarefied institutions at the top and access to midrank schools? How generalizable are the findings of studies of elite institutions to the broader academe landscape? Following up on an idea introduced in chapter 1, how does positioning elite institutions as the unquestioned reference points for generic questions about minority experience in higher education contribute to the normalization of class stratification and thus to the normalization of minority exclusion from those sites?

"A hierarchy we can believe in." It might be desirable to exempt Queer Studies from this "we," the "we" of law school professors, perhaps because queers need each other for sex and love as well as professional connections. But Gordon will not permit us to excuse ourselves by acknowledging the generosity we see exhibited among Queer Studies colleagues, for she has seen "community in the midst of hierarchy" among members of her discipline as well. And though she values that community deeply, Gordon insists that community within hierarchy has not changed the larger system that assigns disproportionate value to some positions and some schools over others. Law professors therefore remain implicitly committed to institutional hierarchies in the very act of forming community on the margins, insofar as those formations aren't able to address the underlying structural inequalities that center the field. How, then, are structural changes in academic hierarchies to be made? How do we stop believing in the hierarchies we don't want to, and claim not to, believe in?

Perhaps we don't want to stop believing in hierarchy. Perhaps we—and now I speak of Queer Studies professors—do not want to chip away at hierarchy within our ranks. A belief in hierarchy would be problematic for a field that, as Robyn Wiegman convincingly argues in *Object Lessons*, has staked not only its intellectual but its professional claim so firmly on progressive (read: antihierarchical) politics and on, as Kadji Amin claims, queer egalitarianism. Ironically, taking seriously the suggestion that Queer Studies harbors an illegitimate desire to believe in hierarchy—to trust it, to depend on it, to secure it—might produce not only a new round of obligatory queer disavowals of hierarchy but also, within that very gesture, a simultaneous disavowal of our unspeakable and unexpurgated belief in hierarchy within higher education. In other words, class analysis might well produce a critical cul de sac. This is one of the dangers of criticality, our prized method of exposing a problem: that we create a critical space to dwell in. But what if criticality prolongs the problem? What if queer criticality loves a hierarchy?[26]

Amin's study of Jean Genet, *Disturbing Attachments: Genet, Modern Pederasty, and Queer History*, reassesses queer's explicit commitments to egalitarianism. In the name of egalitarianism, Amin contends, Queer Studies scholars have forced ourselves into a critical corner that requires the idealization of certain of our objects, none so much as those that threaten to thrust an unseemly queer past into the present. Specifically, Amin argues that Queer Studies has idealized Jean Genet so as to be able to disavow, on behalf of the field, the definitionally antiqueer claims that Genet makes to *in*egalitarianism. In other words, Queer Studies' egalitarian commitments override the erotic messiness of Genet, one of its prized queer objects. This must be so, for how could the field avow its political projects of sexual consent and antiracism without disavowing the pederasty and racial fetishism that continue to charge Genet's writing and politics? Queer Studies cleans up troubling objects by finding them troubling in only the most acceptable queer ways. Against that impulse, Amin seeks to de-idealize Genet and to figure out what such a practice might mean for Queer Studies.

Amin is useful here because he enables me to ask whether de-idealization, or some other version of attending to what we feel we must refuse, might give us a way not simply to critique but to work with Queer Studies' simultaneous avowal/disavowal of class hierarchy. Specifically, how might giving up our dubious claims to an egalitarian or antihierarchical field politics help us to more fully consider Queer Studies' investment in class stratification and professional elitism—not in order to craft that elitist investment into one of our critical objects and thus extend its life through criticality—that is, to reassume the queer oppositional pose—but to try to stop it? Or can that distinction hold? As Hiram Pérez suggests, queer theory "actively untroubles" itself around "the problem of race" in order to institutionally entrench whiteness.[27] What would it mean to stop dwelling in criticality without merely withdrawing from it, thereby untroubling ourselves and entrenching upper-class white silence as the norm?

Stopping requires change, and antielitist change is hard to make happen in the academy. Former American Studies Association president Kandice Chuh examines the historical operations of professional elitism that subtend "pedagogies of dissent," including queer ones, and that make antielitist change difficult. Though the main concern of Chuh's 2017 ASA presidential address was to connect defensive claims of academic freedom to the inscription of nationalism, capitalism, and colonialism in the university, she routes her argument through the history of academic professionalization, for "academic freedom delimits its affordances to a select few."[28] Tenure, that chief affordance of the select few, primarily protects "freedom of teaching and research and of extramural activities," according to the 1940 Statement of Principles on Academic Freedom and Tenure by the American Association of University Professors (AAUP). But Chuh pauses over a second benefit of tenure as outlined in the AAUP statement: "a sufficient degree of economic security to make the profession attractive to men and women of ability."[29] While the first protection (freedom of thought and expression) created disciplinarity as a mechanism of professional hierarchy, the second (economic security for the meritorious) was also essential to the AAUP's goal, according to Chuh, of "establishing an elite professional class."[30] It is easy to overlook economic security, to make professionalization a matter of disciplinary expertise rather than, also and always, a question of material production.[31] Holding her focus on economic scarcity, Chuh asks us to question where the land for land grant colleges came from, and who benefits from its seizure in the "settler colonial regime realized in the university?"[32] In line with Chuh, I raise the question of the materiality of knowledge production not only in terms of money but, more broadly, in terms of the leveraging of status. What have been the status-oriented accumulations of queer theory in the academy? What grants queer theory its professional status, when and where it has status? Where is economic security secured by professionalizing around a queer hierarchy we can believe in? Is it not time to de-idealize our belief in our radical field by confronting its investments in those elitist places, payments, and professional practices that, though disavowed, nevertheless define it? What are the obstacles that might prevent such a class- and status-based de-idealization of Queer Studies?

Such complex articulations of status-based power are difficult to formulate for many reasons beyond the apparent incommensurability of community and hierarchy. One's institutional and personal power is easy to be unconscious of, all the more so in a time when education generally is under attack and neoliberal austerity politics have had repercussions across the academy. But problematically, these generalizations, while apt, rhetorically flatten different perspectives within hierarchy. "It's rough all over." "We're all in the same boat." As indeed in some ways we are. I must admit, however, that I continue to feel shock and not a small bit of disbelief when professors in the humanities and social sciences at elite colleges and flagship campuses (most recently someone from Columbia University, which pays the highest salaries of any school in the U.S. and, even more importantly in New York City, offers generous housing subsidies) talk to me earnestly about the lack of funding for their work. I want their receipts. My colleagues at CSI and I have ours: a $0 annual research budget (i.e., no money for books, journal subscriptions, professional membership fees, computers or software . . . all of which we need to do our jobs); a $75 yearly travel budget (not guaranteed); a $430 yearly budget for the entire Women's, Gender, and Sexuality Studies BA Program; Queer Studies graduate students who teach four classes per semester on different campuses to make ends meet; no new tenure-track faculty hires for the foreseeable future). These are the ways my college's boat is sinking. It doesn't seem to me that we are all in that same boat, and indeed some of the loudest cries of scarcity come from dry land, that is, from the top of the academy.[33] Similarly, instead of Queer Studies professors finding productive ways to communicate about our very real institutional disparities and status-based hierarchies, we risk flattening them or situating the problem of hierarchy elsewhere. For example, we point to other stratifications in higher education, as between STEM fields and the humanities or between research and teaching. This move is not only understandable but easy to make when scholars such as Columbia University's Jonathan R. Cole argue from a nationalist perspective that the freedom to invent "the electric toothbrush, Gatorade, the Heimlich maneuver, and Viagra" undergirds the supremacy of the American research university.[34] Lumped together and degraded by others in such accounts, patent-less disciplines such as Queer Studies are unfavorably compared to the university's true engines of knew knowledge. Why pick on ourselves, why investigate our own status-based divisions, when others so passionately underplay our queer contributions? Why not just keep shouting "neoliberalism!" into the strongest winds blowing against us?

It would be easier to stick together in our differences within Queer Studies if we could see each other, but in a steeply tiered educational landscape, opportunities for sustained engagement across status-based and class-differentiated workplaces are surprisingly few. Perhaps we cross paths on a panel for an hour or two per year. Sometimes, Queer Studies scholars—very often women and people of color, in my experience—intentionally create opportunities for cross-status collegiality.[35] At other times, Queer Studies scholars name their personal class locations and histories in their work in order to make visible their relationships to their subjects and, at least implicitly, to their variously class-situated readers. Putting her identity cards on the table, Linda Garber writes from an explicitly white middle-class position in *Identity Poetics: Race, Class, and the Lesbian Feminist Roots of Queer Theory*. She reiterates her middle-class identity three times in the first three pages of her book, a critical self-positioning that I appreciate and imitate here. Yet claiming class identity in the academy proves tricky. As a reader who identifies as a white middle-class academic, I feel my class relationship to Garber become strained when she mentions her academic pedigree (Harvard undergraduate, Stanford graduate school). My middle-class sensitivities—I am trying to describe my experience now—kick in when there is no pause and no reflection around Garber's straightforwardly "middle-class" educational affiliations. I'm not sure what is happening, but I am confused because this contradiction arises in an intentionally class-conscious book that offers a model for bridging the classed and raced locations of queer theory and lesbian feminism by using the poetics of working-class/lesbians of color, including Audre Lorde and Gloria Anzaldúa. I'm confused because, as we know, Harvard and Stanford do not primarily educate the middle class, and they don't educate students for the middle class. Not knowing Garber, I want to learn how to think along with her. She has, after all, brought up the matter of authorial class identity so often obscured in academic writing. Also, to speak personally, her edited collection, *Tilting the Tower: Lesbians, Teaching, Queer Subjects*, was an important book to me as a graduate student trying to understand what it might mean to do Queer Studies in a concrete way. Yet in negotiating her class relationship to her subject, Garber defers the work of explicitly negotiating the status her university worlds have created for her. Is it more important that Garber is a white middle-class lesbian writing about working-class/lesbians of color, or is it more important that Garber is a Harvard and Stanford graduate doing that work? Garber's attention to queer-class-race positioning, I want to emphasize, allows me to ask these questions. More typically, no such invitation is made in Queer Studies.

Thinking more generally now, how do Queer Studies status agents avoid the contradictions that surely arise between being afforded the most elite education in the world and, at best, making unproblematized claims to white middle-class identity or, at worst, not? My guess is that, compared to their rich students, many White Queer Studies status agents actually feel middle class. Does such a comparison measure in miles differences that scale down to inches when the entire racialized hierarchy of the academy is surveyed? How are we to gauge class in the status-based academy? I do not suggest that we can resolve such contradictions but rather that status-based academic worlds seem to produce them. From a Poor Queer Studies perspective, those contradictions raise a very low-class question: do white middle-class queer status agents underplay the status that their pedigrees give them, thereby refusing to explore the imbrications and resonances of class and race and status and queer scholarly production? Are the places of Rich White Queer Studies home to status bearers who are unconscious of their status or deflect it by foregrounding their middle-class identifications? These questions arise for me not because I personally claim a lower-class status but because I work at CSI. The questions come to me because of my institutional positioning. They come from working below.

The Prestige Pipeline

Despite queer critiques of the employment practices of the corporate university, which continues to hire more adjuncts as it whittles down the ranks of tenure-track faculty, we tend to naturalize who gets a job where. When was the last time you were surprised by the PhD-granting institution of a new hire in Queer Studies? While one might be surprised *that* a Queer Studies hire was made, who gets hired quite predictably aligns with academic pedigree. We have here a window onto higher education's "prestige pipeline," the name I give to the system that produces academic knowledge as a function of its underlying institutional commitment to the overrepresentation of affluence, whiteness, and cisgender embodiment at the most well-resourced elite colleges and flagship university campuses. Protocols of pedigree operate with dazzling efficiency on the academic job market to produce fields of study as sites of exclusion and elitism. Lynn Arner, a leading scholar of the working-class professoriate, convincingly argues that "a monumental determinant of what jobs which candidates will be offered is pedigree.... Select job candidates garner coveted posts not so much through individual merit as through the prestige of their associations," including their institutions, graduate departments, and mentors.[36] The evidence for this system of elite field production is not at all ephemeral. David Colander and Daisy Zhuo find that in English graduate programs (which have substantial overlap with Queer Studies), "the top-six programs get almost 60 percent of their tenure-track professors from other top-six programs and over 90 percent from programs ranked 28 or higher. They get no professors from programs ranked below 63 [out of 130 programs total]."[37] Michael O. Emerson finds a similar answer to the question of who hires whom in sociology, another field with which Queer Studies shares an institutional footprint.[38] We can thus relate the field of Queer Studies and the queer professoriate to the institutional prestige pipeline. And more broadly, we can posit that queer scholars' ideas in the academy form in relation to highly self-selecting and increasingly class-stratified audiences. Now, more than ever, Queer Studies itself has a high-class pedigree.

Not surprisingly, pedigree usually begins at home. In their study of "the new academic generation," Martin J. Finkelstein, Robert K. Seal, and Jack H. Schuster find that "academic careers are increasingly attracting entrants from higher socioeconomic backgrounds."[39] "Prestigious, research-oriented universities draw their professors disproportionately from the middle and upper classes. Faculty offspring do the best of all: they are the most likely to be found in the most honored institutions," according to Arner. Citing the federal National Science Foundation's 2012 Survey of Earned Doctorates, she writes, "Recipients of American PhDs in the Humanities had the highest proportion of parents, of both sexes, with advanced degrees: 43.4% of the fathers and 30.5% of the mothers possessed such credentials, while 21.8% of the fathers and 26.7% of the mothers of PhD recipients in the Humanities possessed only high school educations or less."[40] The fact that familial socioeconomic status and parental pedigree so strongly influence whether and where one goes to college, what one studies there, how far one advances in the academy, and ultimately what tier of the academy one works in has important implications for the professoriate. Arner suggests that PhDs from prestigious schools are perceived by hiring committees to have cultural capital, an especially important "substitute currency . . . when access to capital is limited." By this logic, "it is as if one can hire a piece of Judith Butler by hiring her PhD students."[41]

We must protect tenure, but for whom are we protecting it? Who does the queer academy want, and why? In the early years of Queer Studies, when "professionalization" flashed as a warning of what could go wrong if the field found solid institutional footing, white gay men with high-class educations embodied both change (Queer Studies!) and stasis (and the job goes to . . .). In her 1994 "Queering the Profession, or Just Professionalizing Queers?,"

Sarah Chinn, a CUNY colleague and former executive director of CLAGS, invokes this race, gender, and class intersection as she identifies the stakes of queer professionalization. Citing Ed Cohen's open discussion of his successful job search, Chinn writes that

> Cohen's payoff was one that seemed inevitable for a white male graduate student educated in an elite institution . . . a job at Rutgers, name recognition in a growing academic discipline. This seems self-evident, and Cohen is willing to acknowledge it. Yet his honesty borders on a smugness that belies the rich array of choices he was offered and hardly mentions. What is the payoff for those job hunters without a prestigious Ph.D., for whom a shrinking job market could mean that the result of six or seven or more years of loans and temping and teaching wherever you can is, well, a dissertation that can't open too many doors, no matter what its title?[42]

Things have changed since 1994—and for the worse in terms of the job market for tenure-track positions. What has not changed, however, is the rule of pedigree, the rule of affiliation born of institutional status and socioeconomic status. Indeed, as the field becomes more established, with undergraduate majors and graduate certificates that formalize one's queer qualifications, the rule of pedigree concretizes. Weighty queer academic credentials lend heft, even respectability, to the field. Queer status agents throw their weight around. The power of pedigree both reinforces the preference given to white men in academia and simultaneously masks it, as women and people of color from elite institutions join the white men for whom elite institutions have always worked and continue to work hardest.

Queer Studies rarely critiques itself for overlooking or underserving scholars who have attended undergraduate and graduate schools anywhere other than at a small handful of "top" programs. Missing from view are the many would-be rising stars who are not attached to the field's prominent and privileged thinkers, Queer Studies status bearers whose academic capital is brought to bear when their graduate students go on the job market. These statements seem obvious. They are, in fact, remarkable. As someone whose graduate school advisor, Susan Gubar, was a famous feminist literary critic, I have no doubt benefited from just this kind of attachment. Having entered Queer Studies through feminist criticism around 2001 when I began writing a dissertation on James Baldwin, I have been struck by how intricately, yet casually, ordered is the world of Queer Studies. One perceives a resemblance to the private social codes and unspoken protocols in

Edmund White's *Forgetting Elena*. The more I circulate inside that academic order—not just through research but through face-to-face encounters and through a few cross-class Queer Studies friendships—the more it seems to me that everyone knows everyone else personally, though I know that can't possibly be true. But it is sort of true, isn't it? If we follow the money, we can partially explain these connections as resulting from expensive opportunities for professional engagement, such as annual academic conferences or the more frequent events hosted (i.e., paid for) by one's own high-status institution. But beyond the costliness that makes these highly structured opportunities for career building exclusive rather than inclusive (membership has its privileges), the top of the Queer Studies hierarchy seems reinforced by the affective bonds—one might say the flirtations—that condense around status. Elite Queer Studies relationships often date back to undergraduate and graduate educations at exclusive colleges and universities. It's a small Rich Queer Studies world—like Facebook, in its early days, at Harvard.

More disturbing than affective peer bonding created within the exclusive ranks of Rich Queer Studies, however, is the non–peer bonding between graduate students and the well-placed faculty members to whom they look not simply for intellectual mentorship but for material support. That material support can come in many forms, beginning with admission to graduate programs and, later, the distribution of graduate assistantships. The ultimate form of material support that all scholars who wish to remain in the academy need, of course, is a job. While chapter 3 argues for an explicit link between Queer Studies and working-class undergraduate students' work worlds—an argument that considers the value of Poor Queer Studies for work outside the academy—a distorted form of Queer Studies job training happens at the upper end of the academic spectrum. When one's livelihood depends not only on one's own written words but on the words inscribed on that most cherished work-permit-by-another-name—a letter of recommendation by a high-status advisor at a top school—then we need to ask just what kind of work relationship is getting reproduced, rewarded, and coded as knowledge within Rich Queer Studies. And we need to remember that the payoff of the current system is not simply good work (which is everywhere) or even professional recognition (which can be lovely). The payoff of becoming permanently ensconced at the top of the system of class and race stratification of higher education is that magical ability to forget or ignore or dismiss or doubt the fact that Queer Studies is Rich Queer Studies. The payoff is that one doesn't have to talk about what one's ideas cost to make. A room of one's own and money.

The fact that we don't have many Queer Studies departments further hides what is easily observable simply by browsing traditional departments' faculty webpages: the naturalization of hiring practices that conserve and cohere institutional classes. Ungrouped and unstructured, Queer Studies professors are nevertheless within this system of privilege that imagines itself as merit-based. A "tyranny of structurelessness," to use Jo Freeman's phrase from women's liberation, emerges as we fail to grasp the power dynamics that create very real but unutterable hierarchies in our ambiguous field formations.[43] Worryingly, without widespread formal institutional structures for resisting systemic problems (for it is important to note that structures can operate as brakes as well as grease for the wheels), Queer Studies professors embedded in traditional departments may get more leeway to make Queer Studies hires, even as they get less leeway to hire in Queer Studies in the first place. The imbrication of Queer Studies within nonqueer disciplinary structures can even lead us to wonder whether Queer Studies efforts to fight the good fight, to make new queer knowledge, to resist the pressures of institutionalization also lead to the justification of queer elitism.

I am asking whether our own Queer Studies house is too much in order around status. I am asking, along with Chuh and Chinn, how we might disorder it. I am asking, along with Gordon and Amin, whether we want to.

The Queer Studies Aspirational Mood

I blame, in part, our aspirational mood. Just as we learn to say the words and thoughts that class- and status-based Rich Queer Studies has made for us, so too we aspire in our own work. In aspiration, individual and institutional narratives can entwine to form an odd coupling, especially given, on the one hand, the enduring racism, sexism, transphobia, and homophobia of the university and, on the other hand, the dogged persistence of many antiracist, antisexist, anti-transphobic, and anti-homophobic queer theorists. Yet universities do find uplifting diversity rhetoric useful in their aspirational narratives, and queers do find the springboard of status useful in our upward professionalization, such that there is an aspirational common cause. Aspiring (and frequently perspiring) thus becomes the thinkable mode and method of professionalizing in Queer Studies within the university context.

In such an aspirational mood, researchers (to take one example) think to begin a study of the most LGBT-supportive campuses by consulting a list of top public universities predetermined by a media company that, it is perfectly clear, does less to assess academia than to hold it hostage.[44] That is, we look for the top Queer Studies programs at the top. Everyone look up: "The purpose of focusing on the top-ranked universities in this research is to provide benchmarks and best practices that may lead to development of positive trends in practice *since other lesser-ranked universities and colleges regard the top-ranked as aspirational institutions and role models, more often than not emulating and replicating their efforts and strategies*."[45] This trickle-down vision of Queer Studies (there are curricular and research criteria folded into the definition of LGBT-supportive campuses) becomes even more normative later in the study: "Applying the website evaluation framework and criteria developed in this research to other universities and agencies will identify how the rest of the country is faring in terms of representing their support of LGBT people on their websites. Suggestions for interventions and concrete strategies in support of LGBT people at these institutions will also be made to ensure that they do not stray far behind the top identified in their domains of work."[46] The problem, which I worked to contextualize in the introduction, is that the top schools are the unambiguous drivers of class stratification in higher education, even when we select for the top public schools, which are so often still out of reach for low-income students.[47] If the top schools, public as well as private, leave poor students behind, they also leave poor queer students behind. They also leave queer black and brown students behind. The 2019 "Best College for LGBTQ Students" was the University of Washington, Seattle Campus.[48] Yet black students made up only 3.9% of the student body and Hispanic/Latino students just 7.8% in the spring of 2019.[49] How could such a drastically race-sorted school be "best" for students who need black and brown as well as queer communities? Yet such schools are validated by queer research and marketing machines alike as the top schools for queer students.

Far from singling out any particular research study for special criticism, I suggest that the above example represents a rather mundane instance of the not-so-queer methodological suturing of top LGBT schools and the top schools, period. Cathy Davidson, whose work provides a touchstone for *Poor Queer Studies*, argues that our most prestigious colleges and universities are structured by principles of "exclusion, sorting, selecting, and ranking" and that they have thus succumbed to (and enforced) "the tyranny of selectivity," a power play that limits the possibilities for progressive pedagogy at those rich institutions and, disastrously, shapes the educational status quo across the academy.[50] The educational workplaces with the least motivation to innovate become prescriptive models for what college should be. Deep material and structural resources nurture the psychic privilege that makes the educational tyranny of wealth-based ranking systems irresistible rather than laughable. For savvy queer college applicants, participation in the consolidation of the field of Queer Studies around a very select few colleges and universities that can offer queers the most support becomes the goal, the path toward the queer academic good life to which the best aspire.

And this is no less true for savvy Queer Studies scholars. Queer though we are, we forget what Arner reminds us should be obvious: "It's a simple fact: students who attend the most celebrated colleges and universities are not the most talented and gifted scholars.... Socioeconomic background determines, more than any other factor, who gets into the top institutions."[51] She continues,

> I would remind my colleagues that good pedigree does not guarantee anything: there are strong and weak students in all doctoral programs.... I also would advise working-class Ph.D. holders that, although less prestigious, teaching at big state universities instead of private research universities can be a blessing, for there are many more working-class students and colleagues at such institutions. In such settings, working-class faculty members are typically subjected to less classism and would likely find it more rewarding to teach large numbers of their "peeps." *The downside of this distribution, though, is that these placement patterns reproduce a highly classed tier system.*[52]

I appreciate Arner's upending of assumptions about the naturalness with which we assume and assign value within the academic hierarchy. I like her rejection of classism and her vision of how making good decisions around class-based collegiality might be crucial to professional fulfillment. But it is difficult, if one hopes to see oneself as part of an academic field—if one has been trained or trained oneself in an academic field by immersing oneself in the critical literature that is known to define the field—it is difficult to research and write within that field without imagining oneself in intimate conversation with that field. More precisely, it is difficult to do Queer Studies without reference to the field of Queer Studies as it comes to one wearing its class regalia, its bold signifiers of status that take the form of the field's foundational texts and authors, its vanguard figures and propositions, its privileged places. It is difficult to imagine not being part of those conversations and still being in the field, close to what Erica Rand calls "the queer-theory action."[53] Problematically, the field gets reimagined with reference to what is now its given, classed self. Our bibliographies (including the one at the end of this book) bear witness, as do the titles of conference talks by aspiring scholars, where we see perhaps the best evidence of the ways trickle-down Rich Queer Studies manages the discursive terrain that comes to signify as the field.

From the perspective of Poor Queer Studies, the field of Queer Studies often seems far afield. Yet working-class university worlds undeniably constitute a field within which Queer Studies happens. But what is this second field called and how is it constituted? The dissonance between fields makes me wonder: I'm a Queer Studies professor, but how do I stand in relation to the field that names my position? It's clear that Rich Queer Studies professors and I don't have the same job. But do we even have the same career? The comparison may be more odious than previously thought.[54] This book might be understood as an effort to make the comparison between Poor Queer Studies and Rich Queer Studies a bit more odious so that their class- and status-based incommensurabilities can be exploited rather than invisibilized or naturalized. As a point of reference: in the summer of 2018, several campus-wide emails went out at my college. One informed the community that CSI now had one working lawnmower for its 204 acres (huge, by CUNY standards), which had also flooded due to broken irrigation systems. Another email explained that the electricity was out, again. Individual offices were told that there was no more paper to be had until September, nor was there money for postage for a week. Try to find a working water fountain and you'll end up back at the vending machine paying $2.00 for a bottle of Dasani. At least the Dasani is cold, not unlike the water at the sinks in the restrooms, where the hot water has been turned off. These minor annoyances were preceded in the spring of 2018 by an all-college gathering to review our dire finances and share in creating strategies for coping (though I believe the word "thriving" was also used). Why do my faculty colleagues and I, staff members, and the students need to know these things? Why publicly discuss the sordid topic of coin? Because my college is so poor that these are the issues that literally stand out before us and, therefore, around which we must come to a community understanding. My colleagues and I must understand the tall weeds, the pooled water, the stifling classes, the dirty restrooms, together, in order to do our work. Gayle Rubin suggested at a 2012 public conversation with Carol Vance and Esther Newton that categories such as sexual identity are better thought of as part of the built environment than as part of a false consciousness. Rubin's further point was that we ought to purposefully use and negotiate those categories, which exist, rather than try to achieve theoretical liberation from them. Following Rubin, I would add that the built environment of academe is classed, and that doing Queer Studies in a crumbling, crowded, isolated place inevitably forges a queer-class connection that must be negotiated—not as a mere roadblock, but as an often-broken, flooded walkway that a campus community navigates as part of its shared, class-based, institutional identity work. The physical plant shapes how we're queer, here. Such can become the grounds for comparison between Queer Studies done here and Queer Studies done elsewhere. A queer-class comparative analysis forces the question, At what point do the material conditions of our work at Poor Queer Studies schools so alter what it is possible to do at and as our work that we ought to call our professions by different names? And if we do have the same career, is such a convergence only accomplished using the terms of Rich Queer Studies (rather than, say, the terms of lawn care) as our common language? Are Rich Queer Studies professors and Poor Queer Studies professors, to use Arner's language, queer peeps?

We can partially understand the working relationships of people within Queer Studies by considering the ways Queer Studies engages with workers outside the academy. Referencing Anne Balay's *Steel Closets*, Martin Duberman (founder of CLAGS and longtime CUNY employee, ultimately of distinguished professor rank) exposes a devastating weakness in gay politics. Duberman writes, "The most prominent and prosperous gay organizations— the Human Rights Campaign (HRC) and the National LGBTQ Task Force— seem astonishingly unaware (or unconcerned) that the majority of LGBTQ people *are* working-class.... The blue-collar working class is a foreign culture, speaking an undecipherable language (and it isn't queer theory)."[55] I want to pick up on that last parenthetical, "(and it isn't queer theory)." Here, Duberman suggests that if the HRC and the Task Force fail to listen to blue-collar workers, so too do academics, who tune out those who do not speak the language of queer theory. That this second parenthetical mirrors an earlier one, "(or unconcerned)," implies not simply that queer theorists do not or cannot hear blue-collar workers but that, like high-class gay organizations, they don't care to listen to them. The two parentheticals, in other words, suggest a shared class position between upper-class agents inside and outside of the academy.

Further along in his argument, however, Duberman makes clear that he does not conflate queer theory with the queer academy, writing that "radical voices are still heard today, but ... emanate primarily from queer public intellectuals, mostly based in the universities, and from emerging gay organizations on the local level—groups like SONG (Southerners on New Ground), based in Atlanta."[56] In clearing space between the language of queer theorists on the one hand and, on the other, radical voices in the universities who attend to working-class and blue-collar queers, Duberman partially hollows out queer theory's claims to radicality. I have preferred not to parse out queer theory from Queer Studies in this book, for even those Queer Studies scholar-teachers who do not identify as queer theorists per se inevitably create and benefit from and respond to and ventriloquize the incredibly influential scholarship identified as queer theory. Rather, I emphasize the personal and institutional class and status divides among those of us working in Queer Studies (and, in one way or another, engaging queer theory), a distinction that I think Duberman's larger argument would support. The pertinent question within Queer Studies then becomes, Who is or is not listening to whom—and from where are we listening or not—within our class-stratified field? How do our patterns of speaking to and listening to reproduce that stratification? Our internal field divisions certainly do not replicate the material realities that structure the blue-collar worker/elite queer theorist impasse, but they do replay a mode of class-inflected inattention within our most immediate sphere of influence.

Lisa Henderson, who studies the cultural production of class, suggests that "the project of class recognition in queerness ... seeks to recognize the array, internal density, and social significance of mixed-class encounters, some fleeting, ... some enduring."[57] I want to suggest that Queer Studies has a field culture that can benefit from the "project of class recognition in queerness," specifically by examining "mixed-class encounters." For Henderson, the work of queer-class recognition is nuanced, as it seeks to "articulate the array of dynamic class positioning (upward and downward mobility; class escape, entrapment, and security; genteel poverty; patrician bohemianism; the anxiety of productivity across the class spectrum) in contrast to familiar, more static categories and their presumptive attributes. People might talk more about class in culture if available idioms weren't so categorical."[58] In contrast, my initial framing of Poor Queer Studies/Rich Queer Studies redeploys class terms that seem rigid or stale. My intent in using these overly familiar (yet ever-ambiguous) terms is to insistently locate Queer Studies within its milieu—the unflinchingly hierarchical, class-stratified, category-loving context of higher education. We teach in tiers. We write with resources. Yes, Queer Studies names a category-busting intellectual project, but at a material level it also names a job that is site specific. We have offices (shared or not?), we have classrooms (packed or not?), we have office equipment (printer paper or not?), we have restrooms (hot water or not?), we assign books (affordable or not?), we write books (accessible or not?). These questions of materiality can raise questions about relating—or not—across class-overdetermined academic tiers. They can reveal the power of structural disparities in higher education to condition mixed-class encounters. Yet they are not questions Queer Studies organizes itself around. Why not?

Queer Studies professors' varied individual class histories across institutions, combined with blanket theories that flatten our many class-diverse workplaces into the neoliberal academy, tend to make site-specific class recognition within Queer Studies a murky business. Yet, as Dana-Ain Davis illustrates in her examination of neoliberalism at the local institutional level, much of our actual work happens at the level of everyday interaction with material surroundings, resources, and people, which combine to situate class recognition in Queer Studies somewhere between intimately personal histories and grandly theoretical engagements with capital.[59] In other words, the field of Queer Studies might be better recognized as a class-based formation by tracking the workerly ways by which queer people with idiosyncratic histories use the resources at hand to shape and build intellectual projects.[60]

Comparisons of the material bases of our queer work reveal the utility of asserting new class taxonomies, as when I include in the same top-heavy category (Rich Queer Studies) both elite colleges and flagship public institutions. Douglas Greenberg argues for such a connection, writing that although

> the good news is that students seeking a real education can find one at many kinds of institutions, including both public and private universities . . . , the bad news is that the flagship public institutions are more similar to the elite privates than [some] realiz[e]. Their aspirations are similar, their students are judged by similar standards, their faculties seek (and receive) the same sources of grant funding and honor for their research, they tend to emphasize the undergraduate "experience" rather than undergraduate education, and too many of their faculty would rather train new Ph.Ds. for whom there are few jobs than teach undergraduates.[61]

This is not to dismiss the ways that interpersonal relations and broader relations of political economy inform the class culture of Queer Studies but, rather, to recognize the field as a set of material relations among its queer people and places. Such recognition seems to promise neither the depth of an individual, richly fettered class psychology nor the breadth or critical force of overarching theories of class struggle. But it prompts a poignant question: Are Queer Studies practitioners prepared to recognize ourselves and our relations with each other's work in and through the materiality of our work lives? More ominously, what strategies will we encounter for mis-recognizing the materiality of class relations within Queer Studies culture, including the way elitist values recode power and privilege as meritocracy—and thus beyond the purview of class analysis?

It can be difficult to engage with, speak to, and be heard by exclusionary prestigious institutions from the outside, from below. It can be even more difficult to question them as educational models, especially given what I've called the aspirational mood of higher education. That aspirational mood—an unqueer methodological underpinning if ever there was one—inspires reverence and mimicry. And through its inspirational, indeed mystical combination of common sense and empirical research, it tells us what counts as a worthy model of higher education. In the past decade, my school has adopted tenure standards that prioritize scholarship above all and that are modeled on increasingly demanding expectations around publishing. In literary studies at CSI, the requirement for promotion and tenure to associate professor is one monograph published by a high-quality academic press, plus a handful of articles in peer-reviewed journals, plus presentations at inter/national conferences. Another monograph, plus articles and edited collections, plus a bunch of service work, secures promotion to full professor. Of course, excellence in the classroom is supposedly the sine qua non of teaching schools such as those in the CUNY system, where full-time faculty contracts have, until 2018, required 10.5 hours per week of classroom instruction for four-year college faculty (a 3-4 teaching load) and 13.5 hours per week for two-year college faculty (a 4-5 teaching load). In the broader atmosphere of higher education, convincing educators that high-status schools have something to learn from low-status schools (publish a bit less, for example), which is perhaps Davidson's most vivid argument throughout *The New Education*, becomes not only difficult; it simply makes no sense, not only to educators at high-status schools but to all of us who must revere and mimic their strange rich ways—but on a shoestring. And so a blind spot opens up as a structural necessity of the tyranny of selectivity. At poor schools like CUNY, "faculty, administrators, and students . . . work to deliver and to gain the best and most innovative education possible against financial restrictions that those at well-funded institutions *cannot conceive*."[62] And yet we do so under the pressure not to be, ourselves, models but instead to rise.[63]

Poor Queer Studies becomes inconceivable at our model selective Queer Studies institutions. And likewise, for Poor Queer Studies professors, it is nearly impossible to imagine that the work we do within our material constraints can have meaning for those who teach and write without those constraints. Much of the rest of this book tries to convince readers otherwise by paying attention to what actually happens in Poor Queer Studies classrooms and on Poor Queer Studies campuses. The knowledge made in the places of Poor Queer Studies, including the jokes we invent that enable us to decode the provincial anecdotes of Rich Queer Studies, stays there. And so Poor Queer Studies practitioners make educational virtue out of economic necessity, doing good work on our local level but without the concept of becoming educational models for the field. Both blessing and curse, low-status schools innovate by focusing on the student and "not the professor, not the profession, not the discipline, all of which are central to the status of the research university."[64] While this trade-off helps our students, if it requires various degrees of withdrawal from the broader profession and our disciplines, then on what professional common ground can we meet our more well-resourced peers in order to model our student-centered pedagogies and our place-based queer theories? The inconceivability of Poor Queer Studies as a discipline-changing intervention is near total.

It would seem that I've worked my way into an irony or a contradiction, for not only has this book been published by Duke University Press, a high-quality academic publisher known for its cutting-edge queer theory list, but Duke UP has published Queer Studies books by several of my colleagues at the College of Staten Island, including Rafael de la Dehesa, David Gerstner, and two by Sarah Schulman. Further, Duke has published books by faculty working at other far-flung and much-overlooked campuses within the CUNY system, as have other notable presses. If publishing is one means by which Queer Studies is made conceivable, and if CSI faculty are publishing in Queer Studies at top presses, how can I argue that CSI is not one of the places of Queer Studies? The answer has to do, predictably, with the power of class to organize the potentially knowable into the known or to disorganize the potentially knowable into vagueness, the opposite of a target. Wendell Ricketts, editor of two anthologies of writing by working-class queers, writes that "if 'class' very broadly refers to systems created for the accumulation of power and influence and for the allocation of goods and resources, then it seems clear that who can write, who does write, and whose writing is rewarded with publication and distribution (and, thus, tends to survive) is not random."[65] Agreeing with Ricketts, I would emphasize a contradiction of this moment in the academy. In addition to publication being a reward granted to those who have already accumulated class power at work, being published can actually magnify the risks associated with one's underclass institution location. Beyond the risks of not finding a publisher (I received twelve disheartening rejections before my first book manuscript on James Baldwin was accepted for publication at the University of Michigan Press), Poor Queer Studies professors publish at their own risk. We insert our work into a system of knowledge production that promises to reward us less. Our publishing-based promotions will result in smaller salary increases. Our colleges will not have the resources (including institutional name recognition) to make our work visible beyond on our own campuses. They will not reimburse us for travel when we try to promote our work. In short, the risks of our good work being diminished hang over us. Not all of these problems are unique to scholars from poor schools, but problems accumulate and compound in special ways for us, just as power accumulates and compounds in special ways at wealthy schools. Book publishing can point toward both accumulations at once.

Lucky and Rare

I am arguing that Queer Studies is a field divided from itself along lines of class and status. By indexing such a split between resource-rich schools with high institutional statuses and resource-poor schools with low institutional statuses, I echo several running narratives about stratification and hierarchy within Queer Studies (scholar/activist, theory/pedagogy, lesbian and gay studies/Queer Studies, women of color lesbian feminism/white queer men's studies). Indeed, Queer Studies seems always to have been the field which is not one. And as it has matured, Queer Studies has increasingly made of us insiders and outsiders.

Perhaps the most basic lesson here is that it's a lot harder to think about material resources when you have them—or rather, when you've always had them—than when you don't. Perhaps this is a human failing, but it's certainly a scholarly one, with its deepest roots in the white privilege that is the backdrop of class-stratified education in the U.S. There may also be a lesson here about Queer Studies as a maturing discipline. Has the field of Queer Studies, as an academic formation, become established enough that it can and must forego discussions about material resources of support for its leading practitioners? If intellectual engagement is linked to forms of material support, by foregoing discussions of the latter do we rhetorically level the playing field, as though scholars without academic jobs or material resources (despite having jobs) should be able to keep intellectual pace with well-resourced scholars who come together (on whose dime?) to determine what's queer about Queer Studies now? Does Queer Studies rely now (and for how long) on a trickle-down theory of knowledge production? Just how can queer status agents imagine and manage their institutional privilege once they've got it?

Upward mobility in the academy produces a normative alignment between individual and institution. For bell hooks, academic success breeds conformism in all but "lucky . . . rare individuals." In *Teaching Community*, hooks records her surprise at discovering an inverse relationship between advancement and radical thought, writing that

> like many professors I naively believed that the more I moved up the academic ladder the more freedom I would gain, only to find that greater academic success carried with it even more pressure to conform, to ally oneself with institutional goals and values rather than with intellectual work. I felt enormously lucky that I was able to succeed in the academic world as a radical, dissident thinker. My success, like that of other lucky individuals whose thinking goes against the norm, was a constant reminder of the reality that there are no closed systems, that every system has a gap and that in that space is a place of possibility. All over our nation, conservative repressive institutions are vocational homes for those rare individuals who do not conform, who are committed to education as the practice of freedom.[66]

My provocation in this chapter has been to link upward mobility within Queer Studies to the conformism of class domination, the engine that powers success in higher education today. Quirky, kind, and queer as many Queer Studies professors are, we cannot suppose ourselves to be that lucky or rare.

My point is that Queer Studies status agents operate at the tricky intersection of intellectual and institutional work in that they, often brilliantly, drive queer scholarship in unexplored directions while doing so in ways that can buttress and are buttressed by the sovereignty of status. Moving up becomes an act of fortification, though not uniform protection, for the power play of moving up is also dangerously unpredictable. Because being an insider in the queer academy—having high-status institutional affiliations—does not preclude and, for queer scholars, queer scholars of color, and queer scholars with disabilities, may indeed be predicated upon being an outsider within those institutions, queer status agents are pointedly devalued at various sites within their home institutions. We are of our institutions, even as we are often deeply at odds with them. Surely a multiplicity of intimacies develops around the status of Queer Studies and its agents.

"You Can Write Your Way Out of Anywhere"

I wonder whether we might begin to see a pattern among Queer Studies status agents who, in order to redefine the field, must also continually redefine and readjust their relationship to status and hierarchy. In this respect, Eve Sedgwick may seem like one of the more unlikely figures through whom to trace my narrative of a field divided from itself, given the extent to which she is understood to have helped consolidate Queer Studies as a field. Not incidentally, *Between Men*, Sedgwick's groundbreaking 1985 monograph, insisted on class as one of the structuring elements of a specific, if shifting, set of sex and gender relations that make possible male homosociality as a central libidinal bond in Western thought and culture.[67]

And so I come to Sedgwick as a bad example, perhaps the worst of the bad examples in this book. Yet, inconveniently perhaps, an anecdote about Sedgwick was the starting point for my thinking about status and Queer Studies in this chapter. On October 31, 2015, the CUNY Graduate Center hosted a conference, "Eve Kosofsky Sedgwick's *Between Men* at Thirty: Queer Studies Then and Now." One of the panels at the conference was titled "Publishing Eve." At the very end of the panel during the question and answer period, an audience member, whom I can't identify, approached the microphone to share a brief but striking memory. He said that during the "difficult professional years" in which Sedgwick was writing *Between Men*, she had told him, "You can write your way out of anywhere." For the audience member, this line contains the evidence of Sedgwick's remarkable "confidence and courage," and it shares with her other writing the quality of "creating spaces of jailbreak for a lot of people."[68] The original professional context for the quote was Sedgwick's efforts to secure a tenure-track job after graduate school at Yale (which followed undergraduate at Cornell). One interesting feature of the anecdote ("those difficult professional years") was that Sedgwick's road to stable employment was rockier than might be remembered, and the outcome—ultimately being hired at Duke—was the much-deserved resolution to years of professional nomadism. The road was difficult because, as many panelists at the conference emphasized, almost no way had been prepared for *Between Men*. The space it took up was the space it created. The professional rewards were deserved because, as Robyn Wiegman observes, Sedgwick possessed a capaciousness of mind that produced varied defenses against critical sovereignty, including "an appetite for the double bind, which meant learning how to withstand the insecurity of a present that offered no epistemological grounding from which to adjudicate the contradictions that characterized it."[69] Perhaps my comments below, which position Sedgwick in relation to academic mobility, pedigree, and the class relations of Queer Studies, might best be viewed as an effort to work in Sedgwick's own mode of privileging the double bind.

"You can write your way out of anywhere." I wish Sedgwick had not said that. Perhaps the man who quoted the infinitely quotable Sedgwick got it wrong. If she said it—and is that really so unimaginable?—then the problem is not simply that the statement is not true, as almost anyone in academia would know. The more vexing part of the problem is that the person who is said to have said this line, Sedgwick, actually might not have known that it wasn't true. And that is because Sedgwick seems, inarguably, brilliant enough to have written her way out of anywhere. She wrote her way from Cornell (undergraduate) to Yale (graduate school) back to Cornell (postdoctoral) to Hamilton College (first tenure-track job) to Boston University (second tenure-track job) to Harvard (fellowship) to Amherst (third tenure-track job) to Duke (first tenured job), on her way to the CUNY Graduate Center (distinguished professor), the last move made under the very sad circumstances of the return of the cancer she had lived with since 1991.[70] The writing legacy Sedgwick left provides one of the stunning examples of intellectual mobility in Queer Studies—the ability to think untethered from the theretofore thinkable. Sedgwick links that capaciousness, which was her gift, to institutional mobility. But in doing so she generalizes: "*You* can write your way out of anywhere." But it was Sedgwick who could do so. Why generalize? Her generalization was interpreted at the conference above as an act of generosity or mentorship, a willingness to see others' gifts and to appreciate them as hers were ultimately appreciated. From this view, Sedgwick's generalization is, itself, an act of making space for others. I honor that generosity. But in the class-stratified field of Queer Studies, and certainly in the context of Sedgwick's own professional trajectory, can "out" mean anything other than "up"? Sedgwick's is an aspirational vision. Her readers will be forgiven if we forget that making good on our queer aspirations requires the ability to be seen by institutions. We will be forgiven precisely because Sedgwick was a visionary who wanted others to be seen.

But none of this makes the statement "You can write your way out of anywhere" true from a Poor Queer Studies perspective. Few of us attend Cornell and Yale, not the worst places to write one's way out of. Few of us scoot up to a desk at Amherst, a place where not a few memorable lines have been written. Perhaps at Hamilton (endowment of $1 billion for 1,850 students) Sedgwick hit a queer low, but the point is that she didn't have to stay at any of these abundantly resourced schools. She got out, and she moved up, brilliantly. The further point, given Sedgwick's pedigree, is that we will never know if she could have written her way out of anywhere. She never had to, and that presents Queer Studies with problems not unlike the one posed by Adrienne Rich to her intended audience of straight feminists in "Compulsory Heterosexuality and Lesbian Existence": if one's desire lines up with the normative compulsion to heterosexuality, how does one ever separate that desire from that compulsion? If one's queer (studies) desire lines up with the normative compulsions of the field to rise, how does one separate that desire from that compulsion? And if one's material, place-based advantages line up with one's ultimate professional success, how do we attribute the capacity for mobility to the "you" who writes your way up, always already from near the top?

The truth is that almost none of us will write our way up and out of where we are. If you start writing at the top as an undergraduate and graduate student, you may get lucky enough to stay there. Most queer scholars of color are not writing themselves out of anywhere. Most women are not writing themselves out of anywhere. A few people write themselves out of the top tier into the tip-top tier. To make an example out of any queer scholar is risky business. But that does not let us off the hook for examining Queer Studies' investment in class and status. A class and status analysis reminds us of the myth of Rich Queer Studies. The myth is that anyone can do it alone. The myth is that some particular, special one can do it no matter where that one starts. The myth is that the black and brown ones who have done it have not *really* done it. The myth is that those at the top deserve the affordances of being at the top, even though they may well deserve to be at the top. The myth is that those at the bottom deserve to be there. The myth is that we can do nothing about Queer Studies' class- and status-based stratifications. The myth is that no one on the bottom knows how to make that happen. The myth is that everyone wants to.

chapter three

The Queer Career
Vocational Queer Studies

If the gay activist experiences a sense of liberation through the public avowal of gay-ness, imagine the heightened exhilaration felt when the espousal of one's gay identity takes place within the context of one's life work, when private self and public role come together, and the relevance and connectedness of one to the other is asserted and acted upon. —John D'Emilio, introduction to *The Universities and the Gay Experience*

Isn't this the moment to wrest minority difference away from specialization, . . . away from that mode of expertise that compels us to turn modes of difference into credentials that will put us in the employ of power? —Roderick Ferguson, *The Reorder of Things: The University and Its Pedagogies of Minority Difference*

Students are already workers. —Marc Bousquet, *How the University Works*

Best known for his 1990 study of gay men and lesbians in the military during World War II, *Coming Out under Fire*, gay historian Allan Bérubé made seminal contributions to Queer Studies' understanding of the intersection of queer lives, the racial integration of labor, and unionization. Referencing his work in progress (unfinished at his death in 2007) on the Marine Cooks and Stewards Union, an organization of working-class men and women that integrated black and white, gay and straight, and conservative and radical in the 1930s, Bérubé asks, "How can studying what they did and wrote help us widen the field of queer studies so that it includes working-class intellectuals and cultural workers? And why is this kind of task especially important now?"[1]

Bérubé poses these questions as a struggling queer intellectual laborer. From that position he writes, "The fact that queer work has a history of being unionized gives me some hope in these hard times."[2] Of course, the precarious "now" of the 1990s was only a sign of things to come in the academy, and Bérubé's question penetrates even more deeply in this now of 2020. In their introduction to the historian's posthumously published book, John D'Emilio and Estelle Freedman remember that Bérubé, working as an independent scholar after having dropped out of the University of Chicago without completing an undergraduate degree, "labored with very few material resources to support his research. He enjoyed none of the benefits that a faculty position at a university provides: no salary or health insurance, no paychecks during the summer, no funded sabbaticals for writing."[3] Bérubé keenly felt the strains of working without an institutional home, writing, "I've been very frustrated lately, discouraged about ever getting the time I want and need to write. This business of squeezing it into lunch hour or Saturday nights is for shit.... This frustration from lack of money and time is just about driving me crazy."[4] Frustrated by the challenges of writing and researching from outside the academy, Bérubé illuminates the more general problem of queer intellectual work inside the academy then and now: How to survive the many indignities of being part of the (now majority) contingent academic labor force? How to fund queer writing? How to prioritize research and writing when other work, both paid and unpaid, tends to crowd it out? And how to produce high-quality class-, sex-, and race-conscious scholarship when the tiered system of higher education hides the work of so many from view? These questions are both queer questions and labor questions, but we are not used to asking them in the same breath because "our collective silence about queer work has impoverished both gay history and labor history."[5]

As a professor of Queer Studies—a job title that explicitly names a queer-labor intersection—I'm interested in what Bérubé calls "queer work," defined as "work which is performed by, or has the reputation of being performed by, homosexual men or women."[6] Bérubé calls the work "queer" because he wants to preserve the stigma that attached both to the word and to the work in his Depression-era study. What interests me about Bérubé's research is the thesis that black and white queer union workers of the 1930s were known as queer to their straight union coworkers, with whom they were joined in class struggle. Moreover, Bérubé understands queerness as enabling coalition—a point of engagement at which straight black and white union comrades could defend their black and white queer coworkers precisely as queer workers. The work of academic Queer Studies might be set in relation to that earlier sense of queer union work not only because Bérubé's definition in large measure applies to both work sites, and not only because stigma around and resistance to queer work and workers persists, though changed, but because both kinds of queer work—not only the queer work of the Marine Cooks and Stewards Union but present-day Queer Studies as well—can be thought of as important models for how queerness and class struggle intersect. Both kinds of queer work can be understood as having implications for how queers and queerness can improve work lives. Queer Studies has not fully recognized its potential to contribute to that conversation, in part because Queer Studies, as a field and as part of its field-defining work, has not adequately developed theories and pedagogies that connect it to labor, including nonprivileged classes of labor in the university.

Or it might be better to say that Queer Studies tends to forget the connections it has forged to labor, and this is because class has proven to be a category of analysis that slips away. Andy Medhurst singles out class as a "lost identity" in academia, arguing that although the cultural turn enabled identity-based knowledges to flourish, "the political agendas of Cultural Studies have cohered around a selective agenda of identity politics. Female students, lesbian and gay students, black students can all find in Cultural Studies academic empowerments for their own senses of identity, and this is an excellent development. Class, however, is in so many ways the 'lost identity' of identity politics that it almost never figures on the intellectual maps many politically motivated students draw for themselves."[7] John Russo and Sherry Lee Linkon, the editors of the 2005 collection *New Working-Class Studies*, similarly argue that scholarship on the working classes, with its foundations in labor studies and worker culture of the early twentieth century, had by the 1960s begun to cede ground to the emerging register of multiculturalism. Where working-class studies managed to persist, it "ultimately moved away from a focus on class and put race, ethnicity, and gender at the center of its work."[8] Though class is often named as part of the diversity matrix in higher education, it has proven a more unwieldy object of intersectional study. So while scholarship that investigates queer-class intersections and identities exists, the authors above posit the deeply troubling idea that identity knowledges increasingly erase class (perhaps now coded as white) from their intersections.[9] In these formulations, when Queer Studies competes with working-class studies for work space, working-class queers and theories of queer work fall out of focus and get lost.

The pedagogical implications of the absence of a stable queer-class analysis across race and gender are a primary concern of this book. *Poor Queer Studies* remembers what has been lost by asking simple questions about our classroom practices: What would it look like and what would it mean to intentionally teach Queer Studies to working-class students? When the students in our Queer Studies classrooms are working-class and poor students, how can Queer Studies engage them as working-class and poor students? How might we teach Queer Studies students as, simultaneously, both the manual and intellectual laborers that they may have been or currently are? What would a pedagogy oriented around queer-class solidarity look like, and how would that pedagogy necessarily alter our usual queer pedagogies?

I believe questions like these don't get asked because mainstream Queer Studies likes to pretend that its job is not to prepare students to be workers or part of the working class. When it is thus modeled on Rich Queer Studies, working-class Queer Studies is left in the lurch, as Ian Barnard, who taught Queer Studies at the working-class Cal State Northridge, describes: "Faculty at my institution are enjoined to develop curricula that are intellectually rigorous, yet at the same time we are reminded that because our institution is a working-class university, the primary function of its programs should be to train students for the workforce. This is what students want and what we are beholden to provide."[10] In the institutional tug-of-war that pits the intellectual against the worker, Barnard identifies administrative double-speak as the primary source of tension (Teach! Train!). Yet the student-worker, refigured as pure consumer, is made to bear the representational burden of the problem. Pressure at working-class schools to train these consumerist students for the workforce can then only be heard as the decree of capital, a project that rigorous Queer Studies must reject. I suggest that in doing so, however, the field misses opportunities to be rigorous in other ways, including to rigorously theorize our students' employment within our poor queer pedagogical projects. As I will show, I vigorously support the prevailing and important critical analyses of the neoliberal university in which "student" has become synonymous with "consumer" and from which the student departs an ever-debtor who may well encounter unemployment and/or underemployment. But in this mix we need to find better ways of making the following questions meaningful: How might Queer Studies help students in the workplace? How might it improve all kinds of work lives, including those of students forced to work their way through school? How can the lessons of Queer Studies be leveraged to inform conditions of labor? I am not suggesting—and I am keenly aware that I may be misread here—that Queer Studies should uncritically participate in the production of workers. I am suggesting that capitalism does not set the only or exclusive terms for thinking about students and/as workers, a point I have been able to better conceptualize as I have been reeducated in the Poor Queer Studies classroom.[11] Rigorously retrained, I am able to ask what work might mean and be for students who have taken Queer Studies courses that train them not simply to do but to make "queer work."

When Bérubé poses the question "How do jobs become queer?" one answer becomes obvious. Jobs in the Marine Cooks and Stewards Union became queer because they were union jobs. In other words, queers were protected, together, by a solidarity that exceeded their sexual and gender identity but that was inseparable from it. Queer Studies, by extension, might think of itself as becoming queer(er) by pursuing shared labor, workplace solidarity, and even unionization. I will return to the queer-labor union connection toward the end of this chapter. But one thrust of my argument will be that, even short of the formal queer-work solidarity that unions have a history of making possible, Queer Studies might still understand itself as a form of organized labor. Indeed, it already does, as the extensive literature on disciplinarity should have made clear. The fact that disciplinarity has largely set the terms by which Queer Studies has considered the question of the organization of its labor has, however, kept other formulations of queer work underdeveloped. In this chapter, I queer the world of work—the work worlds of our poor and working-class students and the work worlds of Queer Studies professors. In fact, this chapter bridges those two work worlds, arguing for a greater interpenetration of student-worker and professor-worker.

Like each of the chapters in this book, my argument here is grounded by a sense of place, which is also to say that my queer argument is complicated by the compromises that structure one's place in higher education. Poor Queer Studies schools, like CSI, offer case studies in compromise, often very innovative compromise. I never met Edmond L. Volpe, the college president under which the two-year Staten Island Community College and the experimental, financially imperiled, two-year upper-division Richmond College were merged in 1976 in the midst of New York City's financial crisis to form a "comprehensive college," the College of Staten Island. Yet in reading Volpe's 2001 book about his two decades as the first president of CSI, *The Comprehensive College: Heading toward a New Direction in Higher Education*, I recognize an educator and administrator who struggled amid the "educational realities" of his day[12]—just as the CSI community watches our (very LGBTQ-supportive) president, Dr. William Fritz, navigate through years of drastic austerity budgeting by New York State politicians. The volume reads like a book of compromises, creative and otherwise, beginning with the creation of a four-year college guided less by a proactive vision for how education ought to be done than by the state's now utterly recognizable austerity vision of how little can be done and still go by the name of "higher education." From within that field of vision, the "new direction" that Volpe prescribes is a three-year general education undergraduate bachelor of arts degree that eliminates the major. This recommendation builds on two related but competing interests. The first is Volpe's interest in students being able to more freely pursue their shifting intellectual tastes without specializing in, and being constrained by, a major discipline: "A liberal arts undergraduate program should have a single goal—intellectual exploration. It should provide students an opportunity to explore themselves, their society, their world, and in the process develop a critical intellect and an ability to communicate their thoughts."[13] Competing with that interest is a fact that, Volpe admits, "should have (but never really) penetrated my comprehension as a classroom teacher in a four-year college: *American students go to college to prepare for a career.*"[14] The logic here is rather fascinating. Because the four-year degree has become the new two-year degree—that is, because preprofessional programs (Volpe points to business programs specifically) have become the norm across community colleges and four-year colleges—it would make more sense, if one remains interested in the liberal arts, to educate students less for business (or English or biology) and more through intellectual exploration. Rather than two initial years of general education and two final years of specialization in the major, students would spend three years elevating the state of their general educations. Three, a compromise between two and four. Yet even here, another of Volpe's compromises surfaces. The diverse academic preparations of matriculants at CSI make general education look rather more like an extended period of learning basic skills rather than an added opportunity to pursue intellectual side streets. Is general education more elevation or remediation at CUNY?

It is easy to criticize Volpe's compromises, but we should consider the complexity of merging a community college with a progressive upper-division college, a task surely none of us has faced. I begin with Volpe not because I agree with his prescriptions but because his place- and class-based interventions contextualize my own. They tell the reader a bit about where I am writing from, though certainly CSI has changed since Volpe stepped down in 1996. It is hardly possible now, for instance, to fail to comprehend that students attend CUNY colleges to prepare for employment, even as it is impossible to miss that they are also motivated by opportunities for intellectual exploration. Volpe's reflections also tell the reader that people from out-of-the-way places like CSI are asking big questions and trying to chart new directions in higher education and doing so without basic funding. And they tell the reader that imagining new directions from such a place means not simply negotiating among institutional constraints—that is, compromising—but that compromised visions are still visions and that compromised visions can do a certain kind of visionary work.

If one of the overarching concerns of this book is the question of how Queer Studies can serve underclass queer students, this chapter particularizes that question by asking how the field can inform and improve the work lives of those students: the sex store employee, social service agency case worker, junior high school teacher in training, church counselor, retail salesperson, hourly campus worker, unemployed job seeker. To answer that question we must recognize not only, as Volpe did, that students go to college to prepare for a career but that *poor queer students are already workers,* paid and/or unpaid, and that one of the reasons they are students is because they want to get better jobs and better-paying jobs than they might have gotten without a college degree. We must also recognize a fact that is surely more amenable to the liberal arts orientation of Queer Studies: that poor queer student workers value queer intellectual growth and its labors. "How do I become a Queer Studies professor?" some students ask. Against the grain of a Queer Studies field that has developed elaborate critiques of the neoliberal university, this chapter tries to hold these two desires, to learn and to earn a living, simultaneously in mind. I use the terms "vocational Queer Studies" and "queer career studies" to name a queer-class pedagogy capable of integrating intellectual growth and job training, the product of which is something larger: the queer career. Pivoting between the two common uses of "vocation"—a job and a calling—this model accommodates the realities that Poor Queer Studies students seek employment, that they feel called to queer intellectual labor, that they are paid and unpaid workers already, that a life of the mind and queer work lives are only artificially separated, and that Poor Queer Studies pedagogies can be transformative in helping workers not only to develop queerer ideas but also to apply those ideas at the intersection of work and desire.

Cathy Davidson offers a sustained and persuasive argument about the urgent need for "the new education" to bridge the high and the low: skills-based and conceptually based pedagogies; a student-focused community college ethos and the empowerment that comes with ready access to resources at elite colleges; the real world and the ivory tower; and vocational training and students' pursuit of a world-changing vocation. I was not surprised in reading *The New Education* to see CUNY—a system "so starved for funding that it cannot offer even the most basic courses required for graduation, has decaying facilities, and uses technology from the last century"—used as a case study in how to build those bridges. Situated at an educational extreme, CUNY finds ways to connect and to thrive.[15]

What unexpectedly piqued my interest was the moment Davidson trained her eye on University of California at Berkeley professor Juana María Rodriguez and one of her Queer Studies classes. Predictably, Rodriquez teaches complex queer theories in this course, and Rodriquez is best known for her groundbreaking contributions to Latina/o/x queer theory.[16] But what Davidson picks up on in Rodriguez's queer classroom pedagogy is something the field of Queer Studies has largely overlooked: its relevance to students' future employment. Davidson reports that "Professor Rodriguez has taken a subject area about which her students are passionate, with a commitment that grows out of a deep sense of personal or political identity, and has designed a course that . . . is based on mastery learning [of online editing and digital skills, for example] that will influence how they learn everywhere—in other classes and in their future work lives."[17] Drawing on the example of what I would call Rodriguez's vocational Queer Studies pedagogy, Davidson links interdisciplinary programs best known for their shared project of conceptually reworking traditionally bounded knowledge practices to "the range of complex skills employers routinely ask for."[18] While my project dramatizes the value of Poor Queer Studies happening at low-status colleges, Davidson and Rodriquez remind me that vocational Queer Studies can be envisioned across institutional strata.

We can pursue the potentially controversial connections named by vocational Queer Studies by considering the queer career of the Poor Queer Studies professor, recasting that job in more workerly terms than are sometimes used to characterize the profession and thus framing the job as a model of queer work with which our student workers can make connections, whatever job they have in mind. At a basic level, Queer Studies, like other forms of employment, happens on a job site. Queer Studies practitioners negotiate workplace issues, not only in the classroom but on campus. We forge connections with other queer workers, whether faculty, staff, or students, just as we learn the institutional histories of our Queer Studies locations in order to better orient ourselves to the work ahead. We even become, for better and worse, hyperresponsible for creating a more diverse workplace, more typically called a campus climate. Yet Queer Studies does not, in the main, think of itself as responsible for incorporating into its pedagogies the workerly lessons and strategies that its practitioners have learned are essential to our jobs. Why shouldn't Queer Studies be considered an applied field of study?

The following list offers some examples of vocational Queer Studies. Readers will recognize many of the topics as ones they already teach. The reorientation I propose is to teach these topics as, among other things, preparation for employment. Applied Queer Studies might include classroom pedagogies that examine:

- Employment laws at the local, state, and federal levels, asking students to determine where and how they will or will not be protected from being fired for being LGBTQ.
- The links between un/employment and transgender, people of color, and immigration status.
- The links between these last three and access to education/ graduation as a gateway to employment.
- The ways incarceration practices and LGBTQ, race, and poverty create a system of unemployability and, due to youth incarceration, create absences in our Queer Studies classrooms.
- The connections between gentrification and queer lives. We might ask about the kinds of neighborhoods students want to live in. How will their employment status situate them there? What kinds of queer community are possible in their visions of future employment, housing/neighborhood preferences, and class contact?
- HIV/AIDS as a workplace issue (health insurance coverage, coming out as HIV+ on the job).
- Coming out as a workplace issue.
- Writing a non-heteronormative work document (a résumé, a job advertisement, an interoffice memo, an invitation to a company holiday party, a formal complaint about workplace discrimination, a medical intake evaluation, a visual pitch for a product or service, etc.).
- The overlapping and distinct LGBTQ and GNC (gender-nonconforming) issues that arise at work.
- The ways systems of capital and sex/gender are interpenetrating rather than distinct and therefore require an integrated analysis (drawing on scholarship such as John D'Emilio's groundbreaking "Capitalism and Gay Identity," as well as more recent studies such as *Sexuality and Socialism: History, Politics, and Theory of LGBT Liberation* by Sherry Wolf and *The Reification of Desire: Toward a Queer Marxism* by Kevin Floyd).
- And finally, we might ask the queerest question of all: What makes work straight?

If I were to narrativize this list—that is, tell the story of how this list finds its way into my teaching rather than offer it as a disconnected set of recommendations—I would explain how these bullet points appear in and across the many different classes I teach. Perhaps foremost, I see literature courses emerge from these employment-related examples, a disciplinary connection that is perhaps not obvious. I see, certainly, a queer working-class literature course, but also a lesbian literature course, a disability studies literature course, an introduction to poetry course. Further, the literature I envision teaching in these courses would not necessarily be about the items in the list above in terms of plot or content but, rather, about the production and consumption of literature in prisons, or the publishing industry's shifting marketing strategies around queer literature, the efficiencies of verse compared to prose, or, most obviously, the pedagogy of teaching queer literature at a working-class school. What could be more appropriate than these intersectional queer-class lessons for the future public school teacher, librarian, publicity agent, parole officer?

Just as students can benefit from vocational Queer Studies—the intellectual call to work queer theories into students' current and future workplaces—so too can Queer Studies benefit from students' experiences as workers. By considering their working relationships with queer student workers, Queer Studies professors can expand the ways we understand the work of our own field, particularly opportunities for class-conscious, student-informed intellectual projects. Rather than shying away from the reality that our students are current and future workers (as well as other facts of our working students' economic lives, including student loan debt, racism, first-generation and immigrant experiences, and homelessness), we would do well to devise pedagogies that focus on sexuality and economic inequality precisely by taking our students into consideration as workers as well as thinkers and making common cause with them as such. Their work narratives, for example, can become our classroom texts, as can ours. Saying to one's class, "I have never worked for money outside of academe," would surely open up opportunities for teaching and learning. The queer pedagogy of comparing my current queer career at CSI to the cornfields and plastics factories and stockrooms and offices that comprise the various closeted places of my personal, now-distant, rural work history not only contextualizes the work I do but also produces a flipped classroom in which student-workers are encouraged to discover ways of bringing their own work histories to bear on our Queer Studies class.

As we link the job of the Poor Queer Studies professor to the jobs of our Poor Queer Studies students, we must also consider the implications of such a workerly queer pedagogy. Poor Queer Studies workers—both teacher and student—can serve as models for integrating queerness and class within and beyond the managed university without simply reproducing that for-capital system and without reverting to an idealized liberal arts model of education that takes neither queer poverty nor student employment nor the racist history of liberal arts education into account. This discussion necessarily leads to recent reflections on queer organized labor as an intersectional framework for a kind of queer-class collectivity that Queer Studies seems both to desire and to obscure in its attempts to link sexual, racial, and economic lives. And it points to chapter 4, which takes up the expansive sense of queer pedagogy that develops when students' and professors' queer careers intersect.

Linking Queer Studies to its value for student workers goes against the grain of most queer and neoliberal critiques of the state of higher education today. How dare we consider students as workers in this day and age of the corporate university, when our institutional administrative practices dictate that we relate to students in this very way, as degree-seeking consumers for whom work will be almost completely circumscribed for decades to come as the effort to pay back student loan debt, whether or not they graduate with that coveted degree? No one has better demonstrated this closed system of corporatized education than Marc Bousquet in his withering analysis of the partnership between United Parcel Service and "Metropolitan College" (and its affiliate institutions, including the University of Louisville) in Louisville, Kentucky.[19]

My point is certainly not that Poor Queer Studies should contribute to and help sustain the logic by which college exists for capital. Rather, I think Poor Queer Studies can do its part to throw a wrench into that system. I suggest that it can do this only by starting from the same facts that Bousquet starts from: our students are already workers and instructional faculty are already workers. The question then becomes, Can the work of Queer Studies be, in part, to prepare students to cause queer trouble at work? For poor and working-class students, how might learning about queer labor history, Black fightback, women's unpaid labor, and AIDS activism be framed as essential job preparation? How might Queer Studies educate in the service of those most at risk of present and future unemployment, underemployment, or work with few job protections? How can we connect queer and race and gender and immigration status with the broad field of work in Queer

Studies? How might the fact of our own jobs—professors of Queer Studies at working-class institutions—provide case studies of integrating queerness with work, making change within a heteronormative work environment, and negotiating within significant constraints, such as austerity ideologies, as we nevertheless work queerly for better work?

I want to make one final, pointed comment about my effort here to open up a discussion of vocational Queer Studies. As I referenced above, the predictable rebuttal to this line of thinking will be that framing education—not only two-year or applied four-year degrees but liberal arts education—as job training not only risks but actively promotes complicity in inequitable systems of market governmentality in higher education. It is common knowledge, from this point of view, that Queer Studies and liberal arts education more generally should not be in the business of being a business. I would argue that nothing could be more ironic than this counterargument, since for many of us every day we spent in college and at the university doing undergraduate and graduate coursework and learning the protocols of higher education was job training . . . for the job of professional academic. While many Queer Studies professors have honed skills outside of academe that qualify them to teach (filmmaking, community organizing, psychoanalytical training, sex work, etc.), many of us have only our academic résumés to recommend us. In other words, we have aligned education with employment, the work history of being a student with one's academic position. And, crucially, we have made it our job to create educational mechanisms—queer courses and programs of study—that even better train students to do our jobs. Increasingly, the Queer Studies major becomes the Queer Studies professor (though usually in a traditional disciplinary department). Yet one can easily imagine Queer Studies professors refusing the notion that our field and job training mix. The idea that higher education can be job training only for those of us who become professors (but of course the issue is almost never put in these terms) points to a failure of the queer pedagogical imagination that has the disturbing effect of de-queering careers other than our own. Beyond professor of Queer Studies, and at the many intersections of desire and work, how can we prepare students for the queer career?

The poet Audre Lorde, who earned a bachelor's degree from CUNY's Hunter College and a master's degree in library science from Columbia University and went on to become a head librarian at Town School Library in New York City, started teaching at CUNY in the SEEK program at City College in the late 1960s.[20] She then taught briefly at CUNY's Lehman College before moving to CUNY's John Jay College of Criminal Justice in 1970, where she helped to build a Black Studies program. From 1981 to 1986 she was the Distinguished Thomas Hunter Chair at Hunter College. Lorde discusses the work of teaching at Lehman and John Jay in her 1979 interview with poet Adrienne Rich. In both instances, Lorde was teaching in particularly raced environments. The students at Lehman were almost all white women training to be teachers of black children in New York City schools. The students at John Jay, which had been a police college until it became a four-year college in 1970, were a mix of black, white, and Puerto Rican men and women, black and white police officers (with guns), and first-generation students from all races who were able to attend college thanks to the new policy of open admissions at CUNY.

What stands out to me in Lorde's thinking about pedagogy is that she thoroughly integrates the racial contexts that charge her classrooms with the careers the students are training for. Teaching white future educators was "terribly costly emotionally" to her as a black woman, but that work raised in her mind the question, "What about Black teachers going into ghetto schools? . . . I saw there were different problems, that were just as severe, for a Black teacher going into New York City schools after a racist, sexist education."[21] At John Jay, Lorde was able to do the work she felt called to—"I want to teach Black students again"—but here she was teaching in classrooms where cops sat next to "kids off the block." The work of her courses could not be separated from the students' various relationships to race or to policing, nor from their relationships to the street, nor from their relationships to her as, for the first time, an explicitly out lesbian professor. Just as Lorde was teaching some of her students how to "work with themselves as Black women," she was teaching other students how to work with these students as cops, and she was teaching all of this as someone working from an openly queer black position. Lorde was teaching Black Studies to student-workers, and she was teaching Queer Studies to these student-workers as well. Lorde's example teaches us that queer career studies does not happen only in Queer Studies classes or in isolation from other disciplinary concerns or classroom dynamics, and it does not happen in the vocational vacuum that "training" implies.

Poor Queer Students as Workers

One of the things I want most for the students in my Queer Studies classes at CSI is for them to graduate and get good jobs and bring Queer Studies to bear on those jobs in some way. This is, at least partially, an unqueer desire for a Queer Studies professor to have. I want my students to get good jobs because I see the bad jobs they already have, which is to say that I see the jobs they will always have if they don't find a way to get better jobs. In a recent general education class, almost all of the students (sophomores, juniors, and seniors) work more than twenty hours per week. In all of the classes I have ever taught at CSI save one (an honors course for first-year students in the Macauley Honors College, a tiny subset of scholarship students who receive disproportionate academic accommodations for their achievements in high school), I have students who are parents as well as workers. That many students land in my Queer Studies classes at all is, in fact, somewhat a function of their employment and parenting status. I typically teach night school, so my classes fit into students' work and family schedules.

The fact that my students often love creative and critical literatures—and perhaps more to the point, the fact that I love these literatures—doesn't obscure the fact of their paid and unpaid labor outside of the classroom. They're not interested and interesting thinkers despite working so much. Nor are they necessarily interesting thinkers because they work so much. Their identities as readers don't necessarily problematize their identities as workers, though they sometimes do, and vice versa. Their often-interesting perspectives as students, in other words, stand in unpredictable relation to their current and future employment. Sometimes my students' experiences as workers carve out some of the sharpest angles from which they approach the literature we read and the ideas we confront in the classroom. At other times, students' beautiful minds seem, to use the expected word, "wasted" as they toil behind the cash register at the local CVS or the mall shop. The most unlikeable student I ever taught, who blatantly voiced his self-perceived intellectual superiority over his classmates (something that simply never happens among my students), finally told me his story one day. He'd come back to school after driving a delivery truck for over a decade. He had been, he said, wasting his life, going nowhere. What this know-it-all (who was in fact bright) didn't know was precisely the thing that his condescending attitude was designed to hide: that once he had set himself in motion, the stakes of failure were so high that he spent enormous amounts of energy pushing away from anything resembling stasis, including his peers, the college, and perhaps especially me, someone who had stopped in a place he was trying desperately to leave behind. He asked for a recommendation letter, and then he transferred out to a better school. Poor Queer Studies success stories are often compromised.

Similarly, Lorde's experiences teaching police officers at CUNY's John Jay College of Criminal Justice strikes a chord with me because Staten Island has a palpable police culture, and a segment of CSI students follow parents and other relatives into the family business of police work. One of those future cops was one of my first students at CSI. A former soldier rather than a police officer's son, he had returned from the war in Afghanistan alive and enrolled at CSI (which is perennially atop the Military Friendly schools list). Our class was a standard composition course that I was teaching (to the students' surprise) as a queer theory course, beginning with Freud and ending with Black Queer Studies. I had recently arrived from a postdoctoral teaching fellowship at Duke University, and I was surprised to find myself thinking as the class progressed, "This ex-soldier is one of the smartest and most driven students I've ever taught." Near the end of the term, he told me he was going to apply to the police academy once he'd earned his sixty credits. I stared, incredulous, and then I tried to talk him out of it. The term soon ended, I reviewed his excellent work, and that was that. Until I bumped into him years later working the busy corner in midtown Manhattan where I lived. My block was his beat. He was in his police uniform, and I was uncomfortable. Yet in that moment I thought, "This cop has queer knowledge with him on the job, and that is better than not, for him and for the rest of us." I wondered if I was right, and I wondered what might have happened if I'd taught him as a future police officer. What would have happened if, in that course years ago, I had understood one of my Queer Studies job responsibilities to be queerly training him for the job he wanted rather than trying to talk him out of it because he was so smart? One of my goals in this book is to think through such compromising questions.

I am stopped short by valid criticism as I pursue this line of thinking. I am warned: you have compromised too much. Police are not like other workers. You can't queer a gun, the blue wall of silence, or the enduring history captured in a photo of a policeman's boot on a black woman's neck. The risk of homonationalism—of using queerness to prop up the state—threatens to undermine a Poor Queer Studies workerly pedagogy that does not commit to the difficult task of historicizing the often disturbing work cultures of our students' intended careers. The stakes are high in such Poor Queer Studies classrooms, not only because students sometimes feel very strongly called to particular—and particularly troubling—vocations but also because their material livelihoods are involved. The stakes are also high for the professor, who surely never imagined becoming a queer career counselor in addition to the more predictable stressors of the profession. Far easier to imagine doing one's Queer Studies job when the only job we have to think about doing queerly is our own.

The Queer Studies Workplace

Diversity has been reframed as good for business, and Yvette Taylor references Sara Ahmed's work to make the point that diversity has been reframed as good for the business of higher education as well. Yet there is a hidden, though to many of us glaring, cost to this business of marketing institutional diversity. Taylor writes, "HEIs [higher educational institutions], as increasingly 'enterprising' seek out and sanction 'diversity' as an institutional capital, while effacing unequal experiences and institutional-interpersonal 'mis-fits.'"[22] Taylor explores the costs to faculty for whom marginal class, sexual, and gender identities operate simultaneously yet often quite differently. While lesbian difference can be leveraged by both HEIs and individuals in higher education, Taylor argues that "class is not a 'difference' that can be easily incorporated into a queer research framework or institutional practice, where notions of deconstruction and diversity sit uneasily alongside that which often is still not named, complicating ideas of multiplicity and situatedness inside and outside of academia."[23] Taylor continues, "In situating these political locations and intersections, class is repeatedly 'dislocated' and 'given up': how then to hold on to it, to recognise continued intersections and unequal effects?"[24] Like the working-class studies and cultural studies scholars we saw earlier, Taylor sees class matters being backgrounded within the broader picture of educational diversity, including sexuality studies. To the extent that class differences go unnamed, a queer deconstructive critique cannot grab hold in order to subvert or denaturalize the constructedness of class categories.

I suggest that when and where Queer Studies dislocates or gives up class, Poor Queer Studies can help negotiate a queer-class reconciliation. If we shift our gaze to students, who are at once the largest customer base to which HEIs market their diversity and also, once admitted, one of the most touted indicators of institutional diversity, we see another kind of class dislocation vis-à-vis queerness. We tell minority students to come to college, and we say that the diversity experiences that college offers will prepare students to enter a diverse workforce. Yet, at the level of curriculum, it is precisely the courses that might help students develop a sense of their own and others' sexual, gender, race, and national diversity—intersectional Queer Studies classes being a prime example—that are the least associated with and marketed as courses that will produce a better workforce. For it has not been made clear, either by university marketers or by Queer Studies practitioners, how queer knowledge will make students better on the job. In other words, Queer Studies has not yet realized its potential to respond to student anxieties about future employment, due in part to the undermining and cynical uses to which diversity has been put in higher education. The dramatic but unremarked ramification is that students might avoid Queer Studies because they do not see how it pertains to their employment goals. Queer students, let alone nonqueer ones, whose focus is becoming employable might reasonably enough be tempted to forego learning about the queer differences that partially structure their lives and which their entire educational experience has withheld from them as viable objects of study. To the extent that workerly concerns direct students away from Queer Studies—and to the extent that Queer Studies does not imagine itself as applicable to workerly concerns—a condition of educational heteronormativity emerges. For the work-minded student, Queer Studies doesn't apply. But work and queerness need not be in such an oppositional relationship.

Rather than jettisoning the diversity-as-workforce-preparation argument as antithetical to Queer Studies, the field might attempt to examine—if not exactly make good on—the diversity promises that the university has made, however sincerely, naively, or cynically. Sara Ahmed demonstrates the possibilities for such work in *On Being Included: Racism and Diversity in Institutional Life*. This fascinating workplace report makes it more possible for diversity workers to understand and therefore potentially intervene effectively in their workplace problems or, as Ahmed has more recently argued, to deploy tactics that will gum up the works of the system so that it cannot continue to do its unfair work.[25] Queer Studies more generally might follow Ahmed's workerly lead, look around us at our campus workplaces, and see what we can learn and teach about queer-worker connections and queer-class pedagogies. A key insight of Ahmed's work on the institutionalization of diversity in higher education is that diversity is incorporated or centered rhetorically while agents of diversity are simultaneously individualized, spectacularized (e.g., on marketing brochures, through their hyperpresence on various committees), and, paradoxically, marginalized. The mainstreaming of diversity effects a displacement evidenced, ironically, by the photo op in which diversity shows up and therefore seems to have a place. But the diversity worker is not actually given a place. Rather, she becomes a placeholder for an institutional commitment that goes no place else. Because the diversity bait-and-switch in the academy happens across work environments, the Queer Studies workplace can be used as a pedagogical case study for teaching students how to read their other workplaces. It can alert them to the signs that indicate, for example, that they have been hired to sustain the uneven distribution of diversity work. That lesson becomes particularly important for a university system like CUNY, with its unparalleled racial and national diversity, for our students will inevitably become the workers asked to shoulder the workplace diversity burden. Intersectional queer-class-race-gender studies can provide tools for resisting those forms of diversity work meant to keep their agents running in place.

Out of line with critiques of the corporate university as workforce preparation, I am arguing that the field of Queer Studies can reorient itself to the intellectual work of making better employees in the very real sense that it can enable people to recognize and confront the conditions of their employment that undermine them as queer, of color, gender nonconforming, women workers, and people. With knowledge of others' queer workplace interventions, including queers' involvement in labor unions and adjunct employee labor movements, our student workers might attempt to change their own unworkable conditions. Given their class backgrounds, Poor Queer Studies students will have knowledge about workplace structures and politics that will inform and guide that classroom work. They might therefore learn to queerly position themselves within integrated forms of meaningful employment as opposed to assimilated into bad employment. The diversity worker who can conceptualize diversity's complex functioning in her workplace—this is a good worker, one whom Queer Studies might better recognize and with whom it might cultivate a pedagogical relationship. And importantly, Queer Studies practitioners might ourselves become better queer workers, in the mode of Ahmed, by examining our own workplaces in order to teach, for instance, the ongoing and still active histories of educational homophobia, transphobia, cissexism, heterosexism, and misogyny that have denied and continue to deny students access to the kinds of queer knowledge that Queer Studies works to produce. We might examine with our students, as I am doing here, the material disparities that condition Queer Studies across the academy and the class biases embedded within much of the field's intellectual labor. The pedagogical work of coproducing that knowledge along with one's fellow campus workers might be understood as replicative—as laboring together toward a vision of more just labor.

My Job Is Your Job: Modeling a Queer Career

Though few Queer Studies jobs exist, I want to think about the job of Queer Studies professor as a model for integrating queer and work. The goal of this thought experiment is to see whether that model can be made adaptable and provide a logic of queer-work integration for other jobs. While the academy cannot provide future employment for many Queer Studies student workers, Queer Studies in the academy exemplifies a workplace where work can be modeled as explicitly queer and where, in fact, doing so is a job requirement. We can even say that an imperative exists, for the Queer Studies professor may well be the most queerly integrated worker whom our Queer Studies students not only know but, moreover, have observed on the job (often in great detail). Watching us do our jobs may be our students' most intimate and practical example of a successful queer career, and in this way it may stand out against other career opportunities for them. One goal of Poor Queer Studies pedagogy would be to turn itself inside out as a model—to make other queer career options available and, even more importantly, to help students envision possibilities for queering nonqueer careers.

Though queer career studies may at first seem disconnected from other, more recognizable work in Queer Studies, potential intersections abound. For example, I read Sarah Chinn's conversation with Heather Love about pedagogy and the recent critical intervention of queer affect as remarkably resonant with my present concerns. Chinn asks, "What do you think brings students to a Queer Studies class? What sense do you get of the emotional needs they bring that are different from the ones that would be in force in, say, a course on the modernist novel?"[26] Love responds, "I think students come to these classes for all kinds of reasons," and she surmises that students' investments range from "identification to curiosity and even at times … a kind of ambivalence or resistance." Love continues, "I think there is something deeply important in that context [of students' various investments] of simply teaching in the field—affirming that this material is significant, that it has a place in the college curriculum, and that one could potentially devote oneself to scholarship on this topic, even over the course of a lifetime."[27] I read this exchange between two Queer Studies professors as seamlessly weaving together a pedagogical concern for queer students— with their many articulated and unarticulated affective attachments to Queer Studies—with a second professional understanding. That is, an important part of the Queer Studies professor's job is to attend to students' various queer attachments not by addressing them directly, or even ever knowing them, but by modeling the possibility of professionally attending to our queer attachments, whether those attachments be to a specific object such as literature or to a less recognizable project, including the project of integrating the twin desires to be queer and to do meaningful work.

Workplace protections for LGBTQ employees across the U.S. are spotty. But even if we had airtight laws banning workplace discrimination based on gender and sexuality, with the result that all LGBTQ people came out on the job, we would still lack a theory of queer work as called for by Bérubé. Beyond a few stereotypical associations such as the gay male hairdresser or the lesbian factory worker—two queer-class figures who certainly deserve thoughtful consideration—we still have few ready models of queer workers that we can carefully turn over in our minds and make sense of. Anne Balay, whose *Semi Queer: Inside the World of Gay, Trans, and Black Truck Drivers* joins her earlier *Steel Closets: Voices of Gay, Lesbian, and Transgender Steel Workers*, continues to break new ground in this respect. But for the most part, how the meanings of work and of queerness interanimate each other, or not, remains a fascinatingly open question.

For this reason, Queer Studies can offer a window onto the concept of the queer career, so long as we recognize our classrooms and campuses as sites for producing grounded understandings of queer work. Training—a word that will surely make some readers uncomfortable because of the ways "apprenticeship" language has been used by university administrations to undermine the work status of graduate employees (and thus to counter attempts at unionization)—nevertheless seems a fitting one for teaching students to make use of the lessons, insights, histories, and workerly details of the Queer Studies professoriate across a range of employment opportunities. Job training—let's not denigrate that phrase. Rather, let's recognize it as queer pedagogy. Queer Studies professors might, then, pull back the curtain on our jobs as jobs. As part of Queer Studies, we might explore the employment contexts in which we produce the field, asking:

- What is the job of a Queer Studies professor?
- What does the Queer Studies workforce look like at our institutions?
- How are the jobs of Queer Studies graduate instructors, other contingent faculty, and tenure-track faculty alike and different?
- How does one become a Queer Studies professor?
- How did the Queer Studies professors at a given institution get their jobs?
- What does your job pay?
- What are the expectations of the job?
- How many hours a week do you work?
- Is travel a big part of your job?
- What kind of benefits package do you have?

- Who is your boss?
- What is the relationship between our sexual, gender, racial, national, and class identities and the job?
- How does your queerness interact with your job?
- Does your queerness affect you at work?
- Why did you choose this job?
- Do you want to stay at this institution?

This sort of pedagogy, which ties workerly questions to the field of Queer Studies, might be particularly useful for poor and working-class students who see education as a route to social mobility and who have a sense that queerness might facilitate that movement from a lower to a higher class. But such questions also speak in a common work tongue capable of relating work and workers across class divides. Certainly queer-class pedagogies can introduce students to the inside story of attaining a new stratum of work through queer academic professionalization, but the real project would be for students to discover the insistent queer-work questions for the jobs they want that are not my job—that is, jobs that are not always already queered.

I've articulated a certain praxis of Queer Studies pedagogy in my preceding comments by connecting the field of Queer Studies to life on the job. I want to set this notion alongside one of Samuel Delany's insights in *Times Square Red, Times Square Blue.* Near the end of his book, which is part ethnography of the Times Square/Port Authority area of Manhattan and part queer social theory, Delany ponders the valences of the question, "What makes us gay?"[28] Perhaps it is what we do. Perhaps it is what was done to us. Ultimately, Delany answers this question in terms of the built environment and the practical rewards of social spaces that encourage queer interclass contact. What makes us gay is not the fact of our being but the fact of there being places where being gay can have social meaning, spaces where people can be gay together. To be gay is to be able to live among others within the social constraints that produce (rather than merely oppose) opportunities for gay sociality: "The fact is, I am not interested in the 'freedom' to 'be' 'gay' without any of the existing gay institutions or without other institutions that can take up and fulfill like functions."[29] Much of Queer Studies also understands the right or freedom to be gay to be a low-reward agentic process. And yet, Queer Studies makes us gay (or queer) because it opens a door to rooms, in this case classrooms, in which we do queer stuff together. Likewise, other workplaces can—though they often do not—give concrete shape to LGBTQ being in the world. Employment can be one of those "other institutions that can take up and fulfill like functions" as "gay institutions." Class- and race-mixed work sites, like nonselective colleges, can create opportunities for queer interclass contact. The work of vocational Queer Studies can be to make imaginable new queer rooms beyond the classroom and the porn theater. Queer Studies classrooms already orient students toward one queer career. Thanks to the lessons learned through interclass contact with queer student-workers in my Poor Queer Studies classrooms, I am able to suggest that the field might design queer pedagogies that can train students for the jobs they want, for jobs that they want to make queer, and even for jobs we don't want for them as queers.

This Job Is a Life

But let me back up. This chapter about queer work originally started with another story.

"You teach career studies?" The frequency with which I've been asked this funny little question when I tell people what I do for a living suggests a peculiar kind of misunderstanding. By now I've been faced with this question enough times to know that people ask it, primarily, because they don't know that Queer Studies exists or that studying queer can be a job. This has been true of most of my students, most of my colleagues, most of my friends, and all of my family. In other words, in many personal and many professional contexts, the words "Queer Studies" make no sense. And so a creative mis-hearing sometimes results. "Queer," which can't be heard as a thing to be studied, is replaced by "career," a word everyone knows how to hear. Plus it rhymes. We can even say that a certain politics of rhyme governs this mis-hearing. Unfamiliar with the study of "queer"—or, less interestingly, unwilling to repeat that word—the interlocutor pivots to the more familiar sound. Perhaps they have heard of "career studies." I doubt it. But the idea, the sound of it, at least makes sense. In the face of this mistaken question, "You teach career studies?," I am put in the position of having to name the work that I do more clearly. I say, "No," and then I repeat my job title slowly and loudly, which of course adds to the strangeness of this already strange word. More than once I have needed to spell it out: "q-u-e-e-r." This usually, though by no means exclusively, happens when the conversation occurs over the telephone. The alumni affairs worker who called from my undergraduate alma mater in rural Indiana to update my records was fairly scandalized, I believe, to have typed those letters as I patiently spelled them out. Their ensuing silence is, of course, open to interpretation. In any case, the semiofficial nature of that interaction stands not apart from but in line with the more numerous casual face-to-face opportunities for misunderstanding and clarification that come my way as a professor of—read my lips—Queer Studies.

Multiple vocational queer pedagogies arise in the vignette above. By naming and renaming his job, the Queer Studies professor teaches the fact that queer work exists. One could go looking for Queer Studies courses, programs, even jobs. On a deeper level, he teaches that "queer" and "studies" make a kind of sense together, a different kind of sense than "career studies" makes, not least because queer sense must be made out of the non-sense— the ostensible mis-hearing—that would erase it. Queer sense is the sense made out of antiqueer non-sense, and so this pedagogical moment becomes an object lesson in Queer Studies–as–applied studies in the world. And finally, this scene reveals that the job of Queer Studies professor contains a meta-pedagogical work imperative: in our lives, we live our careers. We explain our jobs, and in the explaining we do our jobs, even though we are not at work. This claim reverses the misconception that minority faculty go to work, talk to students about being a minority, and, if it's a good day, find a few minutes to conduct their "me-search." In fact, my guess is that most of us go home from work only to find that our queer pedagogies have refused to stay at the office. In that our work of making queer sense of the world follows us home, to lunch, on vacation, it can be said that not only do we have queer careers but that we live queer pedagogical lives.

One of the surprises of being a Queer Studies professor is hearing from students who haven't done all that well in class that they want to become Queer Studies professors. I used to think that this career goal was an expression of these students' excitement at being exposed to new ideas. Who can blame them? But I didn't take these claims very seriously or very literally because they weren't backed up by any number of intellectual practices— the tools of the academic trade—that might enable a move into a career in Queer Studies in the academy. (In my thirteen years working at CSI, I've had one student accepted into a doctoral program with a focus on Queer Studies.) What I have come to realize is that there is a much more complex set of meanings around these students' stated desires to do my job and, in doing so, to enter a profession that enjoys a degree of status. I now think that more than trying to chart a viable career path, students are attempting the difficult prospective labor of envisioning an integrated queer-work life. They want to learn how to be professional queers because they want to learn—and who can blame them—how to be whole people. My present point is that for people who work and for whom work is a life constant, wholeness is always in part a function of work. Vocational Queer Studies pedagogy has its work cut out for it insofar as its job is to make queer work livable.

Organizing Queer Studies Labor: Sitting astride the Union

In chapter 2 I argued that Rich Queer Studies brilliantly dominates the field's agenda and activities, distributing queer ideas throughout the academy but without redistributing material resources or disordering the systems of class and race sorting that are the most distinguishing features of Rich Queer Studies' home institutions. In this chapter, I have framed Queer Studies not only as a field but as a form of employment, a job largely defined by the conditions of its work site, including the presence of student-workers. I can now reframe Queer Studies once again by considering it as not just a field or a job but, potentially, a form of organized labor.

In her extensive examination of contemporary LGBT politics, *Irresistible Revolution*, Urvashi Vaid argues that "the new social movements [including the mainstream LGBT movement] are often focused around claims for rights, assertions of identities, desires for community, and assertions of values," and in this way they are distinguished from "the 'old' social movements [that] were grounded in material interest (unions organizing for the rights of workers)."[30] With this political orientation, the rights-based, mainstream LGBT movement has distanced itself from grassroots LGBT organizations' "demands for racial equity, economic support of poor and working people, and social justice—all of which require some form of redistribution (of power, taxes, assets)."[31] Far from sharing a monolithic politics, LGBT activist communities have split along class lines. Vaid argues that because mainstream LGBT organizations have been able to exploit their class-based access to rich donors (of both Democrat and Republican parties), "wealthy people dominat[e] the movement's agenda and activities."[32] These actors and their agendas have relied on odd bedfellows for support. While they enjoyed support from labor, with large unions strongly backing the single-issue charge toward marriage equality, they also tapped deep-pocketed corporate Republicans for donations, thus cozying up with actively antilabor interests.

Although some of Queer Studies' most memorable work involves the critique of normative LGBT politics and, more recently, neoliberalism, the field is not immune from charges similar to the one Vaid makes about mainstream LGBT organizations.[33] Writing in the *New Labor Forum*, Amber Hollibaugh and Margo Weiss argue that "queer studies has mostly ignored the economy" and therefore has not been able to address queer precarity. Now more than ever, queers, including Queer Studies scholars, must "keep our focus on both sexuality *and* economic inequality" if we are to work toward queer economic justice.[34] That project cannot be satisfied by "inserting gay and lesbian people into an existing set of rights and protections but [by] asking questions about power, sexuality, and desire that resist the easy satisfaction of incorporation and instead pursue the difficult work of transformation."[35] One of the implications of this article is that Queer Studies' inattention to the economy (an increasingly arguable claim, I hope) may not simply be a fact of the field but an indicator of the "easy satisfaction of incorporation" of the field within larger liberal fields of power and specifically within the "managed university." That Hollibaugh and Weiss's article appears in the *New Labor Forum* is important, as I turn to the question of thinking Queer Studies through the old social movement lens of material interest. How can we conceive of Queer Studies and/as a form of organized labor that can resist incorporation because of what it knows about power and desire?

In *How the University Works: Higher Education and the Low-Wage Nation*, Marc Bousquet defines the "managed university" as follows: "Understood as a humanly engineered historical emergence of the past three decades, the 'managed university' names a global phenomenon: the forced privatization of public higher education; the erosion of faculty, student and citizen participation in higher education policy, except through academic-capitalist and consumer practices; the steady conversion of socially beneficial activities (cultivation of a knowledge commons, development of a democratic citizenry fit to govern itself) to the commodity form—the sale of information goods, such as patents and corporate-sponsored research, and the production of a job-ready workforce."[36] If the overarching goal of the managed university is to transmit the values of capital, Bousquet argues that its method for achieving that goal has been to create a new form of administrative culture, the chief characteristic of which is its ability to present itself as if there were no alternative to how the university now works—even though we know the university has not always worked this way in the past. The evolution of the so-called job market as an unfortunate but status-quo feature of academic life offers perhaps the best example of how a managerial mind-set penetrates as irresistible cultural condition, "as if 'market-driven' indicated imperatives beyond the human and political, of necessity itself, rather than the lovingly crafted and tirelessly maintained best-case scenario for the quite specific minority interest of wealth."[37] The university has been "wildly successful" in engineering a culture that seems to be made of nothing so much as of necessity.[38]

Bousquet presents a compelling and resonant but perhaps totalizing argument when he claims that administrative culture has displaced faculty culture. He ventures that "one tantalizing question begged by management's wildly successful social engineering of faculty culture is this: Under current conditions, to what extent do the tenure-stream faculty represent the possibility of an opposition, a counterculture? With the spread of acceptance among the tenure-stream faculty of academic-capitalist values and behaviors, and acquiescence to an increasingly managerial role with respect to the contingent, there is little evidence of anything that resembles an oppositional culture. Indeed, it has become increasingly difficult to speak of anything resembling faculty culture apart from the competitive, market-based, high-performance habitus designed for them by management."[39] In this view, managerial power spreads through the faculty via the tenure system of tiered labor, and all tiered systems of labor are alike. Tenure, which in a previous era operated as a lever of oppositional power, shared governance, and faculty culture, now operates, where it operates, as an opposition killer, itself a branch of university administration.

For Bousquet, resistance to the managerial culture of today's university must come from the working majority within higher education. The largest group of workers in higher education is easy to miss until we are reminded that "students are already workers," a fact that accords with my experience of students at CSI, as discussed above. The other majority workforce in higher ed is also in many ways invisible. Contingent faculty often have no offices, no faculty websites, very low institutional status, and, in the case of graduate employees, are often denied the very category that defines so much of their academic life: worker. With only one-third of university faculty now in the tenure stream, contingent faculty—including graduate employees, adjuncts, and part- and full-time non-tenure-track faculty—become the new heart of faculty opposition to power-for-capital in the university, in Bousquet's polemic. Further, the working conditions of contingent faculty give Bousquet a window onto more general economic conditions and allow him to envision contingency as the basis for common cause among workers across strata of labor: "Mobilization of the academic community will inevitably require tearing down the barriers between academic work and other kinds of work. We will have to set aside the often-crippling exceptionalism associated with 'mental' labor generally. Ultimately, the most helpful standpoint from which to initiate action will be one that sees contingency as a global condition engineered by capital for labor, and which understands the university as a dynamic node of post-Fordist employment from the sweatshop to the classroom."[40]

Bousquet's idea that oppositional faculty culture is a relic of the past relies on a definition of "oppositional" that presupposes organized labor to be the only effective means of resisting administrative culture in today's university. Indeed, he names this commitment: "For me, the basis of solidarity and hope will always be the collective experience of workplace exploitation and the widespread desire to be productive for society rather than capital."[41] Though the thrust of my book is that Queer Studies needs to understand its embeddedness within systems of class inequity, my argument for Poor Queer Studies extends from within Poor Queer Studies—because that is where I learned the lessons of this book. So as I make my claims from within the same university system as Bousquet did originally, the CUNY system, I also make my claims from within my field—a field I am trying to reorient by considering its connections to class. And it is from within this field that I have gained an understanding that Queer Studies, as a knowledge project, does not align with the goals of capital, nor is it easily fooled by power's attempts to seem "of necessity." In Queer Studies, we have a word for power's unending and ingenious attempts to portray itself as the only game in town: normativity. That there are many antiqueer normativities—and that these norms often reference and reinforce each other—reflects just how ingenious power can be. That we know this reflects how ingenious intersectional queer theory can be. It is that disciplinary ingenuity that makes this book, which talks back to its discipline hoping for engagement around class issues, possible.

Nevertheless, as an academic formation, Queer Studies certainly faces the dilemma of being incorporated into the university only by agreeing to be managed by it, a deal made by all disciplines. Are there, however, particular disciplines that might be better suited to the task of thinking through institutional power—and the possibilities for resistance to it—than others? Bousquet looks to the field of composition, a move that makes sense given his training in a graduate program in English (my own home field as well). But more importantly, because the economics of composition are nearly synonymous with the economics of contingent workers, the field of composition provides disciplinary grounding for his conviction that "the academy's contingent workforce has a superior standpoint for understanding the system of our work."[42] Bousquet reminds us, and not at all in an offhanded way, that the contingent labor force in higher education and in composition courses specifically is mostly composed of women. Women workers are important to his study. But what does he make of the simultaneous rise of university management and the rise of Women's, Gender, and Sexuality Studies? Of Black Studies? Of Queer Studies? Of Disability Studies?[43] I share Robyn Wiegman's view that "identity studies are distinguished from other areas of contemporary knowledge in the U.S. university by their acknowledged attachment to the political," as well as her simultaneous insistence that "a critical perspective on the operation of the political within identity-based fields has not been sufficiently engaged."[44] If identity studies are not simply political or oppositional to power, they nevertheless offer some of the most refined tools for the analysis of the political even as they also stage a confrontation with the disavowed "operations of the political that constitute [them]" as fields.[45] This is to say that we might linger over the multiple questions of oppositional culture within minority disciplines, the development of which are contemporaneous with the period of administrative ascendancy that Bousquet tracks.

Roderick Ferguson addresses this and related questions in *The Reorder of Things: The University and Its Pedagogies of Minority Difference*. Ferguson offers an analysis of the incorporation of "pedagogies of minority difference" in the form of "the interdisciplines" of Ethnic Studies, Black Studies, Women's Studies, and Queer Studies within and by the university as a way of managing the radical political potential of New Social Movements. Though not in direct conversation with Bousquet, Ferguson similarly argues that we must temper our hopes for an oppositional faculty culture, for the mere presence of the interdisciplines within higher education does not translate as resistance to the new form of capital that the university serves and extends. Indeed, he claims that "we are now in the moment where it is crucial that we develop a critically agnostic relationship to minority difference and culture," for these are characterized by their "maneuverability by dominant systems of power, [so that] we can no longer assume their radical alterity."[46] Yet because Ferguson's work is so attuned to the nuances of disciplinarity, he can imagine not only the constraints upon but the resourcefulness of minority fields such as Queer Studies, as I show further on. This is not to disagree with Bousquet's call for collective action as a solution to the multiple exploitations of workers in the managed university but, rather, to suggest that we might recognize, draw on, and animate existing minority disciplines' countercurrents instead of flattening them by painting with broad strokes the picture of an acquiescent faculty *tout court*.

Ferguson makes clear that without an understanding of "the reorder of things" that was accomplished in the university in response to the social movements of minority difference, we cannot understand the new social reproduction, that is, the work of education.

> If "it is in discourse that power and knowledge are joined together," as Foucault argued, the minority movements of the 1960s and their instantiation in neighborhoods, on campuses, in businesses, and in the state demonstrate how minority discourse occasioned a new union for power and knowledge. This new union would help to rewrite the ingredients for social reproduction, making minority difference, culture, and identity much more than isolated acts, showing them to be the means by which new social relations were produced.... The social changes that brought about these new relations encourage us to assemble a theoretical apparatus that can account for the rise of social relations explicitly shaped by discourses of minority difference.[47]

Minority difference here can be distinguished from Bousquet's vision of an "identity of interest" (synonymous with "community of interest") realized through class consciousness. In Ferguson's study of the post-1960s academy, "minority difference, culture, and identity ... [became] the means by which new social relations were produced." At the same time, the discourses of minority difference and the revolutionary movements that articulated and embodied them were not strictly oppositional to power. Rather, they were rearticulated, or absorbed, by power: "Absorbing those movements meant that capital would use them to reorganize its most fundamental assumptions," including those undergirding its (dis)interest in local productions of difference.[48] Taken as a managerial object of capital, minority difference became productive within, as well as a production of, a form of power newly responsive to subcultural resistance.

Yet even as Ferguson identifies the current "period of hegemonic affirmation" of minority difference within the university, he turns back to minority difference as a deep well of dissent and counterculture. "The question for us," he asserts, "has to be how best to maneuver an especially flexible social artifact to disrupt dominant forms of institutionality." He continues by asking,

> Isn't this the moment to wrest minority difference away from specialization, ... away from that mode of expertise that compels us to turn modes of difference into credentials that will put us in the employ of power? Isn't this the hour to define critical intellectual practice as the refusal to let minority difference be the functionary of institutions? Doesn't that task entail our constant attempt to make minority difference speak truth to a

mode of power that claims to speak in our names? Isn't this the time to boldly confront the fact that resistance is not minority difference's taken-for-granted identity but is instead the redistributive practice that we devise under minority difference's various designations?[49]

I want to stop rather abruptly to demonstrate the generativity of reading Ferguson and Bousquet alongside each other. It is not the project of Ferguson's book about the administrative power of capital in institutions of higher education to fully explore the intersection of pedagogies of minority difference and organized academic labor, particularly insofar as unionization might bolster queer interdisciplinary resistance. And it is not Bousquet's project in writing about the managed university (by, in part, questioning the very possibility of oppositional faculty culture) to explore the intersection of organized academic labor and minority difference, particularly insofar as queer minority difference comes to the academy with such a rich history of activism and social vision for change that, at least partially, eludes managerial power. For Ferguson, minority difference after the New Social Movements is "the means by which new social relations are produced." For Bousquet, the "production of society itself," which is the work of educators, hinges on social-movement unionism, "a nexus of real-world agency through which organized humanity can once again see itself as the engine of history" or, most fundamentally, on "the common experience of selling one's labor in order to live, as well as on the wide-spread desire in the academy and in many sectors of service work to be productive for society rather than for capital."[50] Bousquet's critique of the neoliberal academy is less concerned with the role of minority difference than is Ferguson's, and so he overlooks the interdisciplines as formations capable of resisting the system that absorbs and rearticulates them. But in his related comment "that classroom activities are an insufficient lever for social change, and that it is possible for teachers to deploy radical pedagogy in dominative ways," he frames a key site of university work—the classroom—as an ineffective and even potentially uncritical place from which to rework the university, despite the fact that classrooms are precisely the sites where campus labor ("students are already workers") is already successfully organized and primed to work.[51] Ferguson, conversely, sees the potential for traction or pushback within pedagogies of minority difference, but his trenchant analysis of capital and labor amid the New Social Movements does not address organized labor, the old social movement that is the very model of resistance for Bousquet.

Within the frame of my study, what makes the above missed connections possible is the relatively blank space that exists where two modes of organized resistance, the field of Queer Studies and organized labor, have yet to fully recognize and relate to each other. It is possible, for instance, that higher education's incorporation of minority difference through the creation of the interdisciplines has effaced labor as the structuring difference that capital exploits. With the worker's difference—the labor that distinguishes him and makes him useful to capital—hidden by minority difference, the university divides and conquers potentially interanimating forms of political collectivity. And it is possible that minority difference is effaced by social movement unionism that takes the academy to be, primarily, a site where generic labor is sold, thus preventing these particularly knowledgeable pedagogical formations and the histories of social activism that ground them from participating in mutual struggle with organized labor more conventionally defined.

Bousquet and Ferguson point me toward exciting questions about a new figure, the organized queer academic employee. What is exciting here is that "organized" suggests multiple forms of affiliation—affiliation with academic employees in the broadest sense, across the academy and other employment sectors and including student-workers, but also affiliation with academic employees in a more tailored sense, across Queer Studies employment. How might Queer Studies take its place both as and within organized labor, perhaps by queering social movement unionism as a way of organizing queer academic labor?[52] Queer Studies labor has everything to do with shared queer struggle, even as it also has everything to do with shared economic struggle. In my revision, "Oncologists unite!"—Bousquet's somewhat trivializing example of "an identity of interests based ... on workplace disciplines"—becomes "Queer Studies practitioners unite!" And that, I want to argue, must be heard as a specific and a general call, for if workers across the academy and across sectors cannot understand that call as being "productive for society," then there can be no solidarity. The terms of solidarity, in other words, can be no better and no worse than the terms of "queer work."

Miriam Frank describes the kind of tension I am highlighting in her book *Out in the Union: A Labor History of Queer America*. Tracing the rise of gay businesses and LGBT community workplaces, or "gay hot shops," Frank writes that "gay businesses prospered in the lively counterculture scenes of large cities and college towns starting in the late 1960s. Throngs of young people were living adventurously and forming their own communities, and

LGBT migrants were in the mix. Gay workplaces offered enticing alternatives to straight jobs in a straight world.... [Gay people] still wanted the basics: good pay, safe working conditions, respect."[53] They did not always receive these, even though their employers and bosses were also queer. From the perspective of queer bosses, "plans for a self-sustaining queer economy did not include collective bargaining."[54]

Union organizers took note that even as a gay community workforce coalesced, gay employer/employee differences emerged. Amid this tension, "union agents ... attempted to sign protesters to their locals. They understood the jobs and the unfairness, but what puzzled them was the guarded sense of community at these unconventional workplaces. Why were their interventions generating such intense friction? What was so important about those intricate loyalties that bound customers, clients, business owners, and workers? And what was it that made the obvious next step of unionization not quite right?"[55] Frank's book documents the many ways these questions have been answered as part of the continuous labor history of queer America from the 1960s to the present. She argues that fundamentally the labor movement and the movement for LGBT rights "share an ethic." "Throughout its history," Frank writes, "the labor movement has accompanied its economic programs with the principles of solidarity, often expressed in the century-old motto 'An injury to one is an injury to all.' That call to political unity and human dignity is similarly essential to the modern movement for gay pride."[56]

Frank's study is helpful to my present discussion because it reminds us of the realities of what we might call queer disorganization, the class-based divides among queers (employers and employees, for example) that Urvashi Vaid finds so detrimental to equitable LGBT social movements. But Frank also reminds us of a fundamental desire for queer work among queer workers. Of particular interest to me here, she specifically links queers, teachers, and organized labor:

> The first queer union caucus was New York City's Gay Teachers Association (GTA), which after 1990 became the Lesbian and Gay Teachers Association. It began as a support group in 1974, when coming out in the profession was still taboo. For many years, the pledge of "Closet Rights Respected" was printed on the newsletter's front page. The group concentrated on making schools safe for themselves and their gay lesbian colleagues as well as for gay youth in their classrooms. At monthly forums, topics could be professional (gay-appropriate high school reading

lists) or political (the difficult progress of the gay civil rights bill in the city Council).[57]

Shifting to higher education, we might ask whether the managed university has irrevocably undermined the potential for a specifically queer-labor solidarity, despite the long history of that alliance. Or, might the mutual concerns that have galvanized queer labor coalitions in the past—enacting LGBT workplace antidiscrimination measures, organizing labor at AIDS clinics (which by 1990, "had become the best-funded and leading employers of gay people in the nonprofit service sector"), and securing transgender health benefits—be better understood as precursors to our current moment?[58] In this moment, Poor Queer Studies, precisely because it grapples with workers and working conditions in the academy, might be imagined as a uniquely crafted link in the chain of labor's opposition to managerial power, especially as managerial power—far from absorbing the lessons of diversity—continues to express itself through homo- and transphobic, racist, and sexist workplace practices.

The call to unite around academic work without uniting around the disciplinary concerns of queer academic workers, including students, worries me. We must make no mistake: pedagogies of minority difference are responsible for many of the positive changes that have been made for queers in the academy, not least of which is our ability to work and produce knowledge under that sign. Ferguson and Ahmed show us the complexities of that often slow and stymied diversity work, a fact that, it seems to me, might lead in the direction of organized academic labor. But without an understanding of academic workers as queers of color, women, HIV+, and transgender—many of whom, as I suggested earlier, live queer pedagogical lives—"the obvious next step of unionization [may be] not quite right."[59] For queer workers, who are experts in uniting desire and labor—the old union song still rings true: "give us bread, but give us roses."

The Gay Academic Union and the Duties of Queer Work

In 1973, a handful of gay and lesbian academics began meeting in New York City to think about the university and gay experience. The group called itself the Gay Academic Union, or GAU. The word "union" in this context not only signifies a collective but unites the organization's first two terms, "gay" and "academic." The power of that use of "union" is easily lost today, when readers' first responses might be to criticize the nomenclature "gay" as exclusive rather than to pause over the now-unremarkable juxtaposition of "gay academic." Richard Gustafson's opening remarks at the GAU's inaugural conference in November 1973 therefore provide a historical wake-up call: "Welcome to the first conference of gay academic people in the history of civilization."[60] In a 2016 reintroduction to the conference on OutHistory.org, GAU member John D'Emilio confirms the attendees' experiences of being part of history in the making: "Participants had a strong sense that we were making history by coming together. Though gay and lesbian issues were surfacing in some professional associations, like those of anthropologists, sociologists, and psychologists, this was the first large and free-standing multi-disciplinary gathering of queer academics."[61] D'Emilio's original introduction to the proceedings of the conference even more evocatively captures the spirit of queer work that moved through the lecture hall at John Jay College over those two days in the city that four years earlier had been home to the Stonewall rebellion. He writes, "If the gay activist experiences a sense of liberation through the public avowal of gayness, imagine the heightened exhilaration felt when the espousal of one's gay identity takes place within the context of one's life work, when private self and public role come together, and the relevance and connectedness of one to the other is asserted and acted upon."[62]

I want to end this chapter by recalling the strangeness of gay scholar-teachers organizing together as the GAU. The strangeness lay precisely in members' sense of themselves as gay workers in a common profession. The queerness of the union was rooted in the members' professional identities as much as their sexual identities. The language of personal and collective liberation, typical of the day, framed the group's approach, yet that framework was brought to bear with a specificity determined by the context of the academic workplace. Coming out thus translated into discussions of coming out on the job: "By coming out, it was asserted, we did not just end invisibility. We began to build a collective constituency, an essential element in the construction of a liberation movement. Speaker after speaker seized upon the language of liberation. There was a strong sense of being part of a system that oppresses most people and of a need to challenge that system from top to bottom. Panelists rejected the impulse toward integration into the system as it is. The goal was the celebration and embrace of difference and the assertion of a radical anti-assimilation perspective."[63] The system in question was, as the title of the conference attests, the university. At the same time, that workplace revolution was pointedly linked to social movements beyond the academy. Gay and lesbian academic workers in the GAU clearly understood themselves to be gathered in opposition to a related set of society-wide problems (misogyny, homophobia, racism), but for the first time they understood the queer work of the "gay academic" as providing leverage in those struggles.

In this chapter I have been concerned with making connections among queer workers, primarily among Queer Studies faculty and the students who enroll in our classes, not all of whom are queer but all of whom can and do learn to do queer work. The GAU offers a model of queer-work connections among faculty, but also among graduate students in attendance. And, in a strange twist that helps me to argue for the ubiquity of unpredictable opportunities for vocational Queer Studies, it offers a model of connection among queer academics and the student workers we teach.

I mentioned that the 1973 GAU conference was held at the John Jay College of Criminal Justice. On the first day of the conference, during education professor Edgar Z. Friedenberg's talk, "Homophobia and Society," a bomb threat was called in to the police. Inserted into the text of the conference proceedings, in the middle of the transcription of Friedenberg's talk, is the following:

INTERRUPTION BY CHAIRPERSON: *I'm sure that this is going to come as a big shock to everyone here, but apparently there is someone out there in New York City who doesn't like gay people. So they called up 911 and said, "Hey, guess what! I got in there last night and put a bomb up on the third floor." So . . . I know you're all used to it. The cops are outside. What we have to do is go outside and stand across the street. It's nice and cool out there! Don't panic: they think we're going to panic when we hear there's a bomb.* [Laughter].[64]

What a remarkable statement. What a sense of shared knowledge of the perverse pleasure of not panicking, of campy coolness in the face of a lifetime of threats. The 300 GAU attendees evacuated. Then they walked back into the building to continue their queer work.

We are reminded by this incident that queer academics and working-class students have always gathered together, and often for overlapping though not identical reasons. At John Jay in 1973, these groups gathered together for education, especially as a route to better employment and social mobility (this is the same school in the same era when the out-on-the-job lesbian Audre Lorde was teaching Black Studies to police officers and "kids from the block"). And on a November day, a newly organized queer faculty joined police officers on the job—not in the classroom but outside across the street, everyone standing there in response to a bomb threat. Surely the long history of police violence against queer people, as well as the more recent history of queers fighting back, conditioned the experience of danger and safety that day. Nevertheless, the queers and the cops were on the street together, this time as workers, each with a duty. Historically, the police had honored their duty—to keep queer citizens safe—in the breach. The queer professors' duty—to not let homophobic panic set the terms of their academic labor—was just being realized as, precisely, an issue for organized queer labor. I have tried to suggest here that Poor Queer Studies can reorganize queer labor once again in order to make work queer both in the classroom and beyond.

chapter four

Poor Queer Studies Mothers

We believe education is liberation.

We work to free ourselves.

We create our own models of lived educational structures.

We encourage and support each other and create communities and movements that include crafting, healing, transforming, liberating, and reclamation of agency through truth telling.

We do not distance ourselves from our personal truths while in academic settings because our personal is beyond political, it is quintessential.

—tz karakashian tunchz, "Telling Our Truths to Live: A Manifesta" (in *Revolutionary Mothering: Love on the Front Lines*)

Our visions for tomorrow are most vital when they emerge from the concrete circumstances of change we are experiencing right now. —bell hooks, *Teaching Community*

It's always been me and my mom. —a queer commuter student

In this chapter I reflect on the ways mothers have shaped my Poor Queer Studies classrooms and expanded my understanding of Poor Queer Studies pedagogies.[1] Student-mothers' stories are the centerpiece of this chapter. Those curricular and extracurricular stories, gathered together here, accumulate into queer pedagogical knowledge in unexpected ways. The result is a chapter overflowing with small revelations, as well as the general revelation that Queer Studies without an understanding of its working-poor and working-class student-mothers is an impoverished field. I want to emphasize the irony that the provincial knowledge I call Rich Queer Studies has helped me to grasp and grapple with its own impoverishment in the absence of Poor Queer Studies mothers.

The first thing I should say, however, is that there are too many lessons to be learned from thinking about Poor Queer Studies mothers to fit in one chapter or even one book. Yet relatively little has been done to queer student-mothers, especially recently. As the epigraph by tz karakashian tunchz suggests, however, the volume *Revolutionary Mothering: Love on the Front Lines* offers an important new contribution to the work of imagining queer education and student-mothers.[2] One important realization for Queer Studies is that Poor Queer Studies mothers exceed the field's most well-known knowledge. "Our personal is beyond political, it is quintessential," writes tunchz. In this chapter I try to evoke this knowledge in excess of what Queer Studies knows through the unheard-of-ness of my chapter's title, "Poor Queer Studies Mothers." When we slow down to hear it, a strange phrase can do estranging work. The sound that the phrase "Poor Queer Studies Mothers" makes ("er-er-uh-uh") produces both a halting question ("er . . . uh . . .") and a rhythmic beat that references and remakes the field's original, defining act of unheard-of-ness, the splicing together of "queer theory." Like "quare studies" and "crip theory," "Poor Queer Studies Mothers" discursively queers, in a class-gender-embodied key, the reproduction of the field.

"Poor Queer Studies Mothers" repeats through its gendered final term the phrase's initial act of prefiguring Queer Studies through class. If the phrase "Poor Queer Studies" evokes new queer-class-field meanings, the addition of "Mothers" as a bookend prompts a necessary, open-ended bracketing of the field. Queer Studies, when called by its expansive, emergent class-gender name, is surrounded by "Poor . . . Mothers." Nominally reshaped, the constellation of terms "Poor Queer Studies Mothers" compels us to remember that the field not only operates within but also resonates through the material frames of class and gender. I intend "Poor Queer Studies Mothers" to suggest a field imaginary surrounded by a substantive atmosphere, a field phenomenon. In this chapter, poor mothers' phenomenal and imaginative presences drive concrete pedagogical innovation and praxis.

Not all of the pedagogical lessons in this chapter are learned thanks to mothers, but many are. Not all of my examples are about women, but most are. Whereas csi reports that 55 percent of the student body is female, about 80 percent of my students over the years have identified as women, and that number goes even higher when the students know beforehand that the class will have queer or feminist or critical race content.[3] Not all of the mothers here are women of color, immigrants, or first-generation students, but many are. If, as I argue, mothers draw our attention to the class-gender atmosphere that produces transformative learning among peers in the Poor Queer Studies classroom, they also point us to innovative queer pedagogical relationships that emerge outside of those formal educational environments. Where student-mothers go, Poor Queer Studies goes.

This last revelation, one among many, points us toward a new understanding of Poor Queer Studies as a knowledge project that makes its way along routes determined by the material conditions of poor and working-class and working-middle-class daily life. These class- and race- and gender-based routes run through CSI classrooms but inevitably exceed them, circulating Queer Studies in public but also in domestic spaces. As Poor Queer Studies at a public commuter college makes its way home, into houses, into neighborhoods, into workplaces by traveling with its dynamic students who have busy extra-extracurricular lives, it participates in an expansive queer pedagogical project, and student-mothers provide one of the through-lines of that story of pedagogy extended beyond its normal bounds. By paying attention to Poor Queer Studies mothers and the ways of knowing they enable, we can take up Christopher Newfield's call "to show how real college learning works; *what it looks, sounds, and feels like.*"[4] As I demonstrate in this chapter, learning looks, sounds, and even feels different when informed by Poor Queer Studies mothers.

The Poor Queer Studies Mothers Atmosphere

What is this broader curricular and extracurricular atmosphere, filled with but not exclusively constituted by student-mothers? Like the weather produced only on one side of a mountain, gender-race phenomena created on the underclass side of the higher education hierarchy yield the data "Poor Queer Studies Mothers" analyzes. I thank my CUNY colleague Linda Villarosa for bringing the term "weathering" to my attention in "Why America's Black Mothers and Babies Are in a Life-or-Death Crisis."[5] The "weathering hypothesis" as first proposed by Dr. Arline Geronimus states that "the health of African-American women may begin to deteriorate in early adulthood as a physical consequence of cumulative socioeconomic disadvantage."[6] My student-mothers tell stories of nightmare pregnancies and births. They connect their experiences to Serena Williams's experience of postdelivery medical racism, as told by Villarosa. They further connect their experiences to Williams's experience of racist objectification, as reconstructed by Claudia Rankine in *Citizen.* The Poor Queer Studies mothers atmosphere enables us to take quantitative and qualitative and imaginative measurements of experience.

Christina Sharpe, taking her cue from Toni Morrison, adopts "the weather" to figure the ongoing "singularity" of slavery as a "pervasive climate of antiblackness . . . in which the push is always toward Black death."[7] The weather, like "the wake," enables Sharpe to make present the conditions of the "afterlives of slavery" and to find in those conditions black "knowledge to survive such lived and produced ecologies." Part of that epistemic work is taken up by black scholars who "teach, write, and think about slavery and its afterlives" as a matter of Black Studies yet who, simultaneously, live in the wake and, therefore, with and through knowledge "in excess of those studies."[8] "The question for theory," Sharpe writes, "is how to live in the wake of slavery, in slavery's afterlives, the afterlife of property, how, in short, to inhabit and rupture this episteme with their, with our, knowable lives."[9] My use of "weather" to evoke the Poor Queer Studies environment is neither as precise as Villarosa's, who expertly links broader conditions of racism to specific black mother and child health outcomes, nor as deeply historical as Sharpe's, who offers "wake work" as a form of expansive black consciousness. My hope, rather, is that my attention to Poor Queer Studies mothers can offer a different kind of leverage by navigating pedagogical spaces where black student-mothers are; where black experience explicitly and implicitly frames the knowledge produced; where not all student-mothers are black; where in my case the teacher is white. With black experience and thought in mind and understood as knowledge that can expand what is thought, I adapt "weather" to help me characterize the atmospheric accumulations and accruals around Poor Queer Studies mothers. I need to describe what that atmosphere, that weather, looks like, sounds like, and feels like at Poor Queer Studies mothers schools. On this side of the mountain:

- We see a lot of mothers. We enroll many mothers, many queer mothers, many mothers of queer children, and many children of queer mothers. All of these populations will be students in our Queer Studies classes, and so we need to know what difference that makes to Queer Studies.
- Some women enroll in Poor Queer Studies classes in order to be better mothers to their queer and not-queer kids, or to better perform their duties at their low-paying community outreach jobs. Yet, impossibly, Queer Studies manages to talk about a divide between

town and gown, ivory tower and real world, queer theory and lived experience.

- We know that some of our students will be homeless and that queer women students will be disproportionately homeless, and queer transgender students even more so. A queer student holds back tears: "This is the first time they've kicked me out for good." At CUNY we work with students in families—and particularly single-mother families—where the whole family is homeless. Poor Queer Studies witnesses and responds to inherited precarity.

- Many single women at CSI face the following bind: they want to earn a college degree (often becoming the first one in their families to do so) and therefore attain social mobility. But working against that goal of autonomy and mobility, these women are often subtly and sometimes ruthlessly encouraged by their families, with whom they still live, to graduate so that they can get married and start having children, grandchildren, great-grandchildren. These women are ethnic white or Hispanic, Muslim or Hindu or Catholic. Reasonably, and only seemingly against their own individual interests, the chief goal of some young women becomes *not* to graduate as quickly as possible precisely so that they can forestall marriage or resist increased pressure to marry. This may be especially true for lesbian women who don't want to marry men and for bisexual women who don't want to be forced to marry men. These pressured students, not-yet wives and not-yet mothers, show up in Poor Queer Studies courses. How can we help them linger there? How do we need to queer graduation rates both by graduating Poor Queer Studies mothers and by not graduating Poor Queer Studies women? What are the beneficial links between queer/women students and low graduation rates? What if persistence was a queer academic strategy for staying single and childless in addition to university-speak for a retention metric?

- From this Poor Queer Studies perspective, graduate school and the letters of recommendation we write take on new meaning and new importance. "My family won't make me marry him as long as I'm in school, so I'm applying to graduate school," says a student promised through the tradition of arranged marriage.

- We see a lot of returning students, women who have raised families and return to start or finish their degrees. At CSI many of these students are fifty-something Italian American moms. What does this intergenerational classroom mean for one's queer pedagogy? In my case, I'm not great at classroom discipline, which becomes clear very quickly. In that disciplinary blank space, returning mothers assert themselves. "Show a little respect," they admonish their unruly young peers. It is such an unqueer moment not only because it often works—the younger students obey—but because the resulting classroom pedagogy of shared authority is produced by an unasked-for and even pushy insertion of motherly authority. Furthermore, because some students don't accede to the mothers' demands to "show a little respect," these instances can lead to a mother/teacher bond around failed Queer Studies authority.

- In Poor Queer Studies classrooms we have pregnant students, sometimes already big at the beginning of the semester. She can make it to November, she estimates. It's her third child, so this is a well-educated guess. "Can we work something out for the final in December?" Or I run into one of my students, a first-time, first-generation mom, on the Staten Island ferry as we commute to campus. She's coming from Queens. Her baby watches from the stroller. "He won't sleep, Professor," she says, exhausted. Once the ferry docks, the stroller will need to go on the shuttle bus for the last leg of the commute.

- Students tell stories of familial homophobia, of their mothers' homophobia. Poor Queer Studies thinks about the class implications of that familial homophobia, thinks about poor students who can't leave home, can't come out. The ongoing difficulty of coming out may be one of the shared, cross-class experiences of students at poor and rich institutions. Or perhaps Poor Queer Studies can remind Rich Queer Studies that the closet remains a structuring presence even at this late date, even in the lives of young people. As heartbreaking as the closet, students who are out to their families tell me their parents and grandparents aren't homophobic. "They're just old fashioned." These students can't invite dates inside their own homes. But their mothers are not homophobic.

- We see students whose mothers told them they had paid the tuition bill, though they had not. A student finds this out just before classes start. She will not be a student in Queer Studies this semester. Will she find her way back? (Update: she did.)

- I meet mothers and more mothers and more mothers. Thirteen graduations' worth of mothers. When we shake hands, I sometimes learn that they know me already, but it takes years for me to understand what this means.

Sometimes the weather is fine, sometimes it is rainy. This is true in many places. When a pattern of weather prevails in a given region, we call that a climate. The list above, the Poor Queer Studies mothers weather, repeats. Conditions recur. Patterns form. Poor Queer Studies is a climate created by broad class-gender-race weather patterns, recurrences. Its barometers are mothers. Look to them to know the atmospheric pressures on this side of the mountain. Comparatively, Rich Queer Studies is a microclimate, the dynamic clash of wind and rock at high altitudes. It is measured in lightning strikes ... irreplaceable, irreproducible illuminations. The question is, which forecasts are we watching?

Spelling for Mothers

Working at CSI and CUNY, you meet a lot of student-mothers. Though they are a minority in my Queer Studies classes, mothers are a constant, shaping presence here, as they are at colleges that admit "nontraditional traditional" students more broadly.[10] In the highly scripted (i.e., structurally overdetermined) drama of underclass education, student-mothers appear as regular actors. Since the late 1960s, women's and feminist studies classes, programs, and departments have provided an important, though not exclusive, context for mothers to explore how they are positioned among any number of forces, especially the familial and the educational.[11] If Queer Studies has overlooked itself at working-poor and working-class places of higher education, it has also overlooked the women who, I argue, significantly inform critical queer pedagogies at those schools. It is time to reconsider these student-mothers and the enriching queer pedagogies that accrue around them.[12]

Although it happens infrequently, sometimes mothers bring their children to my Queer Studies classes. Childcare falls through. Domestic abuse makes a home unsafe. Student-mothers and their children become homeless. Other than boring the child, there is little harm that can come from a child's presence in a Queer Studies class. Indeed, possibilities for critical pedagogy open up. In one such memorable class, our queer work for the day involved reading, saying, and considering a related set of queer words. Interrogating lexical and taxonomic practices is, of course, a standard queer pedagogical move that produces critical inroads to larger ideas and issues. Even regular words said aloud in a classroom context can sound unfamiliar enough to lend themselves to criticality. Queer words become all the queerer. It is still surprising how many people have never said the word "lesbian" out loud, outside the context of a joke or a slur. Saying "lesbian" in the classroom clarifies that point quite easily. More politicized conversations arise around words such as "faggot," a term one must find ways to meaningfully indicate when teaching texts such as *Why Are Faggots So Afraid of Faggots?* or *The Faggots and Their Friends between Revolutions.*[13] Typically, a Queer Studies class might historicize language practices and consider the weight of past practices as they pressurize the words we say in today's classrooms. When did "queer" enter the lexicon, and what did it mean then? What does it mean now for people in different local cultures and different generations? What are the politics of redeploying "queer" in our class? Sometimes my students want to establish rules for classroom language use (we certainly have guidelines for civility of other sorts), but perhaps more importantly, they want to be able to reconsider decisions around language use in the moment. Often, I explicitly carve out space for myself at the conservative end of the spectrum, which means that part of my pedagogy is listening closely for words that are about to be said and engaging, though not flatly silencing, students in advance of those words being spoken. This practice reflects my view that whatever words might be said are already in the room, that students and teacher alike can predict or pre-hear those words, but that there is still a difference between an unsaid word and a voiced word.

The specific class period under discussion, the class to which a student-mother had brought her child, created a space for class- and gender-based pedagogical innovation around precisely the issue of queer language use that the class had previously worked on. Near the beginning of the class period, a student spoke up in a new way. Instead of using the word she might have used—the word "sex" can stand in for the actual term—the student, who was not the student-mother, spelled it: "S-E-X." She did this, of course, because there was a child in the room and because she determined in the moment not to say "sex" to a child. And, with a new consideration put in play about what words they might or might not say, other students modeled their own practice after the first student and they, too, began to spell. They spelled curse words, sex words, sexy words. Having momentarily forgotten to spell, they interrupted themselves and each other. They misspelled and respelled. Given the extra time spelling takes, they reconsidered their word choices midspelling. Spelling made them ask, is this a word we can say? Speaking sex thereby became a newly thoughtful act of student teaching and learning in front of each other in front of a child.

When a class spontaneously acts, that action no doubt references some kind of preparation or training. I discussed above some of the preparations for queer language use the class had made previous to this day. In addition, students brought their outside training. They didn't need to invent the strategy of spelling out sex words so that a child would not hear and repeat (and perhaps even understand) them. They already knew that strategy. They didn't need to invent classroom protocols that, whether a child is present or not, help us negotiate the use of sex words in class. We'd already covered that. Nevertheless, they did respond to a classroom situation in a way that they immediately understood to be pedagogically inventive. This was clear because, when it happened, they laughed. They were delighted with themselves because they understood they had recalibrated, on the fly, how that class could work differently under different circumstances. They smiled at the fluid intelligence they had demonstrated. Their laughs and smiles communicated an understanding that they were acting together, responding to each other, riffing on a theme. They realized, too, they were acting for different reasons and with different goals: to protect, to make do, to make new, to see what they could come up with, to have some queer fun. Some spelled because they had siblings or children around whom they spelled at home. Some spelled because they didn't know whether a child that age (around three) already knew or would remember sex words. Some spelled because others spelled. Some spelled because it was more comfortable for them to do so. Some spelled because, once we laughed, they wanted us to laugh more. And some students did not spell, recognizing what it meant in this altered learning environment to speak sex, to say rather than spell queer words in spaces that can quickly censor them, and for so many good reasons.

There are moments in Justin Torres's *We the Animals* that come to mind as I write about my students at CSI. For much of the novel Torres shows his readers, through the eyes and memories of an unnamed boy narrator, a past-tense world "when we were brothers, when we were all three together."[14] Yet near the end of the narrative, the deeply evocative and remarkably spare acts of showing (thematized in Jeremiah Zagar's 2018 film adaptation as the boy drawing in his journal) cannot show all they need to.[15] Torres's retrospective vision cannot help but break form and explicitly urge us to take a special kind of care. "Look," his narrator repeatedly instructs, focusing our gaze. "Look at us, our last night together, when we were brothers still." "Look at us three, look at how they held me there—they didn't want to let me go." "Look, they're opening doors. They're stepping out. Here they go."[16] These moments are beautiful because Torres takes the double risk of showing the violent beauty of a family coming apart and of pleading with his readers to look closely enough to see that the family is, nevertheless, together. "Look" carries a complicated hope in its humanizing optic, one that also asks readers to look at poor, racially mixed brown and queer boys' bodies and make a universal connection. With Torres in mind, I wonder if readers from other kinds of places, other kinds of classrooms, will look at my students' embodied class-gender-race stories at a Poor Queer Studies school and see something violent and beautiful and complicated and universal. Look.

In the present classroom scene, spelling sex words became a pedagogical way forward, a way to carry on that reflected not only a compromise but also, in its response to that situated compromise, a productive praxis. Sometimes someone spelled a word that their peers thought need not be spelled, raising opportunities for critical definition and contextualized meaning making. Is "queer" a sex word? Is "gay" a dirty word? Who is listening? Through these reflections and these stops and starts, the class began to build its own taxonomical method by which to classify and redeploy words in context. Here, they said, is a list of words to spell when a child comes to our Queer Studies class. For each word, there is a reason to spell or to say. Look.

At this point, if we followed a strain of Rich Queer Studies made dominant by Lee Edelman and other "anti-social" queer theorists, we might turn our attention from the child in the classroom to the figure of "the Child," Edelman's symbol for that which is to be protected in the heterosexualized political project of reproductive futurism. Was my class, in keeping a nonmetaphorical child in the dark about S-E-X, nevertheless "kneel[ing] at the shrine of the sacred Child: the Child who might witness lewd or inappropriately intimate behavior; the Child who might find [dangerous] information . . . , who might choose a provocative book"?[17] How unqueer! But perhaps something else was also happening.

Poor Queer Studies pedagogy presents us with small "a" alternatives to both Child worship and to Edelman's Death-driven radical queer critique that, almost despite itself, claims to preserve actual children.[18] We see one of those alternatives by recognizing that what was happening in class that day was not only, and perhaps not primarily, about the child or the Child but about a Poor Queer Studies mother. Pivoting just slightly from worries about the future and the child who will bear it, we discover a second level of critique produced not through abstraction (Child) but through class-based recognition. The students recognized the mother, recognized her as a student-mother, and recognized the class's multiple relationships to her at the intersection of class and gender and education. In that hypercontextualized space created by the recognition of their whole peer, the students were spelling for her. This is a pedagogical relationship. Look.

How did they know to do this? On what basis were they relating to their peer-mother by spelling for her? A sizable minority of students at CSI are parents, so some classmates were spelling for her as mothers and fathers. They were spelling in parental identification with her, which is different from spelling in response to and in relation to her child. Students who were not mothers were also spelling for her, perhaps identifying with their future selves (how many women in that class were pregnant or thought they might be?). But beyond motherly or proto-motherly identification, the students in that class—and here I mean in our very specific classroom, on our very specific campus, in our very specific educational system—were spelling out a class-based relationship with a peer who was in a tight spot.

The class did not know exactly why their peer had brought her child to class that day, but they knew something had not worked out. The students in this day's class, not all of whom were working poor or working class, understood the quotidian socioeconomic dynamics that inform our campus culture and that looked specifically, on this day, like a mother bringing her child to a Queer Studies class. I am not arguing that Rich Queer Studies students would not have responded in inventive and generous ways. I am arguing that my students were actually faced with doing so, and in that material space where class explicitly makes meaning, and gender explicitly makes meaning, and race explicitly makes meaning, the students invented a pedagogy that responded to those interwoven meanings in order to offer a student-mother a smart bit of help. Certainly the students were rejecting queer theory's "fear of ordinariness," which Biddy Martin claims "results in superficial accounts of the complex imbrication of sexuality with other aspects of social and psychic life, and in far too little attention to the dilemmas of the average people that we also are."[19] "Implicit in these [radically antinormative] constructions of queerness," Martin fears, "is the lure of an existence without limit, without bodies or psyches, *and certainly without mothers*, as well as a refusal to acknowledge the agency exerted by the givenness of bodies and psyches in history, or by the circumstances in which we find ourselves with others."[20] In a Poor Queer Studies class such as ours at CSI, we almost never run the risk of denying ordinariness, including the ordinariness of mothers. Nor do we objectify "the ordinary," for our ordinariness is not actually the point. Indeed, ordinariness is not even *a* point—not something that can be made into a critical object with which to push back against or poke queer theory (as Martin claims queer theory has made extraordinariness into an object used to poke at the ordinary). That is not what ordinariness does; it is far more engaged and multifaceted than that. Just as my class was intent on learning with an ordinary student-mother in mind, and a child in mind, students were also intent on relating to the ideas from our extraordinary queer theory texts. They thus understood their on-the-fly linguistic adaptation as an act of citing and rearticulating the queer theory knowledge: sex words can be contested in different ways in different places and those contests can produce new sexual discourses, new ways of talking about sex in context. In our case, a poor queer pedagogical context. The students were in a layered epistemological relationship, in other words, one in which the extraordinary ideas discussed in prior class periods were re-worked with the ordinary socioeconomic tools at hand.[21] What sense could a normative/antinormative explainer possibly make here?

Rich Queer Studies has been good at conceptualizing the deep space of queer nonrelationality, whether that requires no future or the ever futural. It has illuminated the value of moving beyond Child-dominated contexts and ideologies, as well as other presentist constraints, and it has along the way probably done a disservice to ordinariness by pitting radicality against nor-mality. It is in the context of and thanks to the insufficiency of that norm/antinorm framing that Poor Queer Studies can better illuminate the value of situated queer pedagogical relationships in the moment. If one risk of looking away from the future is that we will be drawn back into relationships governed by the normative political sphere called the present, it is also the case that Poor Queer Studies mothers can draw us further inside that sphere to overlooked places where class and gender are the constitutive material of the queer teaching and learning environment. I follow bell hooks in suggest-ing that "our visions for tomorrow are most vital when they emerge from the concrete circumstances of change we are experiencing right now."[22] Elsewhere, hooks turns to Paulo Freire's seminal idea that "we cannot enter the struggle as objects in order later to becomes subjects."[23] This phrase "became a revolutionary mantra for me," writes hooks, because it gave her language for thinking about "the construction of an identity in resistance," specifically her position in the struggle against "the colonizing process—the colonizing mind-set" of white supremacist capitalist patriarchy in the U.S. Working in the class-charged atmosphere created by student-mothers and their peers, my understanding of the relationship between Queer Studies and education has changed. Teaching the visionary field of Queer Studies to students at CSI has enabled me to participate with my classes in the praxis by which subjects turn everyday class compromises into opportunities for transforming queer ideas with and for each other. Look.

Queer Home Schooling

I have just argued for the value of paying attention to underclass students' experiences of teaching and learning with and from and through mothers in the Queer Studies classroom. Following mothers further and elsewhere, we see equally innovative and adaptive queer-class pedagogies being created beyond the classroom. As they emerge in students' family homes, work sites, and social groups, those pedagogies unsettle and sometimes upend recognizable routes that Queer Studies knowledge travels. If, despite student-centered classroom pedagogies, the queered, flipped, or decentered classroom can still manage to reinforce a top-down model of learning, that direction changes when students leave the classroom and become Queer Studies student teachers to mothers, fathers, siblings, coworkers, and friends on and off campus. The boundaries around who teaches Queer Studies to whom and where become elastic and porous. Helpfully, these pedagogies displace the static, dichotomous formulation of queer academy/queer community. As commuters, as part-time students, as night-school parents, as working adults, as returning students, Poor Queer Studies students cannot be pinpointed inside or outside of the university world or the "real" world at any given time. They rewrite familiar split narratives in the queer academy, such as the one between queer community-based scholars and professional queer theorists, a divide that helped to inaugurate the field as a contested and testy one. They rewrite those divisions from the bottom up. While they are not recognized as public intellectuals, Poor Queer Studies students have extracurricular audiences and interlocutors, if not a platform or podium. The term I use to represent that mostly unseen, indicatively underclass work of extracurricular queer student teaching and learning is "queer home schooling."

At graduation, I meet more mothers. Having seen their children's transcripts, some of my students' mothers know that Queer Studies is a class, a field. They know that queerness can be studied. But more than this, they know Queer Studies. I know who taught them. I was shocked the first time my students reported talking to their families about what we do in our Queer Studies classes. The students do this because in most cases they live with their parents and siblings. They live at home and commute to school. This arrangement is the opposite of the phenomenon of helicopter parenting, where the parent incessantly hovers over their child's campus life. Helicopter parents fly in on the weekends, or they fly their children-students home or to a family vacation destination.[24] Laura Hamilton, a professor of sociology at the University of California, Merced, studies gender, class, and higher education.

In *Parenting to a Degree: How Family Matters for College Women's Success*, Hamilton writes that the "parent helicopters" in her study were "defined by their hovering and their readiness with supplies, assistance, and guidance. A constant stream of cell and Internet communications [with their daughters] alerted them to potential challenges, missteps, and emergencies. Mothers were in perpetual action, even across state lines, and did not assume that their children . . . could manage difficult situations without their interventions."[25] While she notes differences among types of helicopter parents, particularly in the ways they reinforce or resist gender stereotyping their daughters, all helicopter parents "carefully orchestrated their daughters' social and academic experiences and did not hesitate to intervene in educational institutions. Their interventions were costly, requiring time, considerable financial resources, social savvy, comfort with authority figures, and cultural knowledge of higher education. These parents were at least middle class [two of the fifteen families were middle class, the rest upper-middle or upper class], college educated, and—with one exception, married."[26] Though helicopter parents surely hover over their children across the tiers of higher education, ease of communications, parental availability, and financial resources make hovering a primarily higher-class educational/familial project. Its upper-class associations are, no doubt, one of the reasons the term "helicopter parenting" has entered the lexicon at all. We can't stop looking at high-end education.

The point of all this is simple: it's not that mothers are missing from our most prominent stories of higher education; it's that poor and working-class mothers are missing from prominent stories of higher education. Guided by its own lights, Poor Queer Studies illuminates a different parent/child relation using a different analogy, queer home schooling. The class connections are as clear as with helicopter parenting. Continuing to live at a parent's home while commuting to college is an overwhelmingly low-income and working-class experience. Interestingly, parental involvement, assistance, and financial support may well be heightened when grown children (or other dependents) live with their parents during college. Yet we have more inventive and popular language to talk about wealthier parents hovering from a distance than we do for poorer parents sleeping in the next room or sitting across the dinner table. What is the name for an involved parent whose child lives at home and commutes to college?

As Hamilton notes, the connection between upper-class parents and college-going children extends beyond financial support and constant access. It also reflects a family bond around education. Parents with "cultural knowledge of higher education" "did not hesitate to intervene in educational institutions." That bond does not exist, we imagine, between first-generation college students and their parents, nor among families with lower socioeconomic status whose children are more likely to live at home during college. We imagine that parents without "cultural knowledge of higher education" do not "intervene." What, then, to make of the administrative assistant who prints out a Queer Studies reading at her workplace for her child who commutes to college while living at home? What on earth? At CSI, students quickly run out of their allotted number of pages of printing from the library computers (350 sides per semester). Printing extra pages costs 10 cents per side. While I avoid assigning texts that my students must purchase, I do ask them to print out and actively read (i.e., write on) the materials I make available online. We also assign papers, often requiring multiple drafts. Students quickly hit their 350-page limit. And so, having no free pages left to print, students turn elsewhere for assistance with printing out "Polishing the Pearl: Discoveries of the Clitoris," "Is the Rectum a Grave?," and "Punks, Bulldaggers, and Welfare Queens."[27] They ask their mothers or fathers to print out our Queer Studies readings, and their involved parents do it. What office talk springs up around *that* work printer?

That talk picks up around the family dinner table. "Do you know what your daughter is reading?," a Muslim father asks his wife after their covered daughter, a student in my class, asks him to print out a Queer Studies reading. These are not helicopter parents, yet their involvement is extensive. Their daughter-student welcomes that involvement because it gives her the chance to teach them, in person, what Queer Studies is, what it means to study queerness, what it means to be a domestic college student who is being educated in Queer Studies at CSI. This is Poor Queer Studies pedagogy, though in some cases the family is not poor. Indeed, regardless of print limits at school, some students ask their parents to print out class readings—or they simply leave them lying around the house—precisely in order to have discussions about Queer Studies. Queer Studies can give college students who live at home a way to talk to their families about queerness, a means of educating their families about queerness, a way of translating queer pedagogy from class to home. And parents have a chance to ask questions.

It is not just the dinner table where queer studies pedagogies get reinvented by Poor Queer Studies students. It's also in the break room at work, where our students do their homework: "A coworker of mine walked by and noticed. He stopped and said, Queer Studies? You gay, Ms. Sanchez?" Poor Queer Studies gets reinvented on the bus: "All semester I have met with one [of my] bus drivers practically everyday. I discuss more about this class than the others I've taken." It's on the subway and the ferry listening to Kai Davis's poem "Ain't I a Woman" on YouTube. In these public spaces, students ask themselves, Do I hide my copy of the hefty *Queer Studies Reader*, or do I read it openly? How does identifying as trans or not make me think carefully about this question? Is this a teaching moment? Is this a dangerous moment? Is teaching transgender studies dangerous? What all can happen here, on this train, where Poor Queer Studies is? My students have taught me that there are all kinds of good answers to these questions. Back in the Poor Queer Studies classroom, we have conversations about where students feel comfortable doing their coursework. These are conversations about how and when to deploy queer pedagogies.[28]

Sometimes students use slow or deliberate pedagogies . . .

- *I have started to teach my mother and younger brother about the issues we have discussed in class, as well as used the readings to fuel those discussions. My family is subtly homophobic, and it is something that has bothered me for years. Using the knowledge I have learned in this course, I have been making an effort to lessen their micro-aggressive behavior. It is important to me that my family learns how to approach conversations without being homophobic.*

- *I have actually taught my best friend more about sexuality due to all of the information I gathered from class. I gave her some of the readings and got into a few conversations with her on the issues that increased over a period of time in our history. At first, my best friend decided to hear what I learned throughout the semester and later she became interested and gave me her own opinion about this class.*

- *Well, I've done a lot of queer pedagogy.* ☺ *After every class I would send the articles to my friends [in her home country] and then tried to get their opinions about what they read. And what I found out is that some texts are actually too shocking for beginners. I remember there was one text in the beginning of the semester where the author described in detail what he did and how he had sex with other men. I think that could be a little too early to introduce. But I might be wrong.* ☺

Some students use more insistent pedagogies . . .

- *The question should be, Who haven't you taught? The first people I talked about this class with were my parents at the dinner table when I finished the article, "How to Bring Your Kids up Gay."*

- *Every Wednesday, after class, my brother always picked me up and I would openly tell him what the discussion would be about. Because we come from a Middle Eastern Islamic background, his views are narrowed (of course) and we would talk until we reach home. Like it'll get real heated and by the time we're home my parents tend to ask what's all the noise. I feel like that's my cue to very slickly non-chalantly say what the issue is. I've been lucky to have a family that never shut me down for questioning and wondering. [But] I've had the Fingers pointed at me....*

- *I not only discuss the material with my wife, more interestingly I discuss it with my co-worker who is a female in the Army. When I come across an interesting perspective on an issue I did not even have any conception of, I share it with her and seek her opinion. I delight in some of her responses because they are as rudimentary as my own initial thoughts, but when I elaborate further on key concepts and points from our discourse of the material, she says things to the effect of "wow, I never thought about it like that." It's rewarding to me to have substantiated knowledge [with] which I can fight discrimination or plain ignorance by a case by case basis wherever I come across it.*

Some students discover reciprocal queer pedagogical relationships ...

- *I have been on somewhat of a crusade. My most prized story is the continuing battle that exists between my lifelong best friend and myself. He is a highly political conservative waiting to enter the stock market before running for office, and I won't give up on him. I spoke about it with my Dad and he is the most sexually progressive white 60-year-old man you could find; and I never knew. Thank you. I fought my mother tooth and nail and she now has a much more open mindset while still carrying around her bible. I ranted to my highly educated and progressive sister who just smiled and said "exactly." Apparently she's just been waiting for me to wake up.*

- *During dinner one night I discussed the documentary on the HIV epidemic [Jim Hubbard's United in Anger: A History of ACT UP] to my parents and told them how interesting I found it and how this wasn't taught to me and about how I had to wait till college to be taught about the history of it all. I even got comments from my mother about what it was like growing up during that time so I wouldn't say that I taught necessarily but that I learned from my mother.*

- *When I first came out to my parents a few years back it broke their hearts. I noticed my mother was more torn up about it than my father was. He was actually really understanding towards my feelings and choices. What he had done for both he and my mom as well as myself was print out articles on LGBT topics.... As he would find these he would have me read them. This was great because I was learning how he was feeling and he was learning how I was feeling. When he had found out I signed up for this class he wondered if it was because I wanted to learn more about LGBT culture or was it because he thought I was in search of myself again. He was right about it in both ways. I was finding myself as well as learning more about queer culture.... He told me how proud he was of me for finding my way in life.... He said he wouldn't be as open minded as he is without the knowledge I have passed on to him.*

These are conversations about integrating school, and home, and work, and New York. More than I ever would have thought, extracurricular sites become an extension of the classroom as well as models for the classroom. At CUNY, mothers and children and families and friends become both teacher and student in the context of queer home schooling. Poor Queer Studies gets reoriented around the complex daily lives of our students. It hovers there, no helicopter required.

Queer Commuters

Living with their families, CSI students learn to negotiate simultaneous home and school lives. Some students engage in queer home schooling, teaching parents and siblings about parts of their Queer Studies coursework, class-room experiences, friendships with LGBTQ people, and even their own sexual and gender identities. In this way, home schooling can queer familial relationships by remaking them into pedagogical bonds that facilitate teaching and learning about queerness. But negotiating the home-college continuum does not always produce queer integrations. In contrast, some Queer Studies commuter students strategically dis-integrate domestic and academic worlds. These students recognize in the urban geography of the sprawling CUNY system an opportunity to create physical and psychic distances between home and collegiate lives. Strategically putting space and time between home and school, they queer the college commute.

A substantial and growing number of poor and working-class students commute two to three hours each way from their homes in New York City's other boroughs (Manhattan, Brooklyn, Queens, and the Bronx) to the CSI campus, located in the middle of Staten Island.[29] These college commuters are overwhelmingly African American/black and Hispanic. Given the socio-economics of race in New York and on Staten Island, these commuters are also likely to be among the poorest students at CSI. Naturally, or so it would seem, many students dread this commute, which is made significantly longer by the transportation nightmare created as New York State has shirked its responsibility to adequately fund and maintain a working subway system throughout New York City (a transportation system for which the state and its governor are responsible). Commuters must navigate a defunded public transportation system in order to navigate a defunded public higher education system.

But some queer students actively seek out and work to their advantage the significant difficulties of commuting to Staten Island. They do this even though there are CUNY colleges closer to home, and despite data that show that CUNY students typically attend the CUNY campus nearest their homes.[30] Some students seek out a longer commute and a more distant campus, and this separation reflects a poor queer educational strategy: confronted with economic barriers that make CUNY the only affordable choice of school, with family circumstances (e.g., child care) that make moving out of the house untenable, and with academic preparations that put a more selective residential college experience out of reach, students choose to attend CUNY while living at home with their families. At the same time, queerness leads them to choose a CUNY campus as far from home as possible in order to approximate the experience of going away to school. Like so many traditional college students, they want their queer independence. This poor queer strategy of extended commuting from other boroughs must be understood primarily as a poor queer of color educational innovation. But students of all races who live on Staten Island deploy variations of the queer college commute, coming to campus whenever possible, staying on campus all day long, scouting out communal queer spaces such as the LGBTQ Resource Center, the food court, or the library that mark a psychic distance from home. Queer commuter students stretch out what are in fact short distances across the city. They stretch out their time coming and going.

They stretch out their time on campus. They say that CSI is the queerest place in their lives, and they want to spend time there. When I say that CSI is the queerest college I know, this is one reason why: from my queer commuter students' perspectives, CSI is inordinately queer. A Poor Queer Studies method takes inordinate measurements, makes relative meanings, along these queer commutes.

The poor queer theory at work here, if it were to be spelled out further, could deeply inform queer micromigration studies. We might investigate how queer student commuters travel relatively short but time-consuming distances from home across local borders, such as those separating boroughs or regions of an urban landscape. Queer commuter students intentionally put rivers and harbors, subway connections and bus stops, bridges and tunnels, unfamiliar neighborhoods and geo-psychic spaces between themselves and their homes. Though the actual distances of queer commutes may be small, they can represent high-stakes comings and goings. Such microcrossings must be understood as layered within larger migration narratives, even as iterations of them, as when a queer immigrant commuter student cannot come to class because she hears of an ICE checkpoint in her neighborhood or along her commute route on a given day.[31] Likewise, remaining in constant daily contact with home-culture communities can enable immigrant student commuters to sustain and problematize classroom (read: overly academic or prescriptive) critiques of, for example, homonationalism.

As commutes lengthen, space and time take on new meaning. A smart and savvy queer student who had the high school grades to attend a better CUNY school chooses to come to CSI, where her internet research has found signs of desirably distant queerness. On the college website she sees queer coursework, queer faculty and staff support, and queer representation. She understands that she can become a smarter queer at CSI. Does Queer Studies know what this student knows? Do two trains + one boat + two shuttle buses = a sophisticated queer calculation that adds up to the knowing-feeling of being far enough from as well as close enough to home to become a smarter queer? Does queer studies know that one effect of a three-hour commute can be the reward of achieving a qualified, small, temporary queer liberation? But also, do we know the pleasures of the reverse commute, of coming back home? The queer commuter student attempts to leave home as far behind as possible, but she also returns home at the end of her day on campus. After all, as one student told me, "It's always been me and my mom." Not everyone has the chance to know—to even consider—the complex rewards of being a queer commuter student.

Poor Queer Studies travels along routes created by class, gender, and race. Though these routes cross borders and boundaries, the key insights offered here are not about border crossing per se. Rather, I have mostly set aside that sort of thematic inquiry, unwilling to risk sustaining the presupposition that border crossing is transgressive and that transgression is the point. In the examples of Poor Queer Studies I have offered here, transgression of borders is not at all the point. Ignoring, flouting, and otherwise negotiating boundaries— classroom boundaries, domestic boundaries, geographical boundaries—are not so much actions to be radically queered as quotidian facts of life under the compromising conditions of underclass education. I have wanted to think about the queer pedagogies that emerge within those class conditions, and I have proposed that Poor Queer Studies might be the collective name for those pedagogies. Poor Queer Studies pedagogies are the ways we find to work with queer ideas when there's a child at the next desk, when you find your mother reading your copy of *Does Your Mama Know?*, or when your slow, purposeful commute makes you both late for class and late for dinner.[32]

Queer Publics

To conclude this chapter, I take up one further implication of the emergent nature of Poor Queer Studies pedagogy: its potential for mediating new publics. In a 2008 contribution to *Profession*, "Outcomes Assessment and Standardization: A Queer Critique," Kim Emery responds to Gerald Graff's earlier *Profession* essay, "Our Undemocratic Curriculum."[33] While she appreciates Graff's stated interest in helping students better understand "how 'academics' is 'played,'" Emery rejects Graff's conflation of a democratic curriculum with academic "transparency," a desirable quality that, according to Graff, requires the standardization of teaching conventions.[34] For Graff, the "pedagogically useful simplifications" that attend standardization include, foremost, shared rhetorics (argumentation being the exemplary case) and shared assessment protocols. Graff frames the chief benefit of academic simplification/standardization not just as a public one; standardization and its transparencies benefit "the public." For Emery, who teaches queer theory, any simple formulation of regularized pedagogy for "the" public betrays a lack of understanding of the peculiar virtues of queer pedagogies that serve nonstandard publics. She writes (and I embellish),

> What we [queers might] say to the general public [in making the case for the value of academe] cannot draw on the shared points of reference

built up over the course of a semester or more [in a Queer Studies class]; thus it will be less well suited to convey the complex, challenging, or unfamiliar concepts that are the substance of [queer] academic courses. The effort will require not less nuance but more—not because we [queers] have something to hide but because we are doing the work for which universities are intended. Advanced education is supposed to advance knowledge, not mirror its current [heteronormative] limitations.[35]

Emery criticizes Graff for his assumption that standardization will lead to transparency between the public and the academy and, more to the point, that queers would want or benefit from that transparency. But what queers might or might not want isn't within the scope of Graff's argument. How queers might be assessed in the saying of what we want would be, ostensibly, more of his concern. How we make our queer arguments recognizable by appealing to standard/shared forms of argumentation would be the real question in Graff's democratic curriculum. Emery's critique is that Graff's idealization of access to rhetorical forms (e.g., argumentation) as the transparent, democratizing conduit to a generic outside public fails to account for the benefits of purposefully nontransparent queer educational practices. Queer education, in other words, does not imagine itself at the service of a general public to which it ought to speak plainly. It is important to note that queer theorist Donald Hall in a 2007 review of Graff's *Clueless in the Classroom* also offers a queer critique of Graff's tendency to overestimate the virtues of the reductive in higher education pedagogy. Though Hall appreciates Graff's idea that everyday conversation offers a template for academic language practices, including argumentation, he suggests that Graff's overreliance on formal and often blunt (or, to use Graff's word, "crude") protocols can, very predictably, lead to antiqueer "debate." Hall explicitly values the engaged pedagogies of "feminist, queer, materialist, and ethnic studies-based educators," who teach students to critique uninformed opinion rather than establish it as a baseline for academic community.[36]

What interests me in the above exchange is the way neither Emery nor Graff quite seem to speak to the ways academics is played in my Poor Queer Studies courses at CSI. (I admit that I privilege Emery's point of view because, in fact, she argues her case much more persuasively than does Graff, who gets stuck in arguing that argumentation should be taught reductively—an idea that undercuts his favored rhetorical device at the knees.) For my purposes, I would emphasize that Graff sets the terms of the debate about academic learning at the level of formal language acquisition, while Emery sets the terms of the debate about academic learning at the level of the meanings we use language to convey, meanings that include the possibility that communication within a queer classroom is not for the public but is, rather, just between us. Graff's concern that the academy doesn't adequately help students to make sense of the diverse curriculum with which they are presented thus ignores the fact that making sense of queer diversity depends upon much more than the ability to speak in academe's own tongue of argumentation. For Queer Studies, the ultimate audience for communication may not be the public imagined by Graff, and so tagging assessment to that public measure ignores the private good of intraqueer classroom rhetorics. "We queers understand each other" can never be good enough for Graff, yet it is often not only good enough for queers but best for them. Another way of saying this is that queer classrooms might very logically and reasonably not privilege shared, public rhetorics and standard forms of academic address as the most important baselines for learning.

I know this, ironically, not because my experience has taught me about the unique or necessary privacy of Queer Studies classrooms but, rather, because it has taught me that poor queer pedagogy cannot be contained either within the private queer classroom or within the standardized public academy. Here I diverge from both Emery and Graff. I agree with Emery that something very valuable and different can happen in the queer classroom, but I have seen time and again that queer work dynamically make its way out into the world—around campus, off campus, and, importantly, into students' homes—just as the world makes its way into the queer classroom. Queer pedagogy is therefore not only not hidden but also always being translated into other academic contexts (partially but not wholly via rhetorical protocols) and, crucially, into nonacademic contexts where there is no shared language of argument and intellectual engagement. This quality of poor queer pedagogy, its class-based movements, therefore doesn't stake its claim on the entry of its interlocutors into a standardized and shared academic system of meaning making but, rather, precisely on the ability to translate queer ideas into other languages for other audiences. The poor queer pedagogical condition, revealing itself as it moves beyond the classroom to be a superinstitutional methodology, agitates against the very standard systems of assessment that Graff insists are inevitably its lingua franca.

Graff only imagines an intra-academic conversation, renaming that broader academy "the public." Emery, perhaps, too narrowly conceives an intraqueer conversation. As a professor whose students mostly identify as straight and commute to and from class from their homes where they live with their parents, my perspective necessarily differs from Emery's and Graff's. I hear stories of dinner table pedagogy. My students report back that they reteach our Queer Studies classes to their parents, siblings, and non-student friends outside of class. They invent pre-K pedagogies at a moment's notice in class. To enact these pedagogies, CSI students often rely only minimally on a shared academic tongue, as many are first-generation college students. Following Graff in part, my Poor Queer Studies classes work to gain facility with the standard language of academe. We practice "inventing the university," to use David Bartholomae's concept.[37] But we also create and practice speaking in a shared, nonstandard Queer Studies tongue. My students' poor queer pedagogies require them to hone their skills of translating our classroom discussions, filled as they are with standard and queer academic languages and rhetorics, into nonacademic and nonqueer languages and rhetorics: cross-cultural ones, religious ones, familial ones.

When we imagine queer pedagogical models of queers talking only to queers, we don't see this pedagogical innovation—one I never expressly intended to teach and was surprised to discover in my students. And when we imagine educational models that assume a generic, standardized, simplistic public as our ultimate audience, then we invisibilize the truly democratizing impulse that characterizes a poor queer pedagogy that is both unrecognized and unlimited by standard academic protocols and both unconstrained and unprotected by an imagined privacy.

Not every Queer Studies class has the benefit of Poor Queer Studies mothers' presence and pedagogy. Many professors who teach traditional college students—now the minority of college attendees—and especially those who teach at elite institutions cannot help but dwell in this learning deficit. The old pedagogical adage, "Teach the students in front of you," which is to say, meet the students where they're at, proves to be double-edged in Rich Queer Studies classrooms once we realize just how undermined are the possibilities for liberatory pedagogy when the students in front of us come to be in front thanks to the antiliberatory, elitist mechanisms that gather enormous resources together to the exclusion of student-mothers. Peer-motherless, the students who will become the next generation of Rich Queer Studies educators are trained up by each other with an orphan ignorance that goes by the name of knowledge. Elitism structures their intellectual impoverishment. And in that absence, we might ask just how queer must a Rich Queer Studies professor be to not become the parent figure in this high-class family drama?

chapter five

Counternarratives
A Black Queer Reader

In the church I come from—which is not at all the same church to which white Americans belong—we were counselled, from time to time, to do our first works over again.... To do your first works over again means to reexamine everything. Go back to where you started, or as far back as you can, examine all of it, travel your road again and tell the truth about it. Sing or shout or testify or keep it to yourself: but *know whence you came*. —James Baldwin, *The Price of the Ticket*

It is a big leap from working class, to Ivy League schools, to being a tenured professor. And *a part of* that leap and *apart from* its specificities are the sense and awareness of precarity; the precarities of the afterlives of slavery ... the precarities of the ongoing disaster of the ruptures of chattel slavery. —Christina Sharpe, *In the Wake: On Blackness and Being*

Primer, n.
2a. An elementary school-book for teaching children to read.
 b. *fig.* Something which serves as a first means of instruction.
 c. A small introductory book on any subject.
—*Oxford English Dictionary* Online

Pedagogies of Black Queer Literacy

This is a chapter about remediation, about learning what we should have already learned: to read black queer literature. It is a chapter about a classroom experience of learning to read again, of collectively coming to terms with the enforced illiteracies and educational impoverishments that make minority pedagogies of rereading generally urgent. And this is a chapter about a collection of stories and novellas—John Keene's 2015 *Counternarratives*—that both exposes this state of black queer illiteracy and functions as a primer for addressing it. My opening claim is that *Counternarratives* is a black queer reader, a book that helps us to "do our first works"—of reading, of teaching—over again. My opening invocation of James Baldwin, a crucial touchstone for Keene, helps me to err on the side of the literal in nominating *Counternarratives* as a black queer reader, for the collection teaches us to revisit some of our first work with language—making sense of the world through story—and thereby to reexamine ourselves as readers. Enacting a fugitive pedagogy, a practice of education that has at once been banished from normative instruction and at the same flees from its constraints, Keene puts counternarrative in the service of black queer literacies.[1]

The "we" above is important. It assumes a general illiteracy and therefore advocates for widespread reform. I do not come to that position theoretically but rather through my experience teaching black queer literature at the College of Staten Island in the City University of New York system and, previously, at an elite private college and at a flagship state university. No matter the institution, higher education does little to teach its charges black queer literature or literacies.[2] And if the students at CUNY, one of the most diverse educational systems in the country, have not been guided toward fluency in reading black queer texts; if my classes exhibit what we describe to ourselves as black queer "illiteracy feelings," though we are presumably the right audience for that literature, then the problem is not simply ours. No, this is a cross-class, cross-status, cross-institution problem—which is to say, given the racial architecture of the academy, a cross-race problem. In response to this epistemological crisis, black queer remedial reading should be understood as a general educational requirement.

All of the texts in my undergraduate Black Gay Male Literature course in a recent semester exposed the structured educational deficit of black queer illiteracy, as have numerous works in other classes I have taught at CSI, including The Lesbian Novel, Queer Studies, Writing HIV/AIDS, and The LGBTQ Short Story. *Counternarratives*, however, offers a flashpoint for illuminating and addressing the systemic failure to teach black queer reading practices, for it conducts a radical formal experiment in crafting literacies of black human being in the New World that help us to read anew. Literacies of black human being can be understood as a set of abilities, taught to us by narrative or, rather, counternarrative, for comprehending what has been made an obscured and often unreadable intersection: black human. And in Keene, always, black queer human. Two framing questions immediately arise. How is it even possible that the mundane formulation "black queer human" can signify as unreadable or illegible? Second, how does Keene use his collection of fiction, and specifically the concept of counternarrative, to intervene in this state of illiteracy? The first question points to the construction of an epistemological crisis surrounding black intelligibility, a crisis that is not new but that has received renewed critical attention. To answer the second question, which is my primary concern, I use a pedagogical lens, the experience of teaching *Counternarratives* in my Black Gay Male Literature course at CSI.

That Keene situates his experiment explicitly in the New World, beginning in 1613 and ending in the near-futural twenty-first century, speaks to the "firstness" of the work he does over again and to the historical and geographical distances he is willing to travel to do it. Spanning four centuries, Keene's counternarratives formally encode black literacy practices that open out onto a capacious understanding of black meaning and world making by people, to adopt poet-scholar Tracie Morris's formulation, "who do with words": "We know fantastic world-making through words when we see them. We always make new worlds. We refashion them out of the sounds we said at the beginning of humankind. We make them out of all the atoms of sounds even those spoken to harm us. This is what we do: Out of all these building blocks we wail a world, create joyful noises, the first thing and new things with words."[3] Central to Keene's embodied and learned black epistemological project, queerness becomes part of the building blocks, the very syntax or organizing principle for making black people meaningful through language. *Counternarrative*'s service to blackness therefore contributes to the larger project of queer-of-color writers "to know and be known," with special attention to the ways black bodily experiences and black intellectualism inform the creation of and access to knowledge.[4]

A reader, also called a primer, is typically understood as a text of first instruction. As primers go, *Counternarratives* is therefore unrecognizable. I should state the obvious: *Counternarratives* is a difficult read. Fundamental matters of character, setting, and plot are only circuitously revealed, and even then textual questions are not easily answered without a rudimentary knowledge of Portuguese, of the history of the African slave trade in South America and the Caribbean, and of global black intellectual and creative culture in the late nineteenth and early twentieth centuries. My class was not familiar with the people and places that Keene, who is also a translator of Portuguese, French, and Italian, writes about, from Mannahatta and Juan Rodriguez to the *quilombos* of colonial Brazil to the Catskill creek where musician Robert Cole committed suicide in 1911. The narratives jump through time, yet they also follow an exacting and indeed overwhelming chronology as dates abound and genealogies meticulously unfold. Which figures are historical, which fictional? Who was Miss La La? Mário de Andrade? When was the Counter-Reformation? Was there really a United States Army Balloon Corps? My class googled furiously as we read. What words and worlds and people were these?

We do not come by our trouble reading *Counternarratives* naturally in the U.S. Rather, our primers and textbooks have educated us away from facility with its varied—not alien—knowledges. Whereas recognizing and curiously misrecognizing black queer narratives could have been taught as common literacy practices, instead, according to Donald Yacovone in his study of three thousand U.S. history textbooks dating from 1800 to the 1980s, "the assumptions of white priority, white domination, and white importance underlie every chapter and every theme of the thousands of textbooks that [have] blanketed the country. This is the vast tectonic plate that underlies American culture. And while the worst features of our textbook legacy may have ended, the themes, facts, and attitudes of supremacist ideologies are deeply embedded in what we teach and how we teach it.... To appreciate why white supremacy remains such an integral part of American society, we need to appreciate how much it suffused our teaching from the outset."[5] Priming students for white supremacy has been an educational project sustained by the simultaneous pedagogy of queer erasure. Without the teachers and texts he needs, Joseph Beam thus describes the work facing black gay men as "making ourselves from scratch."[6] We cannot read or write when reading and writing are preempted by the violent question, continually put to writer and pornographer John Preston throughout his life, "How dare you even think these things?"[7]

How, then, does a black queer story make its way into being and then survive to be read, especially as an instructional text? My class had been thinking about that question a good deal throughout the semester as we read or viewed other works by black gay men. A narrative does not survive without readers who can make sense of it. And to make sense of black queer literature, one needs the full range of imaginative writing, including other works of black queer literature. My class needed other texts at hand as reference materials, and in fact we started to think of Keene's book as itself a reference work, a black queer take on erudition that, in antielitist fashion, implicitly tethers modernism's use of allusion (we thought of T. S. Eliot) to its entwined colonial and racial projects. The politics of intertextuality, in other words, were on full display rather than hidden. Moreover, *Counter-*

narratives became more legible in the context of this particular Black Gay Male Literature course because the reworking of history in the book was framed for us by the history of this book's production within the world of black queer publishing. As I will explore shortly, it is not simply that this book was a long time in the making (Keene's previous novel, *Annotations*, was published in 1995) but also that it extended the work of other collections of black gay male writing and joined their struggle to exist.

By contextualizing Keene's book, which my class read at the end of the semester, within a black queer literary tradition, we were able to rearticulate and confront our illiteracy feelings, those affective experiences of not being what Robert Reid-Pharr in *Archives of Flesh* calls a "wide-awake reader."[8] Following Sharon Holland, I have elsewhere explored the utility of using tradition as a framework for understanding gay, same-gender-loving, and queer black men's writing.[9] Here, I do not argue that this is the only or even the best way to contextualize Keene's collection, but I do want to suggest that positioning it within a tradition enabled my class to key into particular black queer reading practices. For example, from a specifically black queer reading perspective, we had become familiar with what Valerie Traub, in *Thinking Sex with the Early Moderns*, calls the opacity or obstinacy of sexual knowledge. Traub argues that the epistemological value of sex, especially over time, lies precisely in its inscrutability: "The opacities of eroticism—not just those aspects of sex that exceed our grasp, but those that manifest themselves as the *unthought*—can serve as a productive analytical resource. . . . These structures of occultation and unintelligibility *are also the source of our ability to apprehend and analyze them*."[10] We took Traub to heart by making the very name of our course, Black Gay Male Literature, into an obstacle that could be productively used for rethinking racialized and sexualized epistemological standpoints. Black queer naming practices had been a steady source of debate in the course (in *Tongues Untied* and the short documentary "Passing"), as had encoded writing strategies (in Harlem Renaissance poetry); the contestations around masculinity and same-sex desire (in *Moonlight*); the power of white, middle-class hetero- and homonormativity to put brown and gender-nonconforming bodies at lethal risk (in *Giovanni's Room*); and the need to create life-giving historiographies of queer black lived experience (in *Looking for Langston*). Is the phrase "Black Gay Male Literature" good for thinking sex across these texts, we asked?

Following Traub, the sexual opacities we saw in *Counternarratives* stood in often ambiguous but productive relation to the sexual knowledge we had produced earlier in the course. Keene sets many of his counternarratives prior to the development of late nineteenth-century sexual and racial tax-onomies. A bachelor plantation owner lounges between the thighs of his seated Haitian slave, who elsewhere in the story "moved through the house as if it were his."[11] Near the end of a long list of items found in the mas-ter's trunk, Keene—without explanatory comment—places a "large carved and polished rosewood implement, like an arm-length squash, that smelled vaguely of the outhouse."[12] A young white mistress mistakes her slave's du-tifulness for devotion and, instrumentalizing her property, "would practice her affections" upon her. In the "The Aeronauts," Red, a black man with a perfect memory who works in the service of a Union engineer during the Civil War, takes an unintended solo flight in an Army hot air balloon. The savant Red navigates his way from Washington, DC, back to his male sweet-heart in Philadelphia, and the two form a model of long-term romantic companionship. In "Acrobatique," the fetishized queer black female body, object not only of the white male artist's gaze but of the intertwining cat-egorical compulsions of scientific racism and sexology in fin-de-siècle Western Europe, is pushed higher up her acrobat's rope (represented by a slim vertical line of text) as much by the stares as by the voices of the men in the carnival audience below.[13] The perspective is reversed at the story's close by another vertical line of text. This time "Miss La La," whose real name was Anna Olga Albertine Brown, stares down the rope, fixing her eyes on the small white man frantically sketching her, "Degas, le blanc, down there."[14] In all of these textual instances and others, my class confronted imperfect ana-logues to many of the sexual/racial issues we had been discussing all semes-ter. By recasting *Counternarratives* as a black queer reader that produces but also rewards illiteracy feelings, I am nominating it as just the sort of text that can be used to think sex and race from what Traub calls an analytic "dis-position," or the methodological approach that makes room for "the value of ignorance, intellectual curiosity, and disciplinary humility."[15]

Like Keene, Traub gives us language to discuss the capacity of power differentials to produce sexual knowledge and ignorance. But certain igno-rances get more critical traction than others, which remain obstinately un-thought. In the politics of knowledge creation, sexual impasses are not only encountered and explored; they are made into things to be encountered and explored, which immediately raises the question, Which opacities count? In her consideration of *Thinking Sex with the Early Moderns*, Anjali Arondekar critiques the way geopolitics has been made to signal an opacity that is unresponsive to and ungraspable by inquiry.[16] Arondekar argues that the global South in particular represents a place where the West's responsibility for knowing often stops. Western scholarship merely stages the opacity of geopolitics as a method for disengaging from the global South, a strategy brought into relief by the different ways opacity is elsewhere invoked as the very invitation to investigation, as with the opacities of the histories of Western sexuality. Arondekar concludes that "our historical challenge, if I were to think sex with geopolitics, impossible or self-deconstructing as it may be, would be to neither inhabit opacity, nor to mobilize it for the accretion of value, but to interrogate the contradictory and unsettling directions in which it continually operates."[17]

I find Arondekar's critical entanglement of sexual and geopolitical opacities helpful for thinking about *Counternarratives*, for Keene holds his gaze on precisely those places that Western inquiry turns away from, including the geopolitical terrain of slavery in seventeenth-century Brazil, Hispaniola, and even Mannahatta, terrain that is often produced as that which is too unfamiliar to engage. Keene is coming at questions of geopolitical, racial, and sexual opacities from the perspective of a writer of experimental fiction. In the role of experimental artist, Keene succeeds in undercutting the staged opacity of geopolitics—the leveraging of ignorance in the face of non-Western history—and he does so through narrative form that explicitly replays and reinscribes the tensions around knowing and unknowing. In other words, *Counternarratives* enacts a double staging of opacity, preventing readers from taking their reprieve from the geopolitics of the global South by obscuring, rather than clarifying, the way unknown stories are told. In effect, the geopolitical opacity is interrupted by the formal opacity. We are made to reflect on how we do not know, not simply that we do not know. Craft allows Keene to crack into the hard double shell of epistemology, the rules for deeming some people and places uninterestingly opaque and others interestingly opaque.

As my students and I considered the obstinacies that Keene marshals in *Counternarratives* in order to write in the service of black queer literacies, we also studied the obstacles related to acts of black queer literary production. We combined that inquiry with our self-study, asking, What are the particular contours of the dispositions used to think about black queer literature in our underclass setting? How do class and race stratifications in higher education inform the ways sexual impasses and opacities are not only encountered and explored but made into pedagogical things? How was *Counternarratives* made to be a thing to be explored, especially given that

Keene teaches at Rutgers University–Newark, one of the most diverse colleges in the country? How did we come to explore his book as part of our located project of becoming better readers of black queer literature?

One particular relationship between *Counternarratives* and another black gay male literary text enabled us to work through these pedagogical questions and understand ourselves as increasingly competent black queer readers. Earlier in the semester the class had read large portions of the collection *Brother to Brother: New Writings by Black Gay Men*. Conceived by Joseph Beam, completed by editor Essex Hemphill, and originally published by Alyson Publications in 1991, the book represented the flourishing of writing by gay black men in the 1980s and 1990s. Like Beam and later Hemphill, and like significant portions of their black gay male readership, many of the writers in *Brother to Brother* died from AIDS. The book fell out of print. To imagine the absence of *Brother to Brother* was a powerful exercise for my students in recognizing AIDS as a tool of unknowledge. "Out of print" marked an intentional obfuscation, an illiteracy-producing state meant to make black gay male art and identity resistant to understanding.

The survival of this collection of black queer narratives, poems, and essays was not guaranteed. But Lisa C. Moore, who founded RedBone Press in 1997, recognized the immense value of the collection to queer black literacies and lives, and she reprinted the volume in 2007. Moore has visited CSI twice to talk with my classes and the larger college community about the work of editing the new edition of *Brother to Brother*, once in the spring of 2009 and again in the spring of 2017. By her second visit I knew I was teaching, in part, vocational Queer Studies as described in chapter 3 and therefore asked her to explore with us not only the need for this book in the world (in both the 1991 and 2007 contexts) but also the work of editing, of publishing, of founding a press, of keeping black LGBTQ literature in print. So while Moore gave my class special insight into John Keene's work, which was the explicit topic of our Queer Studies course at that point in the semester, she also talked about her job. Before turning back to the Keene/Moore connection, I pause to once again make the case for integrating Queer Studies with career studies as I did in chapter 3. One hundred people attended the black queer publishing discussion with Moore, a fact that points directly to my students becoming publicity agents for her talk. Instead of creating a bibliography of books published by RedBone Press and an accompanying list of critical sources—an assignment that most any academic would agree teaches an appropriate research skill—the class incorporated that research with graphic design, creating and printing posters (twenty different ones in all) that made the same critical moves but in a visually compelling way and with the important benefit of advertising the event to the campus. At Moore's event in our large lecture hall, the class's posters were projected on the giant screen behind the lectern, thus giving the students the sense that their good work was part of the background that made the event possible and successful. In their anonymous feedback, my students reported a range of responses, many of them connecting Moore's personal experiences of being a black lesbian to her professional labor of founding a publishing company. For some students, that narrative was quite powerful. As vocational Queer Studies would predict, the students who focused their responses on the intersection of Moore's identity, her passion for black LGBTQ literature, and her work as a publisher were the students for whom the event was the most interesting and meaningful.

Working at that intersection of personal identity, the need for black queer literature, and transformative vocation—that is, working at the intersection where Poor Queer Studies, as predicted by chapter 3, becomes an undeniably applied field of study—Moore told the story of how the 2007 edition of *Brother to Brother* came into being. She recounted learning how to navigate the challenges of securing permissions when authors had died, of the struggle to find next of kin when some families had abandoned their queer children. She told of locating men who had stopped writing or not, moved or stayed, lived in one way or another. Some of *Brother to Brother*'s authors were easy to find. John Keene was one of them.

Keene comes out of a history of writing by black queers where survival was not guaranteed and, as Audre Lorde attests, not intended. His presence in the 1991 and 2007 editions of *Brother to Brother* cemented for my class the connection between Keene's work in *Counternarratives* and Moore's work at RedBone Press. Their projects are bound together by a shared knowledge that black queer stories are not meant to survive and cannot survive if we do not put the books in each other's hands and begin teaching ourselves and others, once more, to read.

Reading for Queer Blackness

Unprimed as we are by our educations, we might expect that reading *Counternarratives* would be not only difficult but impossible. Even the collection's table of contents, which might have served as a key or legend for the thirteen stories that follow, defamiliarizes in its formal innovation. On the one hand, its shape suggests a highly intentional ordering and collection of its constitutive stories (see box). While the titles of the first story and the final eight stories are very short (usually one or two words), the second, third, fourth, and fifth stories obey an entirely different titular logic. They are far longer and more convoluted.[18] As one of my students pointed out, with these longer titles stretched wide across the top of the page, the table of contents forms the shape of a cross. Or a bird in flight. Or a totem figure, possibly androcentric. This is an unruly primer, a study of language both fixed and in flight. And while a cross makes sense thematically given the presence of Catholicism in the collection, any organizing principle revealed by this shape is at least in part undone when, unannounced by the table of contents, Keene divides the body of the collection into three spatially and visually uneven parts: I. COUNTERNARRATIVES II. ENCOUNTERNARRATIVES III. COUNTERNARRATIVE (this last composed of a single, nonlinear, apocalyptic story, "The Lions"). Though Keene distributes maps throughout the text, they are too small to read. If the promise of a map is to orient, Keene's maps (as well as his musical and literary allusions, his epigraphs, his typography) break that promise and instead become tools of a defamiliarizing methodology. As form breaks proliferate, *Counternarratives* seems intent on actively reimagining what is possible when writing and collecting short fiction together. Or, to recall Morris, Keene wants to "wail a world" through black queer experimental form.

The somewhat familiar kind of readerly problem posed by historical fiction (as exemplified by my class's questions of fact and the strange allusions in the long chapter titles) was compounded because we couldn't recognize Keene's black queer historiographic method. He doesn't, for instance, simply rewrite history, though putting narrative in the service of black queer literacies means, in part, telling stories about black people that have been suppressed or untold as a condition of colonial rule and therefore as a condition of that master fiction, the historical record. Keene's work of countering story goes further, undermining ideological assumptions of Western narrative: not just that the whole story has been or can be told, or that extant stories cohere into a grand teleological narrative, but that we already know how to read stories both told and untold. In fact, *Counternarratives* suggests that the stories we know how to read actively proscribe our ability to read otherwise. Ultimately, the black queer historiography of *Counternarratives*—its story-making method—teaches us to read fiction that does not depend narratologically on the underlying storytelling principles of anti-blackness and

Mannahatta

On Brazil, or Dénouement: The Londônias-Figueiras

An Outtake from the Ideological Origins of the American Revolution

A Letter on the Trials of the Counterreformation in New Lisbon

Gloss, or the Strange History of Our Lady of the Sorrows

The Aeronauts

Rivers

Persons and Places

Acrobatique

Cold

Blues

Anthropophagy

The Lions

anti-queerness. If *Counternarratives* is formally original even to the point of disorientation, and indeed reviews of Keene's collection frequently position it as unique, "unlike anything I've read before," it is necessary to grapple with the context of that disorientation and its pedagogical implications. Only in the face of the widespread inability to read and teach narratives working in the service of blackness must Keene craft stories of such formal innovation as to work the disorientations experienced in the absence of anti-black narrativity into counternarrative.[19] One of the lasting lessons of the primer for my class was that our educations have not taught us to read for, toward, and in the service of queer blackness.[20]

If counternarratives put narrative in the service of blackness by writing black and racialized nonhistories back into the historical record, they also do so by countering some of the West's most familiar stories, revealing them to have been told in the quiet service of whiteness. Counternarratives thereby show whiteness to have been a structuring concern of narrative in the Americas since the sixteenth century.[21] Keene tells readers something about the white stories we've been taught, something those stories have hidden in order to be told, something we have helped to hide by retelling and embedding them in the American literary canon. Put in the service of blackness, counternarrative whiteness is not allowed simply to be. This does not mean that all of the white characters in the collection are bad, as though telling the story of white traumatization of black bodies could be sufficient for rendering blackness intelligible. It means, to the contrary, that whether white characters are foregrounded, backgrounded, or absent from these stories, whiteness is made visible and thus newly intelligible, given narrative meaning and narrative consequences, and that the very connection between white legibility and white meaning is made from the perspective of the most skilled interpreters, those characters with the most urgent need of expertise in seeing and making meaning out of whiteness: characters who know the mundane banality and life-saving urgency of black literacies.

Arguably, Keene puts counternarrative whiteness in the service of blackness most powerfully in "Rivers," a story that accomplishes a breathtaking reorientation of perspective. This story, placed at the center of the collection's thirteen stories, marks the moment in *Counternarratives* when my students literally gasped. "Rivers," one student commented, was the story that the first six stories made possible to tell, which is to say that it revealed something about what those earlier stories were up to. The crucial epiphanic moment in "Rivers," discussed below, therefore becomes a meta-epiphanic moment midcollection, a moment when the unfamiliar fictions of the historical, geopolitical, and linguistic pasts of those earlier stories with long and confusing titles and plotlines meet the familiar fictional near-present in a renarration of Mark Twain's *Huck Finn* from the perspective of Jim. "Rivers" also makes possible the counternarrative work that follows it, and so is linchpin to the black queer method that makes meaning out of the purposeful collection and ordering of stories.

Typical of the genre of short fiction, "Rivers" ends with an epiphanic moment that opens out onto dramatic interpretive possibilities. The pretext for Jim's recollection, quoted at length below, is an interview about his service in the Civil War with a reporter who, standing in the place of the adoring American reader, would rather hear about "the time you and that little boy . . ."[22] Instead of that famous story, Jim, who as a free man has renamed himself James Alton Rivers, tells an untold war story:

> Creeping forward like a panther I saw it, that face I could have identified if blind in both eyes, him, in profile, the agate eyes in a squint, that sandy ring of beard collaring the gaunt cheeks, the soiled gray jacket half open and hanging around the sun-reddened throat, him crouching reloading his gun, quickly glancing up and around him so as not to miss anything. . . . And I looked up and he still had not seen me, this face he could have drawn in his sleep, these eyes that had watched his and watched over his, this elder who had been like a brother, a keeper, a second father. . . . [I] raised my gun, bringing it to my eye the target his hands which were moving quickly with his own gun propped against his shoulder, over his heart, and I steadied the barrel, my finger on the trigger, which is when our gazes finally met, I am going to tell the reporter, and then we can discuss that whole story of the trip down the river with that boy, his gun aimed at me now, other faces behind his now, all of them assuming the contours, the lean, determined hardness of his face, that face, there were a hundred of that face, those faces, burnt, determined, hard and thinking only of their own disappearing universe, not ours, which was when the cry broke across the rippling grass, and the gun, the guns, went off.[23]

In the black queer counternarrative, James Rivers is something of a swindler and sexual libertine, not the Uncle Tom figure of Twain's novel. Using Roderick Ferguson's queer-of-color framework in *Aberrations in Black*, Rivers reads as a model of black nonheteronormativity, a model of queer blackness.[24] This queer black James Rivers of the counternarrative does not try to protect Huck. He shoots him. And it seems, given that he narrates "Rivers" long after the war has ended, that when "the guns" go off, River's bullet finds its target, since Huck's clearly does not. More importantly, James Rivers does not just kill Huck. He deindividualizes him. Huck's story changes from the prototypical narrative of an American boy's ambivalent entry into manhood to a dangerously typical narrative in which the decision to fight and kill for slavery and racial supremacy makes all Confederate white men into the same character, each assuming Huck's face. What, I asked my class, do we make of all those faces, all those soldier Hucks?

Initially, the class of thirty-five—only three of whom, myself included, shared Huck's white male face—fell into the trap that black queer illiteracy sets for us.[25] We read Keene as humanizing the Confederate soldiers by making their faces into mirrors of Huck's, the flawed, redeemable man-boy. Perhaps James Rivers sympathizes with them all or wishes it were possible to save them? But as Huck's face becomes imaginable as the face of the South, the counternarrative inverts this interpretation, revealing that we have used a strategic pro-white literacy practice to misread the boy protagonist by mis-humanizing him. Huck is but one racist in the monstrous horde that wears his same face. Indeed, this is what he has always been. We have been willfully misreading that face as universal rather than as capable of "thinking only of [its] own disappearing universe." If James Rivers is to be real, the thing to be done with Huck has always been to kill him.

This counternarrative epiphany raises an important philosophical point, an ethical point, about our relationship as readers to narratives not countered. "Rivers" sets the stakes of its own absence and the absence of *Counternarratives*, the stakes of *Huck Finn* existing alone in the world. In the absence of counternarratives, we can easily humanize Huck and dehumanize Jim by attributing to him superhuman sympathy rather than the human choice to kill. For those who love to read, including the room full of English majors with whom I read *Counternarratives*, to the extent that this new awareness causes us to revisit our literary love objects and our affect-laden histories of reading, the radical confrontation of racialized reading practices occasioned by encountering *Counternarratives* may well rise to the level of reading crisis. And liberation.

Counternarratives thus raises questions that seem at once remedial, as a typical primer does, and philosophical, as a typical primer does not: How do I read this book? What kind of book is this? What have I been reading? How have I been reading it? What does it mean to read as I have been reading? And what explains the informed illiteracy—or the ignorances created by dominant knowledge practices—at the intersection of black queer human that makes a black queer reader necessary in the first place?

Counternarrative and Black Queer Human Being

Why should "black queer human" fail to signify and thus need to be made readable by a book like *Counternarratives*? Robert Reid-Pharr's critique of humanism in *Archives of Flesh: African America, Spain, and Post-Humanist Critique* offers one explanation. Reid-Pharr argues that "the Western philosophical traditions to which we have all been forced to pay obeisance represent not vessels of truth per se, but instead the quite specific discursive protocols and institutional procedures by which examination and discussion of human being has been delimited."[26] The "human" in humanism turns out to be not the expansive figure championed by "complex rhetorics of pluralism" but instead a narrow and filtered fellow, a mechanism of shrunken possibilities for thought. With murky inclusive language practices supplanting analyses of structural exclusions, "'the Black' can be imagined much more simply and comfortably than he can be addressed."[27] To address "the Black" in and through fiction would be to put literature in the service of blackness as part of a fugitive epistemological project that resists both his exclusion from humanism and the general impoverishments produced by humanism's crude tools for thought.

Reid-Pharr reanimates protocols for knowledge making that center the experiences of black human being. Helpfully for my present chapter, his study calls for the invigoration of "the African American Spanish archive," a project I take to be near the heart of Keene's book as well. Tracing "rhetorics of flesh," a kind of embodied literacy that has been used by black people to "access alternatives to the most vulgar of the humanist protocols," Reid-Pharr reveals "not only enslaved persons' awareness of their presumed status as chattel but also and quite importantly their resistance to this status, their self-conscious articulation of counternarratives of human subjectivity in which enslaved and colonized persons might be understood as both historical actors and proper subjects of philosophy."[28] Using the word "counternarratives" for a second time in his introduction, Reid-Pharr takes pains to "remind readers of some naughty truths. Slavery and colonization produced the wealth that allowed for the development of capitalism and spawned the ideological protocols that produced ridiculously clumsy concepts of racial and ethnic difference. At the same time, however, they also produced any number of (un)bounded, (un)authorized counternarratives in which the many contradictions of racialism and capitalism were made patently visible."[29] Mikko Tuhkanen, in his review essay of *Archives of Flesh*, homes in on Reid-Pharr's sustained critical practice of undoing ideologies of race, describing his intellectual project as *"vulgarizing modernity."* Reid-Pharr's vulgarizing method extends as well to bounded sexual identities and nomenclatures associated with modern knowledge production in the West that operate as markers not only of imprecision but of anti-black epistemological violences that are countered by black philosophy, including (counter) humanist queer epistemologies.

I find Reid-Pharr's call to rethink Western knowledge projects and protocols to be in compelling dialogue with *Counternarratives*, a text that like *Archives of Flesh* indicts humanist philosophies as too thin to narrativize black intellectualism in the New World. It does so by providing a virtual catalog of fugitive epistemologies that emerge from the lived experience of black people under conditions of slavery, colonial expansion, and, in the U.S. context, emancipation. Keene is ingenious in the number of ways he writes embodied black philosophies into *Counternarratives*. Real-life philosophers appear in several stories (including Du Bois and Santayana). Colonial economic philosophies advocated by unnamed narrators ("Growing markets have no margin for mercy"[30]) and political philosophies of celebrated Western thinkers (for example, David Hume, philosopher of freedom) punctuate the text. But they serve as either ironic or grotesque annotations to the experiences of those black characters living on the page whose captivity and freedom are rendered illegible in political philosophy's classic terms of the social order. Similarly, archival materials reproduced in close proximity (an advertisement for a runaway slave followed several pages later by an inset of the Declaration of Independence) suggest a fundamental incommensurability, in this instance between slave and man, at the heart of Western humanism.

Keene even more boldly philosophizes in interludes where characters aren't philosophers by training. In "Our Lady of the Sorrows," Carmel is a slave girl and a polyglot: "I found myself intermittently reciting lines of Scripture, switching from English to French to Spanish to Kreyòl to Latin to Greek to myself in order not to fall asleep."[31] She has invented a sign language that she and her mistress, Eugenie, use exclusively to communicate and that she teaches to several other slaves at their convent in Kentucky. Carmel also speaks a visual language, a "mode of drawing" described as a "queer constellation of imagery and signification" that creates shadowy doorways to other realms: "As for whatever lay on the other side of those drawings, with their arsenal of augury and admonition, I had not yet developed a theory of knowledge by which to understand them. Or rather perhaps I had, but lacked a language to characterize and describe them. It struck me that the spells and the drawings themselves might be a language, but this seemed so exploratory and fantastic, that I set aside further consideration of it, and instead reflected, when the thought struck me, on the process of my experience and practice of those episodes."[32] Why does the possibility that her spells and drawings might constitute a language seem "so exploratory and fantastic" to Carmel, whose Haitian mother was renowned for her skills of divination before her death and with whom Carmel increasingly attempts to make "night visits" as the story progresses? Rather than name her gifts a language, Carmel reflects on "the process of [her] experience." Carmel understands her gifts as potentially having epistemological implications, but she defers exploration of a theory of knowledge and instead turns back to and invests value in the everyday phenomenological experience and practice of her supernatural gifts. Yet, effectively, she develops a theory of consciousness and perception of her power: "At another window that looked out onto the town below I could see the flames, at the base of the hill, ascending, like a wave of gold, towards the convent. Lamp and candlelight from the room seared through the dark. It was as if I were painting and in the painting at the same time, as if the inside and outside were fusing into one rich, polysensory perspective, and I almost had to stop for a second to steady myself."[33] This is a philosophy of some sort, but a sort not recognizable to Western traditions.[34]

Yet Keene does not simply jettison Western thought and replace it with an idealized, non-Western black thought. The fugitive epistemologies created in *Counternarratives* form not by rejecting Enlightenment philosophy wholesale but by engaging it. Philosophical ruminations on themes such as duty and freedom thus emerge from within black experiences of New World slavery and clearly in conversation with liberal rhetorics that shape them: "Under the circumstances, are there any benefits to dedication, devotion, honor—responsibility?"[35] And later, "Within the context shaped by a musket barrel, is there any ethical responsibility besides silence, resistance and cunning?"[36] "Persons and Places" explicitly reminds readers of the long tradition of African American and Spanish American philosophical interanimation rather than isolation. The story is structured temporally, hinged on a fleeting moment as Keene pairs black philosopher and leader-to-be in Harlem Renaissance intellectual and artistic circles W. E. B. Du Bois and the American-educated Spaniard George Santayana. These thinkers, with their overlapping but misaligned orbits, later morph into a more convivial interracial couple in "Blues," which extends the story of a moment glimpsed between Du Bois and Santayana into the story of an evening shared by self-described "poet low-rate" Langston Hughes, a virtual philosopher of black working classes, and Mexican poet and playwright Xavier Villaurrutia. Julian Lucas notes that this story is "a fantasy spun from the slenderest evidence: [Villaurrutia's] dedication of an erotic poem to Hughes and the knowledge that their time in New York and Mexico city overlapped."[37] A half-longing, half-suspicious instant of eye-catching between black and brown (or, to use Reid-Pharr's preferred term, "off-white") men in "Persons and Places" becomes in the "Blues" counternarrative an evening of dinner then sex that indexes a fleeting genealogy of embodied homoerotic black intellectualism and cultural production in the West.

Resonating with Reid-Pharr's posthumanist philosophical intervention, Keene invents a counternarrative method of making queer black experience into vital knowledge. But if, as Reid-Pharr suggests, the protocols of black human being have not yet been fully collected and made legible as archives of flesh, it stands to reason that the work of counternarrative method will not be instantly recognizable either. Keene's counternarrative work must be shared and shouldered by the wide-awake reader of the new archives. I have framed that intersection where counternarrative invention and wide-awake reading practices resist traditional humanist (il)literacies as a site of pedagogy. And if introducing any work of literature into the classroom for the first time can feel like equal parts voyage out and con job, *Counternarratives* seems even more urgently to raise the pedagogical question, How do I teach this unrecognizable, highly original collection? I suggest that the book's uncommon originality can be understood as the very basis for its common value as a pedagogical text, for as a boundary object for black queer literacies it teaches new and indispensable ways of reading. In other words, by purposefully distancing the reader from the text, the book argues that we all are obligated to do the work of becoming wide-awake readers. Though not "an elementary school-book for teaching children to read," *Counternarratives* enters the pedagogical gap created by standard white and straight reading practices in order to teach readers to counterread both black narratives and the white racialized stories that have overwritten them. By framing *Counternarratives* as a black queer reader, I hope to stage an unsettling pedagogical confrontation between readers' current presumptions about their own literacies and *Counternarratives'* unintelligibility. "Illiteracy feelings" thus name the affective, intellectual dis-ease that comes with the realization that one is not, yet can increasingly become, a wide-awake reader.

Secret Pedagogies and Inverted Worlds

My attention to the pedagogical implications of *Counternarratives* as a black queer primer and my discussion of the particular pedagogical scene in which I first taught the book play to my personal and scholarly interest in thinking about queer pedagogy as it intersects with minority race and class formations. But I am also pointed in that direction by a special character-istic of *Counternarratives*: it thematizes fugitive pedagogies. Secret educa-tions and upstart knowledge practices help to structure this book. Slaves are polyglots, linguistic savants, self-educated readers. They invent languages and teach them to others. In fact, roles of the learned Provost and the illiter-ate slave are inverted in Keene's counternarratives, and powers of mind do not gather under pale heads alone. Queer black and brown readers, writers, and scholars animate this text, appearing as characters within individual narratives and as authors of Keene's eclectic epigraphs. The collection is explicitly concerned with black learning, fugitive study, and embodied epis-temological struggle, especially as it relates to black ontology. My treatment of the book as a black queer reader attempts to gather together the various pedagogical moments of the text and then name the sum of the work they ask the reader to do: to read in the service of black knowledge practices, including black thought, teaching, intellectualism, and genius, and thereby to connect black knowing and black being.

The opening story offers a fitting preview of the fugitive pedagogical work of the entire collection in that it enacts a reading practice of enter-ing language anew. Inverting official narratives of colonial exploration and expansion, "Mannahatta" tells the story of Jan/Juan Rodriguez, who in 1613 became the first documented nonnative American to live on what is today called Manhattan Island in New York City. Rodriquez, born in one of the Caribbean's oldest cities, Santo Domingo, was part African and part Lusita-nian/Portuguese. As told by Keene, Rodriguez's story not only subverts a specifically racialized history of firsts by making the first American immi-grant black—and what an impact this simple detail could have on thinking about U.S. immigration today. It also reconceptualizes the logic of settler encounters with first people, in this case the Lenape, who were the origi-nal inhabitants of Manhattan Island. The Lenape envoy who serves as Ro-driguez's primary contact "had, through gestures, his stories, later meals and the voices that spoke through fire and smoke, opened a portal onto his world. Jan knew for his own sake, his survival, he must remember it.... He could see another window inside that earlier one, beckoning. He would study it as he had been studying each tree, each bush, each bank of flowers here and wherever on this island he had set foot. He would understand that window, climb through it."[38] Rodriguez the settler refuses the role of colonial explorer. He plans, rather, to desert the Dutch colonizer's ship on which he serves as translator for trading with the Lenape and to return to the surroundings he commits to memory. Through Rodriquez, Keene conceives of multiple modes of translation happening parallel to imperialist language practices. Rodriguez will not use his linguistic talents to further extract value from the first people. They have offered language as a portal, a series of portals, through which he might pass and, so passing, perhaps commune. The metaphor of passing through windows, of being swallowed up into the language of another, replaces colonial visions of expansion and its metaphors of civilization.[39] Fugitive pedagogy emerges as ecology, a naturalization—an expression in and through nature—of language.

Counternarratives further upends colonial narrative practices by thematizing the methods by which fugitive narratives are produced by technologies that range from the mechanical to the fantastical. How stories come to be told is of paramount importance, and in Keene's experiment in black literacies, knowing how to read means knowing the history of a story's emergence. For instance, multilingual slaves and free black lyricists inhabit many of these stories, exploding racialized assumptions about facility with language. Further, Keene inscribes the mechanisms of communication into his stories, richly detailing how narratives are recorded, transcribed, transmitted, handled, received, revealed, and read. Similar to the way slave songs were complex oral/aural systems that functioned on multiple levels of communication, counternarrative scaffolds diverse black literacies, articulating linguistic competence or mastery of multiple languages to deep understanding of the epistemological and ontological operations by which power differentials are structured by dominant language practices of colonial rule and slavery, including controlling access to the means of production of written narrative. Counternarrative methods are, therefore, neither merely mimetic nor technological concerns but a metatextual flashpoint for conceptualizing the inverted language practices that enable black resistance and produce black human being.

In "Counterreformation," the fugitive cipher symbolizes the power of counternarrative technology to invert worlds. Using the colonizer's own technology of encoded communication—a letter hidden within the binding of a book—the black fugitive writes not just in the language of the Portuguese colonizer but in the secret language practice of the colonizer. And it is via that secret language practice, moreover, that he readdresses the colonizer, personified here as a regional leader of the Catholic Counter-Reformation, in epistolary form. The letter, dated June 1630, begins:

DOM FRANCISCO,

I write you in the expectation that you will soon discover this missive, concealed, as you regularly instructed the members of the professed house in Olinda, during the period that you led it, within the binding of this book that has been sent to you and which you, having discovered the letter, have just set down. . . . The most valuable of all, however, is this written missive, as you will certainly soon agree. As you also shall see, you will gain full access to it only by the application of another trick you conveyed to those in your care, underlining how well your lessons took root, like cuttings, even in the distant fields. Thus the special care I have taken. If you should see fit, do let the lit candlewick linger upon this document once you have read it, as that would be in the utmost order, though it is of no matter to me, for it should be declared that I am beyond the reach of those laws, earthly or divine, that would condemn you, on the very fact of possession of the written account I shall shortly begin.[40]

Dom Francisco, and by extension Keene's audience who shares his readerly perspective, is here confronted by multiple ignorances. Though we soon learn that "this letter sails to you, in its clever guise, out of an abiding desire to convey to you the truth of what occurred at [the outpost monastery in] ALAGOAS," initially we do not know what the letter is about.[41] The author, whose identity we also do not know until we reach the letter's closing signature, opens with a rumination on the technology by which Dom Francisco's ignorance is presently exposed. Exhibition of detailed knowledge of a technique for encoding story soon gives way to the story itself, "that series of events, unforeseeable at least to some of those who lived them, that inverted worlds."[42]

As events build to the climactic inversion of worlds, the "civilized" priests who run the monastery in colonial Brazil and who are the local caretakers of the Catholic Counter-Reformation are revealed to be the rapists and torturers of the "uncivilized" African slaves, who themselves stand accused of all manner of sexual perversion and sodomitic abomination. The inversion of the civilized/uncivilized binary is personified in the narrator, who ultimately reveals himself as N'Golo BURUNBANA Zumbi, one of the former African slaves at the monastery at Alagoas. Because Burunbana, a Jinbada spirit worker, is "such a one who is both," who sometimes appears male and sometimes female and whom "sometimes the spirits fill and mount ... as one and the other," he offers an easy target for the priests' accusations of defiling the monastic order through the performance of lascivious acts and diabolical rituals.[43] Yet, in Burunbana's gender multiplicity, his status as "such a one who is both," we see the collapse of the distinction between his role as narrator and vessel for knowledge. He calls himself his people's "instrument, their conduit and gift."[44] Burunbana has the ability to counternarrate his own story, to manipulate the communications technology and thereby invert the function of the colonizer's cipher to serve his own purposes. He explicitly stakes out his own narrative position: "I ask only that you understand given all that has transpired since you last spoke face to face with any of those at that now accursed house, that some who have been condemned to the most foul contumely do reside, nevertheless, in Truth, and so this missive proceeds from *that strange and splendid position*."[45] In this expanded system of black literacy, fugitive Truth narrative stands not on the periphery of knowledge or in simple opposition to it or, even, outside of it altogether but rather at its fullest point of saturation. Burunbana knows, for example, that the new provost of the monastery, Juaquim D'Azevedo, also goes by a false name, one that hides his Jewish identity and his true intentions, the secret education of Jewish boys in the town whose families are also passing as Roman Catholics. Fugitive literacies intersect as, reading future and past, Burunbana oversees D'Azevedo's escape from the monastery so that he can return to the practice of his faithful pedagogy.

When Burunbana reveals his identity to Dom Francisco at the letter's close, he does so with an impossible reference: "for as my sister will write in the distant future, 'it is better to speak / remembering / we were never meant to survive.'"[46] Burunbana speaks Truth here with the words of Audre Lorde, black, lesbian, mother, warrior, poet, whose lines from "A Litany for Survival" are pulled back in time from the twentieth century to the early seventeenth century. Keene's reference to Lorde reiterates the earlier message that the "strange and splendid position" from which Burunbana counternarrates his story is not only black but also queer—and also literary. Through *Counternarratives*, queerness becomes part of the textual fabric of the emergent black meaning-making project. Lorde's poem also enables Keene to set the stakes of this short story by linking the word to survival. The fugitive narrative is always also a story of its own survival. Black queer story is never, simply, there to be read.

Reading Together

Counternarratives' sustained exploration of fugitivity and Maroon pedagogies returns me to the discussion, prefaced in the introduction, of Poor Black Queer Studies in today's academy. With the concept of fugitivity, we can negotiate the complex intersections of race, class, desire, and knowledge making that, on the one hand, recommend Poor Black Queer Studies as an urgent analytic and, the other hand, force a confrontation with the places and practices of another field formation, Rich Black Queer Studies. Just as one object that emerges from Poor Black Queer Studies' entwined class and race critique of the stratified academy is the excluded poor black queer student (and professor), a second, less-studied critical object emerges as well: the field of Rich Black Queer Studies. It would seem paradoxical that Black Queer Studies, grounded in the renegade formation of Black Women's Studies, has made its stunning advances under the regressive conditions of austerity that have gripped higher education and that have disproportionately hurt poor black people. That paradox is partially resolved, however, when we consider that Black Queer Studies has thrived in large part by making its name at the same elite, exclusionary colleges and universities at which Rich White Queer Studies has thrived.[47] While it is necessary to assert that Queer Studies has always been Black Queer Studies in terms of its intellectual genealogy, it is now also an inescapable reality that White Queer Studies and Black Queer Studies are linked not only conceptually, historically, or theoretically, but prestigiously. That is to say, Rich Black Queer Studies and Rich White Queer Studies navigate the hallways of the same expensive, high-profile, selective institutions that so disproportionately and intentionally exclude poor and black students. Nevertheless, these fields cannot be said to *share* those hallways. The experiences of their practitioners are often deeply asymmetrical. A Poor Black Queer Studies analytic therefore requires that we tease out the complexities of class within Rich Black Queer Studies, a field that must be simultaneously set in contradistinction to Rich White Queer Studies, even as we necessarily locate it at its privileged educational work sites. *Poor Queer Studies* refuses to pit race, class, and queerness against each other, even as it necessarily asks how Rich Black Queer Studies participates in class stratification in the academy in its own ways and with its own impacts and with its own race-queer-class negotiations.

The immediate concern is whether it makes sense to indicate such a class tension within Black Queer Studies. It likely doesn't make sense *not* to posit a Poor Black Queer Studies/Rich Black Queer Studies relationship if we maintain the method of rethinking our intellectual projects—in this case, Black Queer Studies—by taking institutional pedigree, status, and material support into consideration and if we simultaneously understand, as I believe we should, Black Queer Studies as the field of Queer Studies. Yet invoking processes of hierarchy and exclusion in the naming of Rich Black Queer Studies risks suppressing the ever-urgent critique of the ways whiteness so deeply governs class and race exclusions in the academy and, moreover, the way white queerness continues to govern class and race exclusions within Queer Studies. The pervasiveness of racism in the academy, the power of racialization to upend class distinctions, means that professors of color share an experience across tiers of higher education. At the same time, professors of color across the academy do not share common experiences of class and status. The material conditions of their work lives, their educational histories, and their relative institutional power compared to each other are often strikingly different, even though they may have very similar structural relationships to wealth (or to deeper socioeconomic histories of racial capitalism). In this way, Rich Black Queer Studies is produced differently than Poor Black Queer Studies, even as it is produced differently than Rich White Queer Studies.

For me, this tension is captured by the epigraph from Christina Sharpe's *In the Wake: On Blackness and Being.* In her opening narrative about black family, death, precarity, class, and education, Sharpe writes, "It is a big leap from working class, to Ivy League schools, to being a tenured professor. And *a part of* that leap and *apart from* its specificities are the sense and awareness of precarity; the precarities of the afterlives of slavery . . . the precarities of the ongoing disaster of the ruptures of chattel slavery. They texture my reading practices, my ways of being in and of the world, my relations with and to others."[48] Here, the socioeconomic status "working class" stands in more recognizable tension with the institutional statuses "Ivy League" and "tenured professor," conveying a precarious journey for a black woman raised working class and working poor "in the wake of [racism's] purposeful flow."[49] But "working class" does so much more in this passage than mark a distant starting point for a professor who has traveled through elite institutions, for it also stands between the present-day, privileged educational endpoint and the much more distant but still present and still deadly past of chattel slavery and its afterlives. In one respect, "working class" operates as a foil to the larger narrative of slavery's ongoingness, for Sharpe is no longer a part of that class. Nevertheless, in the deeply personal/theoretical narrative with which she opens *In the Wake,* Sharpe describes living apart from the secu-

rity her class mobility, through education and prestigious academic affiliation, might be assumed to have purchased for her. Endless examples prove
that both in the academy and out, black academics' university-associated
class status and the privileges of pedigree may be erased, ignored, or disbe-
lieved.[50] Sharpe reveals how the classroom and the archive alike threaten to
become places where "the fact and structure of [black] subjection remain,"
appearing as the lack of empathy here, epistemological/methodological violence there. What do these black-queer diminishments and status-ruptures,
which are of a piece with life-threatening "precarities of the afterlives of
slavery," do to our ability to analyze class stratification in higher education?
In what ways do actively antielitist places and practices give us necessary
leverage for thinking through class stratification within Black Queer Studies, and how, simultaneously, does the wake of Atlantic chattel slavery *always* disrupt a flatly economic analysis of elite Black Queer Studies, given
the capacity of slavery's precarities to, in Sharpe's words, texture black reading practices, ways of being, relations with others?

My question about the necessity of a Black Queer Studies class analysis is
not, then, meant to negate other stressors experienced by black queer academics. In 2018, ten years after participating in the Black Queer Work(ing)
Group at Yale, Omise'eke Natasha Tinsley writes from the University of Texas
at Austin that "academic institutions haven't been able to force black queer
faculty out, but undervalue and undermined us in ways we never foresaw.
Why was Yale hemorrhaging black queer faculty [by the early to mid-2010s]?
Why did UT just promote a professor whose work attacks queer families
while those of us who live in them remain underpaid? Why does a next generation of black queer scholarship feel less possible now than ten years ago,
and why have some in our field attacked friends when we have common enemies to fight?"[51] The academy continues to commit (to) anti-black and antiqueer and antiwoman wrongs. Put differently, where there are resources,
resources will continue to flow toward the commission of those injustices,
even as resources sometimes flow against them. This is to say that no high-
class solvent will erase the stain of institutional racism and queerphobia.
There can be no way to balance the wrongs enumerated by Tinsley with
the fact that her words bridge two very different, enormously wealthy and
well-resourced universities, Yale and UT Austin. The calculus of class and
race in the academy is far more complicated than that. It is nonetheless true
that Tinsley's voice comes to us from—and is correlated with a pattern of
voices speaking across Black Queer Studies from—privileged sites of speaking. Jafari Sinclaire Allen, Tinsley's collaborator, friend, and interlocutor in

the above conversation, partially captures this tension in describing himself and his cohort as "those of us situated in the Master's house of the tenured professoriat."[52]

And so I repeat one of my early claims: we both are and are not our institutions. To explore the tension between Poor Black Queer Studies and Rich Black Queer Studies, we need to ask, how is Black Queer Studies tethered to status, to class-based demographics, to its material conditions of production? But also, how do scholars across university tiers live in the wake? And further, with Keene's work fresh in mind, is it possible that queer blackness names an opportunity to contravene those classed structures? Tinsley and Allen, even as they inhabited that problematic, elitist place of Rich Black Queer Studies, Yale University, more dramatically model an impulse toward black queer sociality. They discover and cultivate ways to "care about black queerness," and here they use the language of "love." Allen writes, "I do not want to be misunderstood here, especially because I think some may mistake our love ethic and the insistence on Black/queer sociality in our issue [the 2012 "Black/Queer/Diaspora" issue of GLQ] as a description of a club of folks who cosign and adhere to the same politics. We know that's far from the truth. Agreement is not sine qua non of love. Nor is proximity, really. It is our willingness to begin again."[53] That persistence, called love, strikes me as consonant with the kind of cross-class ethic that I find so worthy of illumination in this book, even as difficult questions remain about the structural changes such an ethic enables or accompanies.

But I also want to pause in order to be clear: Black Queer Studies bears no special responsibility or duty to address the imbrication of Queer Studies with higher education's class-stratifying imperative. Black Queer Studies ought not be used to exemplify this broad problem, nor ought it be burdened with the hope or the promise that it can fix that problem. This problem is everyone's. But Black Queer Studies might lend specificity to our understanding of the dilemma we all face, for Black Women's/Queer Studies has a history of facing, if not reconciling, its own class-based contradictions.

In their "Plum Nelly" introduction to the Black Queer Studies issue of *Callaloo* (2000), Jennifer DeVere Brody and Dwight A. McBride write, "If 'queer studies' as a category has already raised an entire set of questions and issues for scholars, artists, culture producers and readers to address about identity, sexuality, desire, and gender, *'black queer studies' has only upped the ante given the fraught relations among and between these often overlapping kinds of black and queer communities.*"[54] Citing its many disciplinary influences, the authors suggest that precisely because it is located within and amid and between critical schools and approaches, "'black queer studies' pushes for a greater degree of specificity in both the questions being formulated and on the conclusions being reached at the margins of American society."[55] Brody and McBride's characterization of Black Queer Studies as both fraught and specific enables me to frame a particular queer-class question: How does Black Queer Studies require me to "push for a greater degree of specificity" in my thinking about Poor Queer Studies, including greater specificity about how a Poor Black Queer Studies analysis must struggle against not only the class and race norms of the academy and Rich Queer Studies but also within—and against—Black Queer Studies produced at elitist institutions of higher education? In other words, can Poor Black Queer Studies up the ante once again by sustaining the queer-class-race tension not only between itself and Rich White Queer Studies but between itself and Rich Black Queer Studies? For without doubt there exist, to rephrase Brody and McBride, fraught class relations among and between these overlapping black and queer academic communities. Operations of class and status in the academy might be particularized by thinking through disparate sites of Black Queer Studies and by articulating the fraught relations that emerge within Black Queer Studies when teacher-scholars confront vastly different material conditions in our work lives.

As my discussion of Ruth Gordon and law education in chapter 2 made clear, class- and status-based divisions creep in even when community values are deeply felt, expressed, and lived. Academia structures or builds-in those hierarchical divisions and tensions. No less does this happen when academic fields of study explicitly reject classism as part of their intersectional work. Academic fields of study happen within the academy, after all. Saidiya Hartman's report on the 1994 conference "Black Women in the Academy: Defending Our Name, 1894–1994" celebrates the groundbreaking nature of two thousand black women academics coming together to share their work and work experiences. But Hartman refuses to overlook—indeed, she holds her historian's critical gaze on—class and status tensions among the participants at the Massachusetts Institute of Technology–hosted conference:

> As women approached the microphone, they introduced themselves, usually by institutional affiliation. Automatic applause followed the declarations of the questioner's pedigree: professor at some elite university, doctoral candidate at rival elite institution, etc. This continued throughout the conference.... Nonetheless, these institutional self-declarations prompted a woman to introduce herself on the last day of the conference

as having a pedigree of another order. She remarked that for two days women had been introducing themselves through the recitation of elite genealogies. This forced her to consider what kind of coalition was possible among us as black women given our class differences and the failure to address that difference. What unity existed between black women? How could we build cross-racial coalitions given the great differences between us, and the suspicion and mistrust that accompanied recognized differences of class, color and privilege? The woman broaching these questions stated that she had been raised in a housing project by a single mother who had worked very hard to insure her children a future. When she went to college, she had been surprised and wounded by the class and color violence she experienced there at the hands of upper-class and fair-complexioned black women. As a professor she said she witnessed the same forms of discrimination and self-hate amongst her students, and at the conference, too. Then she began to cry.[56]

Hartman records several reactions to the distressed woman at the "Black Women in the Academy" conference: "Someone from the Black Women's Health Project guided her away from the microphone and presumably advised her about what services were available through the project." But love is not all. Hartman continues, "Unfortunately, her tears enabled those uncomfortable with or disinterested in the issues she broached to dismiss it all as 'private.' As well, by the third day of the conference so many women had cried at the microphone, that many had grown impatient with all the tears. Were the questions she introduced unrelated to issues of community or coalition? Were these issues 'private matters' or central to the conference?"[57]

The closing speaker at "Black Women in the Academy," Angela Davis, argued that black academia must risk its internal differences by speaking up about them. Davis urged her audience, "As we approach the close of the only century that people of African descent have spent on this soil which has not seen slavery, we need to find ways to connect with and at the same time be critical of the work of our foremothers. There is no contradiction here. The most powerful way to acknowledge and carry on in a tradition that will move us forward is simultaneously to affirm historical continuity and effect some conscious historical ruptures."[58] There is no contradiction, in other words, in understanding class contradictions to exist among black women or, by extension, black queer academics. Davis affirms this liberatory idea by referencing Audre Lorde: "The last point I made had to do with our positionalities as women of color. As not the only women of color, I should say. When we think of ourselves as women of color, that means we are compelled to think about a range of issues and contradictions and differences. Audre Lorde's work continues to challenge us to think about difference and contradiction not as moments to be avoided or escaped—not as moments we should fear—but rather as generative and creative."[59]

For Lorde, difference provides "a fund of necessary polarities between which our creativity can spark like a dialectic." Lorde famously writes that "only then does the necessity for interdependency become unthreatening. Only within that interdependency of different strengths, acknowledged and equal, can the power to seek new ways of being in the world generate, as well as the courage and sustenance to act where there are no charters."[60] The word "charters," easy to overlook in this visionary passage from "The Master's Tools Will Never Dismantle the Master's House," can refer to documents that grant privilege and, fortuitously here, to documents that create or incorporate a university. The pressing question then becomes, how can the spark between queer-class differences uncharter or ungrant privileged university formations, starting with Queer Studies itself but always with an eye toward the university world beyond? I have suggested that literary documents such as *Counternarratives*, with its experimental nature, its formal strangeness, its imagining of black queer genius, and its expansive black queer pedagogies, can serve as a queer-class charter for new ways of reading and teaching in the academy. Reading *Counternarratives* as a black queer reader made possible among my students the enactment of "the interdependency of different strengths" that is anathema to hierarchy and stratification and that looks like keeping books alive, putting them in hands and, together, doing our first acts of reading over again. But how to share Poor Black Queer Studies charters in ways that not only cross institutional class lines but name and struggle with the contradictions of those crossings? We must look for extant models of such work, and we must theorize the contradictions of a broad queer-class-race project.

E. Patrick Johnson is such a model, for much of his work considers the ways Black Queer Studies is implicated in class hierarchies. In a 2014 essay, "To Be Young, Gifted, and Queer," published in an issue of *Black Scholar* that reassesses the field of Black Studies, Johnson traces the line of the new Black Studies through a small handful of young Black Queer Studies scholars. Johnson's edited collection, *No Tea, No Shade*, elaborates on that work, reflecting a broad range of young Black Queer Studies scholarship. I have noted elsewhere the exciting shift in Black Queer Studies over the last two decades beyond its initial—and still vibrant—work in literary and cultural interpretation (and specifically its attachments to James Baldwin) to other fields and objects and methods.[61] Johnson, as an author and an editor, has been one of the champions of that expansion. But if the *what* of Black Queer Studies has dramatically expanded, has the *where*? How do class and institutional status operate within Black Queer Studies as that field evolves and gives critical leverage to scholars eager to pry open areas closed off by traditional academic practices?

Because Johnson has made his path to and through the academy part of his ongoing academic project, I am not surprised that he begins his *Black Scholar* essay with the story of one of his teachers. The narrative of Black Queer Studies, for Johnson, begins with a student-teacher relationship and then unfolds not only as a tale of innovative theories but as a story line of ever-expanding pedagogical relations between a Black Queer Studies mentor (indeed, founder and luminary) and the young mentees he is clearly privileged to learn from, just as he is privileged to guide them through the academy's ever-shifting terrain. Johnson writes that "over the course of a career, academics get to witness change and innovation in their field of study. For some this can be a frightening proposition if they are not willing to move with the field."[62] The old Black Studies (my term, not Johnson's) becomes the New Black Studies in part by supporting the "young, gifted, and queer" among its ranks. Likewise, more senior academics must be able to follow those new scholars whom they support in order to "move with the field." But what if the direction the field and its (new and old) practitioners are asked to move is down? Can Black Queer Studies not only look around (see: diaspora) and down (see: down low) and behind (see: prison bars) and under (see: sex work) . . . can the field not only continue its multidirectional looking but can it, in fact, get down—through rankings and tiers and pedigrees and publishers and, most broadly, through raced class statuses—as one of its innovative, constitutive moves?

I view Johnson as an architect of Poor Black Queer Studies because his scholarship foregrounds class analyses and the material productions of black life, including in the university. In particular, Johnson's autobiographical criticism offers a compelling example of the way we make and navigate academic places in the world by drawing on knowledge learned through the body and in places far from the halls of academe. Thanks to the pedagogies taught to him at home and in black community in segregated, rural North Carolina, Johnson is able to find/create in performance studies a transgressive, disordered discipline to house what traditional academe codes as his "excess (for example, blackness, queerness, working classness, southern-ness, performance methods) and [his] lack (for example, pedigree, writing ability)."[63] Class and race and queerness are not only topics in Johnson's work but quare ways of knowing that enable him to move across hierarchi-cally structured differences in the academy and, through his performances, beyond. Interclass contact is part of the narrative, part of the lens, part of the method, and part of the politics of Johnson's quare studies—or what I am explicitly calling Poor Black Queer Studies. I want to strike a cautious note, however. For in a larger Queer Studies field that has proven resistant to class self-critique, it seems possible that foundational black queer-class concepts such as quare will be read exclusively in terms of race so that, for example, quare merely puts the black in Queer Studies, even though Johnson insists in all of his work that class, too, is part of quare's critical DNA. Though we have multifaceted lenses for viewing black queerness, will we deny their class refractions? As Johnson's work eloquently attests, Black Queer Studies offers models for tracing the narrative arc of research through the parochial and the working-class.[64] We need now to follow Johnson's guide to ever more insistently bend that arc through all of Poor Queer Studies.

One further model of the potentially productive contradictions inher-ent in many queer-class-race projects is Stefano Harney and Fred Moten's theory of the undercommons in the U.S. university. For reasons that I hope will become clear, I am both instinctively drawn to and put off by—that is, kept class-distant from—Harney's and Moten's formulation of the un-dercommons as a way to conceptualize the place where readers come to-gether to engage with each other and with unchartering texts. Concepts such as the undercommons, or any number of queer theories that posit subversive spaces or collectivities, appeal because they hold out the prom-ise of a thoughtful togetherness and an intellectual interdependency simply called "study" in *The Undercommons: Fugitive Planning and Black Study*. The undercommons therefore resonates with this chapter's pedagogy of reading strange and unread and even outlaw texts, together. Collectively reading unchartering texts can produce forms of cooperation and sharing that seem to me to echo the real labor of the undercommons as Harney and Moten describe it: passionate pedagogy beyond the role of the critical academic, the university actor who, through his complicit antagonism of the system, reproduces the system and therefore perfects the negligence of professionalization within the university. Moten and Harney ask, "Does the critical academic not teach how to deny precisely what one produces with others, and is this not the lesson the professions return to the university to learn again and again? . . . This is the professional course of action. This enlightenment-type charade is utterly negligent in its critique, a negligence that disavows the possibility of a thought of an outside, a nonplace called the undercommons—the nonplace that must be thought outside to be sensed from inside, from which the enlightenment type charade has stolen everything for its game."[65] To steal back from the university, "to abuse its hospitality, to spite its mission, to join its refugee colony, its gypsy encampment, *to be in but not of*—this is the path of the subversive intellectual in the modern university."[66] To be a subversive, a criminal, a thief: these become "the only possible relationship to the university today."[67] On the inside, one finds an outsider community. Given my earlier thinking about black queer reading as a practice of general education, it should not be surprising that I am drawn to the undercommons as a name for the place in which to learn/share the fugitive reading practices offered up and demanded by *Counternarratives*. I have argued that Keene, no enemy of expertise, makes outsiders even of professional readers. Like Moten and Harney, I am drawn to a place where readers come together as outsiders, "outsiders" signifying not so much an intentional, politicized (or radical) position as a readerly relationship, even among the studied.

At the same time, I fail in trying to identify the nonplace of the undercommons as a place of Poor Queer Black Studies. Perhaps this is because Moten and Harney, helped by an introduction by the well-placed Jack Halberstam, flatly posit the undercommons as a queer place, a move made easier without the burden—at least in the undercommons essay—of connecting queerness to the sexual or the gendered lives of poor people in the academy. They can therefore thread together in the nonplace of the undercommons the figure of the subversive intellectual and queer study while invisibilizing the very things that *Poor Queer Studies* has tried to make visible: first, the active presence of actually existing poor queers studying in the academy and, second, the elite authorizing conditions of Rich Queer Studies'—and now, it seems, the undercommons'—production. Here, they reproduce queer's dependence on its claim to radicality by claiming an even more radical place for it: no place. Queerness thus affirms its radicality, its criminal character, its street cred, in the undercommons. And just as queerness gets reradicalized by associating with placeless black study, the undercommons gets authorized by queer's diffuse perversities. But this act of mutual buttressing of outsider black and queer philosophies does not come cheap. There has to be something to steal, after all. How much are readers to make of the undercommons' accommodation of standard professional practices in a book that persuades us that professionalization "is a state strategy?"[68] For example, does the "subversive intellectual," someone distinguished by the capacity "to become unreliable, to be disloyal to the public sphere, to be obstructive and shiftless, dumb with insolence in the face of the call to critical thinking," not reproduce the state strategy of class stratification in the university by writing an authorizing/authoritative queer introduction to *The Undercommons*?[69] Does the authority of Rich Queer Studies escape criticism, now that criticality has been debunked as weak antagonism? If only we all had no place to go.

I also wonder about the unspoken class frame used to represent subversion as prophecy. When radical pedagogy is relocated not merely underground but to a nonplace of secular mysticism, attention to the material conditions of pedagogy falls away. My impulse in this book has been the opposite. Moten and Harney adopt the language of "uncanny . . . cadence," "revelation," and ultimately "prophetic organization"—the language of a churchless divinity—to describe their feeling that "something else is there in the undercommons." Here, they exceed the love ethic of Tinsley and Allen. The prophetic organization of the undercommons (characterized as an already existing atemporal call and response) is meant to be understood as an unchurched fantasy or secular prophecy, an idea that Halberstam's introduction takes up by coupling Maurice Sendak's *Where the Wild Things Are* with Jay-Z's and Kanye West's song "No Church in the Wild" as pertinent referents. But this break from structure through feeling is unconvincing. Just as "the wild" disorganizes itself in relation to rather than beyond the organization of "the church," the undercommons disorganizes itself in relation to rather than beyond the organization that bids it to speak: the university and, more to my point, Rich Queer Studies.[70] Hearing the attractive call to queer subversion, to insolence, to wildness in the undercommons, I recall the mysterious revelations and secret pedagogies transmitted by *Counternarratives*, and I believe for a moment that my classes at CSI are refugee colonies and gypsy encampments. Perhaps we are outside, out here on the forgotten borough. But if that is true, it is not only because we study *Counternarratives* together but because we read together at CSI—a hyper-located college place with materially produced underclass pedagogies, a place from which so much has been stolen.

At times, the formulation of the undercommons resonates with the labor of Poor Black Queer Studies, while at other times the nonplace of the undercommons seems to describe something utterly disconnected from that labor. I haven't been able to determine whether this nonplace engenders a consideration of the material conditions of black queer study or, on the other hand, foils it. Because the undercommons operates as a site for an important articulation of black fugitivity, I am worried about the implications of finding the latter to be the case. Nevertheless, I am hesitant to follow such an act of radical displacement, for by the time the undercommons becomes not just uncanny and strange and secret but prophetic, I am no longer able to share in its mysteriously unclassed work. Yet insofar as Poor Black Queer Studies pedagogy describes the crucial sharing of teaching and learning, and insofar as prophetic organization describes a yearning for a new form of social study, perhaps there is common ground. I therefore question but do not abandon the undercommons. Instead, I look for models of being of and not of the university that rely less on claims to immaterial prophecy, less on the figure of the undoubtedly queer subversive intellectual, and less on a nonplace imagined from above. For me, that trifecta opens up too great a class- and status-based gap for Poor Black Queer Studies to fall through.

I am arguing that the subversive intellectual in the undercommons—the radical outsider who is in but not of the university—only problematically assumes such dispossessed relation to U.S. institutions of higher education. The labors of what Ruth Wilson Gilmore and others call "activist scholarship"—a commitment that differs from the work of the undercommons but nevertheless sheds some light on it—is always constrained:

> So here is another conundrum: it is consistently true that the engaged scholar of whatever political conviction works in the unavoidable context of dynamics that force her into self-conscious inconsistency; she must at times confirm and at times confront barriers, boundaries, and scales (Gilmore 2007a; Katz 2004; Loyd 2005). This is treacherous territory for all who wish to rewrite the world. Plenty of bad research (engaged or not) is produced for all kinds of reasons, and plenty of fruitless organizing is undertaken with the best intentions. Activist scholarship attempts to intervene in a particular historical-geographical moment by changing not only what people do but also how all of us think about ourselves and our time and place, by opening the world we make.[71]

Gilmore helps us to perceive a conundrum or "self-conscious inconsistency" in scholarly theories of subversion, including the undercommons. I suggest that the radical act of positioning oneself beyond politics must fail to be consistent, even if only in that the "under" is imagined from over, from above, from a place of authority.[72] How, then, can either the undercommons or activist scholarship be meeting places for those variously constrained by their academic locations in Rich Queer Studies and Poor Queer Studies?

As I turn to this book's conclusion, my critical compromise with the undercommons is this: I will look for opportunities—irreplaceable, from my professional perspective—for working less mysteriously across the peaks and valleys of Queer Studies, while at the same time learning to believe, if not grasp, Moten's, Harney's, and Halberstam's powerful calls for wild solidarity.

epilogue

Queer Ferrying

The field of possibilities—and even the field of possibilities that it is possible to imagine, to say nothing of the field of possibilities that can actually be realized—is tightly circumscribed by one's class position.... Only if you actually manage to move from one side of the border to the other, as happened in my case, can you get out from under the implacable logic of all those things that go without saying in order to perceive the terrible injustice of this unequal distribution of prospects and possibilities. —Didier Eribon, *Returning to Reims*

I remain convinced that there is no transformation or change in the academy unless black feminists engage in a kind of itinerant movement from front to back, to inside, to outside again and again, and unless there are parallel movements, going and coming—in the streets, down the alley, and in the house—whereby dynamic mutuality and exchange coalesce and contest. —Cheryl Clarke, *"But Some of Us Are Brave* and the Transformation of the Academy"

Poor Queer Studies as Public Practice

Queer-class-race stratification in higher education is mundane. It happens everywhere you look, which makes it look about right. *Poor Queer Studies* has tried to perspectivize—to create new perspectives onto—the ways university life, including intellectual life, is sorted out for queer students and professors according to their class and race. The field of Queer Studies has been my window onto that question. Queers are not all of the same class, of course, but queers of the same class get sorted in the same ways. In this, we are as normal as could be. More affluent queers are sorted into top undergraduate schools and top PhD programs, first as doctoral students and then as faculty. Poor queers of color are sorted out of college altogether, or into predatory for-profit schools, or into desperately underfunded community colleges and unranked four-year schools, like many of those in the public CUNY system. Of course, some underclass queers beat the odds, and classist, racist norms can fade from view in the bright light of their exceptional successes. Queer Studies, like much of academia, can thus construct its identity around the myth of meritocracy that disguises the unqueer protocols of academic elitism. The fact is that academic formations like ours thrive at the intersection of resources and opportunity, a combination increasingly found only at the top of the steeply tiered university system in the U.S. Unfortunately, being a historically despised people is no excuse for taking advantage of inequitable class and race systems in this way.

But, hypothetically, if *all* queers managed either to defy the class-race rule of academic hierarchy or to be born straight into its rewards, class stratification in higher ed would become, ironically, even more of a problem for Queer Studies than for normal fields. This is because if queers were to disproportionately benefit from schools that hoard resources, we would be disproportionately responsible for fixing the problem that we either miraculously overcame or that we were mundanely propped up by. In reality, we are not disproportionately rewarded compared to straight peers, a fact that likely breeds quietude among our queer-class normals and our queer-class exceptionals alike.

Many fair-minded people want the U.S. to have a system of broad, affordable access to quality higher education. More than any other recent political figure, senator and 2016 and 2020 presidential candidate Bernie Sanders galvanized a movement for making college "tuition free and debt free."[1] Sanders remains a leader in the "fight to make sure that every American who studies hard in school can go to college regardless of how much money their parents make and without going deeply into debt." In line with Sanders's vision, calls for free (or affordable) college often take for granted the democratizing potential of this vital institution. College serves the public good. But most plans for tuition-free and debt-free higher education, including Sanders's, have been quite clear in situating the debate as a question of free/affordable access to public colleges and universities, not private ones. College isn't only a public good; the good work of democratizing education is to take place in public institutions. The chief drivers of educational inequity—rich, elitist, exclusionary, private colleges and universities—remain untouched by these calls for public-minded reform. Cathy Davidson argues in this same vein that at some of our "wealthiest institutions . . . of higher education, the definition of innovation does not include equality and actually exacerbates inequality. That is an abrogation of the true responsibility of nonprofit, tax-exempt higher education. If higher education does not serve the public good, higher education does not deserve public benefit."[2] Yes, some mega-rich schools are public, but overwhelmingly it is private institutions of higher education that are exempted from the democratizing mandate of "free college for all." They choose the few over the many, and we reward them for it.

Though making public education free would probably increase college enrollments and, probably, move some students from expensive for-profit colleges to newly free public ones, such a stance would preserve and even re-inforce the separate, very different sphere of private education that currently takes up so much real estate at the top of the best colleges lists and in the public imagination. Public education for all really means public education for the masses that wouldn't have gone to selective private schools anyway. "Public" therefore operates as a class- and race-sorting framework. Even more importantly, free public education may have another consequence: it may more starkly define the differences not only between public and private but also between tiers of public institutions. Everyone deserves access to a free public college education, but who deserves access to the best free public education? Who deserves the worst? Christopher Newfield, in accord with Davidson's assertion that all students deserve innovative, student-centered, antielitist education, argues that scaling up local examples of successful ex-perimental pedagogy would, beneficially, "yoke mass-scale free college to the intensities of the liberal arts and sciences in new combinations." The problem isn't that "intensive learning doesn't scale. It's that scaling costs money that the political and business systems won't spend.... Absent a major change in political economy, the new education will not be funded."[3]

What if too many students wanted the same great public education? Who would get it? The ridiculously low acceptance rates at top private schools, where Queer Studies lives its best life (see chapter 2), make equal access im-possible under current conditions. But the slightly higher acceptance rates at merely good schools—including moderately selective public schools—only replay the problem a bit further down the ladder of race-based institu-tional elitism. Not surprisingly, many students and educators want a better education and a better workplace than the system is willing to give. That desire would be no less thwarted were all students given access to grossly underfunded public college education, an education guaranteed to be not merely insufficient to the task because it is done on the cheap (a condi-tion under which some students will, miraculously, succeed) but, in both the short and long term, abortive of students' desire to succeed through educa-tion. One further complication: proposals for free public education often require students to matriculate in their home states. As a result, free or low-cost in-state tuition may keep poor queer students and queer students of color tied to their ultrawhite state university systems, even though these students may have a greater need or desire to escape those racially homogenous environments. Unfortunately, flagship campuses—beacons of public education—sometimes play a special role in the most egregious patterns of race sorting in higher education.[4] Why would we ask queer students/students of color to jump at the chance to be funneled into those "good" public schools, even for free?

Why isn't the call among progressives, including queer progressive intellectuals, for equal public education for all? More pointedly, why do we not call out in one voice for our queer teaching and research to be done as part of an equal-access, open-access, public educational project that does not reproduce class and race stratification? To admit my biases, I want this for queers most of all. With all of our talk of queer publics, why are Queer Studies professors, as a field-based collective, not refiguring ourselves as public servants charged with educating people regardless of income, class, or status? What would that discipline look like, and where? One of Queer Studies' most frequent and seemingly powerful critiques calls for a reversal of the neoliberal corporatization of the university. We offer compelling reasons for wanting to pull the university back from its insinuations with market and with capital. But as long as higher education operates by the current system of race and class sorting, as long as the rich get access to one kind of education and the poor get access only to another, and as long as Queer Studies follows the line of educational hierarchy rather than steps out of line to form collective resistance, our critiques of the neoliberal academy will be far queerer than the worlds they actually create.

As my inability to fully situate myself in the undercommons in the previous chapter showed, I often struggle to do what queer theory does best: take a theoretical leap. I have come to the point of arguing for cross-class Queer Studies collective action only by piecing together the details of my queer work life. I have wanted to show where my ideas come from. Rather than end on a theoretical high point, then, I want to conclude by saying a few more words about how I came to learn what I've learned in this book. That is, I thought I'd reflect a bit further on what made it possible for me to write this book as a way of making future work conceivable. The condition of possibility for this project turned out to be methodological, though that word might suggest more intentionality than is right. The fact of the matter is that many of the insights I gained here are the product of schlepping.

In the introduction I offered a brief history of my institutional travels: undergraduate at Wabash College; graduate school at Indiana University; teaching postdoc at Duke; tenure-track job at the College of Staten Island, CUNY. I now expand on the final coordinate in that trajectory. A more robust accounting of my professional comings and goings in the past thirteen years would note that CUNY has afforded me the opportunity to do Queer Studies from multiple locations. My primary appointment is at CSI, but I frequently have reason to be at the Graduate Center in Manhattan (across the street from the Empire State Building), home to most of the doctoral work at CUNY, and the jewel in the CUNY crown. Like other faculty from the campuses, I am sometimes asked to teach at the Graduate Center, though without official affiliation. I advise master's theses and have been allowed to sit on two dissertation committees. Teaching at the Graduate Center grants me access to its Mina Rees Library, including its print holdings and electronic databases. This book certainly would have been much harder, and perhaps impossible, to write without that library's online resources (which are not shared across the CUNY system, as each differently resourced college maintains its own database subscriptions). Cross-campus access to the Graduate Center's databases has been an enabling material condition of my queer professional livelihood. For six years I was on the board of directors of CLAGS: Center for LGBTQ Studies, the first academic center of its kind, housed at the Graduate Center. While CLAGS is best known for its cutting-edge conferences, its extensive and varied programming, and its community engagement, another of its chief contributions to queer scholarship has been almost wholly overlooked: CLAGS offers Queer Studies scholars from CUNY's community colleges and unsung four-year colleges the opportunity to join with scholars from top universities in the work of building the field of Queer Studies. Not just a "center," CLAGS is a far more important structural feature in queer academia: a bridge between class-based queer academic worlds. The same is true for another CUNY-affiliated entity, the journal WSQ: Women's Studies Quarterly, published by the Feminist Press and housed at the Graduate Center. For three years I coedited WSQ with my CSI colleague Cynthia Chris. The editorial board of WSQ brought together faculty from across the world, but thanks to its CUNY affiliation this group included many faculty from within the CUNY system. Board meetings, issue launches, and collaborative editorial work provided opportunities for cross-class, cross-institutional engagement among board members. My involvements with CLAGS and WSQ reflect structural possibilities for participating in Queer Studies at the vanguard. I cannot emphasize this strongly enough:

these academic structures have made a queer career imaginable, even when I lacked imagination.

But having the Graduate Center as a resource is only half the point, for the Graduate Center could never have provided me the resources I needed to write this book. The whole point, the fact of this book, is that academic formations such as the Graduate Center, its library, CLAGS, and WSQ facilitate dynamic movement between centers and margins. And this is an incredibly under-exploited way of structuring the fieldwork of Queer Studies: through class and status crossing over and exchange. Class-based exchange among differently placed scholars has structured my engagements not only with colleagues from CUNY's many two- and four-year campuses but with distant colleagues from around the world, many of us with strikingly different institutional statuses. I therefore move, to speak personally, between my local commitment to Poor Queer Studies at CSI with its many queer faculty, staff, and students and the energetic institutional space at the Graduate Center that feels like one of the beating hearts of queer scholarship. And this professional straddling across New York Harbor, one foot firmly planted at CSI (through tenure, significant classroom teaching, administrative responsibility, student mentorship, collegiality, its own substantial Queer Studies scholarship, and our class-based community understanding) and the other foot planted (less firmly) at the Graduate Center in the city, provides the perspective from which I can theorize Poor Queer Studies. The need for such structural crossing-over among scholar-teachers working at different types of colleges and universities can guide the field of Queer Studies not so much beyond as *between* the elite institutions that have so brilliantly dominated its history and the work sites of Poor Queer Studies.

I call this cross-institutional knowledge-producing movement "queer ferrying." Queer ferrying is an asymmetrical mode of field building with important implications for queer pedagogy and for training of future Queer Studies professors. Queer ferrying can help us to teach our current and future selves about the need to plan for and enact queer pedagogies as cross-class pedagogies. It gives us a heuristic, part model and part method, for connecting queer-class work sites across the academy, an especially important function if the places where we do our graduate training and the places where we end up teaching possess very different class and race coordinates. Poor Queer Studies also invites us to create pedagogical methods around the concept of queer ferrying, particularly insofar as that concept is capable of recoding operations of institutional differentiation (the "here" and the "there" determined by status, rank, cost, reputation, support) as operations of institutional integration. Such "pedagogies of crossing," to adapt in a literal way Jacqui Alexander's phrase, would facilitate queer-class linkages because students would see how scholars do Queer Studies differently when they are faced with different institutional resources, student demographics, regional locations, and career goals. A methodology of queer-class ferrying can help us recognize and communicate across those differences. Inventing and adapting queer methods in relation to and relating across institutional status—which closely relates with socioeconomic class in today's educational landscape—can teach students about their own intellectual investments, including what they prioritize in research and how they connect research to their own often-unarticulated class locations. Directors of graduate studies, graduate admissions committees, and graduate pedagogy instructors can be (and need to be) Poor Queer Studies facilitators.

Queer ferrying, as a pedagogical method for producing relationships that resist class and race stratification in higher education, will be challenging. The question of what and how to teach seems to be more pertinent at some colleges and universities than others. Paula Krebs, executive director of the Modern Language Association and from 2012 to 2017 dean of the College of Humanities and Social Sciences at Bridgewater State University, suggests that the job of a regional university professor is often a mystery to job candidates coming from R1 graduate training and, often, small private undergraduate colleges. She therefore identifies the need for pedagogical programs that can help graduate students prepare for academic careers in and beyond the R1 universities for which they are almost exclusively trained.[5] Krebs recalls, "I interviewed a job candidate the other day who—like many applicants I meet—had no experience at all at our kind of institution.... Now, that wasn't entirely his fault. He had graduated from different types of institutions—a small private college followed by a large research university. And like many job candidates I see, he didn't know what he didn't know." Candidates who know the importance of connecting their professional work to the local communities from which the regional university draws most of its students pique Krebs's interest. "I'd trade that for any number of refereed journal articles," she maintains. Krebs certainly doesn't foreclose the possibility that her faculty will publish articles in refereed journals, but she puts that professional metric in tension with the work of connecting to the needs of the community, imagining a trade-off between the two. Connection over publication, a potentially surprising order of concerns. "I'll bet your graduate advisers never told you that," Krebs continues. "They don't know everything. Their job is at a research university. And they've been grooming you for the job they have. The one I'm offering isn't that job." Krebs claims a regional seat of knowledge here, located at odds with—and outside the imagination of—the places where knowledge is produced through doctoral training.

I want to pick up on one of Krebs's main points. The regional is often invisible among the professoriate because, practically and conceptually, doctoral training does not professionalize us toward the local, even if that is where the jobs are. It professionalizes toward the national, the R1, perhaps the well-regarded private liberal arts college. The regional is also invisible because the intellectual work most valued there stays there. Job candidates therefore come to located knowledge practices unwittingly and ill prepared, to hear Krebs tell it. Katie King reflects on the dynamic by which feminist theory travels far and wide when it appears unmarked by the local but remains hidden when it is marked by the local.[6] Deborah Gordon's epigraph to King's study is worth repeating in the context of Queer Studies, which has an even more limited professional GPS: "The places we struggle and resist in relationship to different institutions are also something that we need to know more about when we speak to one another. Our disciplinary and academic locations are part of the context we need to be sensitive to. Otherwise, we run the risk of mistaking the most well-funded of feminist discourses for all feminism."[7] Whatever happens in a regional Queer Studies classroom, it happens better when it is imbued with local meaning. While queer theory has claimed a certain everywhere-ness and everything-ness as part of its expanding critical project, Krebs reports a failure within the professorial pipeline to prepare graduate students to do anything but the kind of work produced and reproduced at a relatively small set of highly class-prescribed institutional locations.

I appreciate Krebs's efforts to prioritize regional knowledge production. I further propose that another important approach, beyond preparing graduate students for work at regional colleges, would be to prepare them to integrate their institutional histories. In this model, the goal would not be only to understand how we produce knowledge from any one place or for any particular place but to become better at thinking about how to produce knowledge from place to place, or between places. A relational approach such as this would enable us to recognize Queer Studies beyond the academic production sites where graduate students and even assistant professors undergo their Queer Studies grooming, their professional conditioning, preparation, and consolidation. Until fairly recently, this proposition would have made little sense, as no one was systematically groomed in or for Queer Studies. Even among my cohort of PhDs—who did our coursework at the end of the 1990s and earned our doctorates in the early years of the new millennium—there are those of us who never took a Queer Studies course. But the Queer Studies groom game is strong at this point. The question becomes, How will Queer Studies learn to mediate its many provincial institutional knowledge places, allowing them to meet, relate, and reciprocate?

Because my interest is in cross-class ferrying, this question of what makes sharing and communication possible across sites of Queer Studies is a central concern. There is a strong headwind, and the queer provocation to "cross class!" will certainly be no easier to pursue than the queer provocation to "be interdisciplinary!" Problematically, even at individual institutions, it can be difficult to discern how class works and therefore how class lessons can be shared. Further, class and race contradictions abound. But queer ferrying can orient us to our queer-class-race work, even in the midst of the powerfully disorienting forces of the neoliberal academy, by allowing us to think expansively about our field relations. This has been my lucky method: envisioning institutional class difference as, potentially, queer connective tissue rather than a divisive fault line in higher education. That method has been revealed to me as I sat on the boat that is not simply part of my commute to and from work but, in fact, is part of my Poor Queer Studies job. Rather than a one-way narrative of decentering Rich Queer Studies, I offer *Poor Queer Studies* as a narrative of crossing the field. The queer compass guiding this study needs the coordinates it has me schlepping and shuttling constantly between, my home campus on Staten Island and the looming edifice of the Graduate Center that concretizes at least one well-known version of Queer Studies. This professional shuttling enacts a certain kind of knowledge production not thinkable at either margin or center. The only possible metaphor for this ferrying back and forth is, of course, not a metaphor at all but an actual ferry, the Staten Island Ferry, symbol of the Poor Queer Studies commute. Huge, orange, and free, it connects my work on two very different islands, giving me a perspective on Queer Studies done here and there.

The examples above give me hope that queer-class ferrying among academic worksites happens more frequently than we know. But until an idea has a name and a mode of public transportation, we cannot respond to its call, organize around the work already being done, and together concretely imagine the work to come. I have suggested here that we might mobilize around Poor Queer Studies. While that ferry may be slow, the view is all the better for it.

notes

Introduction

1. Woolf, *A Room of One's Own*, 18.
2. Jenkins, *Moonlight*.
3. In an interesting essay, Suzanne Sowinska also thinks about working-class relationships to the academy in terms of food, recalling meals missed ("claiming I wasn't hungry when I was" [152]) and of meals eaten ("I can imagine that most students from middle-class backgrounds have not had the experience of enjoying dining hall food—because it is like 'eating out' every night" [155]). See Sowinska, "Yer Own Motha Wouldna Reckanized Ya."
4. The City College of New York, the first of what would become the twenty-four campuses of the CUNY system, was originally founded as the Free Academy of the City of New York in 1847. The Free Academy's first president, Dr. Horace Webster, described the mission of the Free Academy in terms of a class- and status-conscious experiment in democratic education: "The experiment is to be tried, whether the children of the people, the children of the whole people, can be educated; and whether an institution of the highest grade, can be successfully controlled by the popular will, not by the privileged few" ("Our History," City College of New York, https://www.ccny.cuny.edu/about/history).
5. Here and throughout the book I have chosen to capitalize this unheard-of discipline, Poor Queer Studies, in order to draw attention to the substantive work of conceptualizing the field through the lens of class. I do so with Rich Queer Studies and Black Queer Studies as well. Queer Studies is capitalized for consistency and does not indicate the uncritical elevation of that standard naming of the field.
6. Mullen, *Degrees of Inequality*, 2.
7. Mullen, *Degrees of Inequality*, 5.
8. Mullen, *Degrees of Inequality*, 157.
9. See, for example, Cahalan and Perna's Pell Institute study of higher education equity in the U.S., *Indicators of Higher Education Equity in the United States*. Renny Christopher's 2005 essay, "New Working-Class Studies in Higher Education,"

offers a succinct analysis of slightly earlier research on how contemporary college students "are distributed through our multitiered higher education system" (210).

10. Cahalan and Perna, *Indicators of Higher Education Equity in the United States*, 11.

11. See Harper and Griffin, "Opportunity beyond Affirmative Action," 43–46.

12. Laymon, *Heavy*, 191.

13. For fascinating related scholarship on the white supremacist foundations of the American university, see Harris, Campbell, and Brophy, *Slavery and the University*.

14. For a helpful visualization of the data from the National Center for Education Statistics, see Ashkenas, Park, and Pierce, "Even with Affirmative Action, Blacks and Hispanics Are More Underrepresented at Top Colleges than 35 Years Ago."

15. Cooper, "Afterword," 382.

16. See Lavelle Porter's 2019 study, *The Blackademic Life*.

17. See Carnevale and Strohl, "White Flight Goes to College," 2.

18. Glynn, *Opening Doors*, 47.

19. Chetty et al., "Mobility Report Cards," 1.

20. Carnevale and Van Der Werf, "The 20% Solution," 10–11.

21. For another measure of economic mobility by higher education institution, see the Obama-era Department of Education's "College Scorecard" at https://collegescorecard.ed.gov/. For a comparison, see Looney, "A Comparison between the College Scorecard and Mobility Report Cards."

22. The most recent such commitment is called the American Talent Initiative (https://americantalentinitiative.org/). Institutional members of the initiative are those colleges and universities that enroll the lowest percentage of poor students and the highest percentage of rich students. More established programs include the Jack Cooke Kent Foundation (https://www.jkcf.org/) and QuestBridge (https://www.questbridge.org/).

23. Giancola and Kahlenberg, "True Merit," 37.

24. See Stephanie Saul's *New York Times* article "A Push to Make Harvard Free Also Questions the Role of Race in Admissions." College endowments held $516 billion in 2014, with 74 percent of the money held by 11 percent of institutions, according to a December 2015 Congressional Research Service report by Sherlock et al., "College and University Endowments."

25. Hoxby and Avery, "The Missing 'One-Offs,'" 3.

26. Hoxby and Avery, "The Missing 'One-Offs,'" 9–10.

27. Hoxby and Avery, "The Missing 'One-Offs,'" 44.

28. See, for example, Benjamin Wermund's investigative report "How U.S. News College Rankings Promote Economic Inequality on Campus."

29. See Jonathan Rothwell's memo of December 18, 2015, from the Brookings Institute, "The Stubborn Race and Class Gaps in College Quality": "But simply going to college is not enough. A great deal hinges on the quality of the education on offer. First-generation, black, and Hispanic students are getting a lower-quality education than their more socially advantaged peers. Gaps in college quality reflect disparities in education in the preceding years, of course. But right now, if anything,

the college years see those gaps widen even further—which puts the ideal of equal opportunity even further out of reach."

30. Herman Gray, drawing from the work of Clyde Taylor, notes that resistance to elitist knowledge practices can morph into reproduction of those practices. See Gray, *Cultural Moves*, 114–16.

31. See, for instance, Garber, *Identity Poetics*.

32. See Kadji Amin's *Disturbing Attachments* for an insightful rendering of Queer Studies' commitment to egalitarianism.

33. Renn, "LGBT and Queer Research in Higher Education," 132.

34. Hoad, "Queer Theory Addiction," 139.

35. The most frequent exceptions to the rule of locating Queer Studies at rich schools are the large public universities where much terrific queer work has been done and where, simultaneously, resources have been unconscionably drained by state governments. Most of that queer work happens in the humanities and social sciences. Yet many of these schools are flagship institutions where national reputations can be made and status traded upon. Anthony Grafton, in his survey of books on the American university in the *New York Review of Books*, thus sees schools such as Rutgers-New Brunswick, Ohio State, Indiana, Florida State, Iowa, and the University of Wisconsin at Madison joining with more recognizably elite institutions such as Virginia, William and Mary, and Berkeley to make up "the top, the shiny part of the iceberg that rises above sea level." See Grafton, "Our Universities." William Deresiewicz similarly expands the definition of elite education to include "second-tier selective schools" in "Don't Send Your Kids to the Ivy League."

36. Rand, "After Sex?!," 272.

37. I take up the queer-labor intersection more fully in chapter 3 and Harney's and Moten's black-queer-class notion of the undercommons in chapter 5.

38. Henderson, *Love and Money*, 5.

39. Henderson, *Love and Money*, 5.

40. See Gluckman and Reed, *Homo Economics*. A more recent collection is Jacobsen and Zeller, *Queer Economics*. See also Follins and Lassiter, *Black LGBT Health in the United States*.

41. See, for example, Jessica Fields's description of her work with women in prison in "The Racialized Erotics of Participatory Research."

42. Freud, "The Sexual Aberrations," 88.

43. Escoffier, "Inside the Ivory Closet," 105.

44. Duggan, "The Discipline Problem," 179.

45. Morton, "The Class Politics of Queer Theory," 472.

46. Morton, "The Class Politics of Queer Theory," 472.

47. Bérubé, *My Desire for History*, 242.

48. For a fascinating example of how an individual discipline can be implicated in the larger trend of class stratification in higher education, see Christopher Findeisen's "Injuries of Class." Findeisen argues that MFA programs purport to contest establishment values while continuing the mass exclusion of poor people from higher education: "When we look closer at how the last forty years have altered American history, we see that Kmart realism [which refers to a Raymond Carver-esque style

of writing difference] becomes symbolic for the [writing] program era not for how it marks the presence of the lower classes in higher education but, more powerfully, for how it replaces them—allowing lower-class culture to proliferate without any meaningful increase in lower-class enrollment" (291).

49. Stein and Plummer, "'I Can't Even Think Straight,'" 181.

50. As sociologist Amin Ghaziani and I argue in *Imagining Queer Methods*—an argument made possible thanks in part to the work of Stein and Plummer—recent interdisciplinary reorientations within Queer Studies away from theory and toward questions of queer methods and methodologies can both reveal and galvanize interclass, cross-institutional queer formations that aren't part of the typical story of the field.

51. Wiegman, *Object Lessons*, 7.

52. Cohen, "Foreword," xiii.

53. Cohen, "Foreword," xii. I elaborate on the necessary imbrication of Poor Queer Studies and Black Queer Studies in chapter 5, especially as that pairing represents the class-race foil to another field formation, Rich Black Queer Studies.

54. For an excellent primer, see Love's essay "Feminist Criticism and Queer Theory."

55. The special issue of *GLQ* in which Love's comments appear (as part of the feature "Queer Studies, Materialism, and Crisis" by Crosby et al.) is titled "Queer Studies and the Crisis of Capitalism."

56. Bérubé, *My Desire for History*, 243.

57. Oldfield and Johnson, *Resilience*.

58. Other anthologies of working-class academics also point to the multiplicity of tensions around changing class, including feeling like you haven't, ever, and feeling like you have, irrevocably. Carolyn Leste Law, coeditor along with C. L. Barney Dews of *This Fine Place So Far from Home: Voices of Academics from the Working Class*, writes that "ambivalence, more than any other theme, is the common denominator in the stories . . . that are collected here" (2).

59. Love, "Doing Being Deviant," 87.

60. Love, "Doing Being Deviant," 90.

61. See Gabriner, Schiorring, and Waldron, "'We Could Do That!'"

62. See White, "Beyond a Deficit View."

63. *Oxford English Dictionary Online*, s.v. "poor," n.d.

64. See Ahmed, *Queer Phenomenology*.

65. See the CSI Institutional Profile, compiled by the Office of Institutional Research, https://www.csi.cuny.edu/about-csi/institutional-effectiveness /institutional-research/institutional-profile.

66. "2018 Social Mobility Index," CollegeNET, accessed June 6, 2019, http://www .socialmobilityindex.org/; "Economic Diversity and Student Outcomes at College of Staten Island," *New York Times*, 2017, https://www.nytimes.com/interactive /projects/college-mobility/college-of-staten-island.

67. "The 'protected classes,' delineated in Executive Order 11246, include American Indian or Alaska Native, Asian, Black or African American, Hispanic or Latino, Native Hawaiian or Other Pacific Islander, and Women. Updated federal guide-

lines further expanded these protected classes to include two or more races. As of December 9, 1976, the Chancellor of the City University of New York identified Italian Americans as a protected group at the University" (6). "CUNY Affirmative Action Plan for Italian Americans," accessed June 6, 2019, http://www2.cuny.edu /wp-content/uploads/sites/4/page-assets/about/administration/offices/hr/central -office-human-resources/FINAL-2016-Italian-American-AAP.pdf.

68. Christopher, "New Working-Class Studies in Higher Education," 213.

69. For more on the excellence of poetry faculty at CUNY, see Harris, "How CUNY Became Poetry U."

70. "America's Top Colleges," Forbes, 2018, https://www.forbes.com/top-colleges /list/12/#tab:rank.

71. Interesting to me is that I assume my colleagues will easily discern that I am not romanticizing our work by making it "poor." I assume this because, of all the affective energies at CSI, a shared romanticization of our work does not seem to be among them. "Poor" works against the "theft of pride" that Willy Staley, in "When 'Gentrification' Isn't about Housing," associates with the psychic gentrification accomplished when the language of poverty becomes a metaphor used in the "repackaging of [poor] people's lifestyles." Also see Kathi Weeks's "Down with Love" for an analysis of the ways injunctions to love our jobs draw on a discourse of romanticization reminiscent of unpaid domestic labor in order to attach workers ever more intimately to waged work.

72. Love, "Feminist Criticism and Queer Theory," 346, 345.

73. Gilmore, "Forgotten Places and the Seeds of Grassroots Planning," 36.

74. See Love, "How the Other Half Thinks," in the collection *Imagining Queer Methods*, as well as Ghaziani and Brim, "Queer Methods: Four Provocations for an Emerging Field," in that same volume.

75. Manalansan et al., "Queering the Middle," 1.

76. Manalansan et al., "Queering the Middle," 5.

77. Hartle and Nellum, "Where Have All the Low-Income Students Gone?" Other studies put the college attendance rate for children from poor families even lower, at 25–40 percent. See Chetty et al., "Where Is the Land of Opportunity?"

78. "76.1 percent of low-income students graduated on time in 2014, compared to 89.8 percent of non-low-income students (a 13.7 percentage point difference)," in "High School Graduation Facts: Ending the Dropout Crisis," America's Promise Alliance, June 5, 2018, http://www.americaspromise.org/high-school-graduation -facts-ending-dropout-crisis. Also see "Driver 1: Low-Income," in *2015 Building a Grad Nation Report*, America's Promise Alliance, October 4, 2016, http://www .americaspromise.org/report/2015-building-grad-nation-report#driver-1-low -income; and "Table 1. Public High School 4-Year Adjusted Cohort Graduation Rate (ACGR)," Common Core of Data, NCES, 2016, https://nces.ed.gov/ccd/tables/ACGR _RE_and_characteristics_2014–15.asp.

79. Manalansan et al., "Queering the Middle," 6.

80. Somerville, "Locating Queer Culture in the Big Ten." I deeply appreciate Somerville's kindness in emailing me a copy of this essay, and I want to recommend it as a readily adaptable model of pedagogical innovation.

81. Kramer and Flanigan, *Staten Island.* The late Professor Kramer retired from the college in 2000.

82. Wabash College would be an ideal object of analysis using Jane Ward's study *Not Gay: Sex between Straight White Men.*

83. The college opened its first residence halls in 2014. Currently, 4 percent of all students live on campus. Also, trees were planted along the college's main walkways sometime around 2008.

One. The College of Staten Island

1. Brim, "Larry Mitchell," 11. Thanks to *The Gay and Lesbian Review Worldwide* for its permission to reprint Larry's obituary here.

2. "Richmond College [an experimental, upper-division (junior/senior) college that would merge with Staten Island Community College in 1976 to become CSI] developed the first women's studies courses in CUNY, and in 1972 the college was one of only two schools on the East Coast that had a program leading to a degree in Women's Studies. The college was also willing to explore the creation of degree programs in new disciplines such as Computer Science, Puerto Rican–Latin American Studies, Afro-American Studies and Urban-Community Studies." See "A Guide to the Richmond College Records, 1963–1978," College of Staten Island Archives and Special Collections, http://163.238.8.180/finding_aids/CM-2.pdf.

3. A fortieth-anniversary facsimile edition of Mitchell and Asta's *The Faggots and Their Friends between Revolutions* was reprinted by Nightboat Press in 2019, with new essays by Morgan Bassichis and Tourmaline.

4. Two other pertinent, meaningful instances of following have helped me piece this project together. My graduate advisor, Susan Gubar, explored the changing field of women's and gender studies by writing a fictionalized, pseudo-Woolfian account of life in and around her home institution, Indiana University. *Rooms of Our Own* remains my favorite of Susan's many books, and by envisioning a field of study through a specific institutional setting, it provides a model for my own project. Second, in my sixth year at CSI, I discovered that my colleague in media culture, Cynthia Chris, and I were from the exact same place in Indiana, having lived for a time within a few miles of each other as children. As I followed Cynthia into the coeditorship of WSQ: *Women's Studies Quarterly*, a deeply collaborative role in which we worked together for three years, I was able to make further connections between the ways a sense of shared queer-class history informs my ability to imagine Queer Studies at CSI.

5. See the following Queer Studies field narratives and assessments: Valente, Merryman, and Blumenfeld, "25 Years On"; Sara Ahmed's *On Being Included*; Roderick Ferguson's *The Reorder of Things*; David Halperin's *How to Be Gay* and "The Normalization of Queer Theory"; Hawley, *Expanding the Circle*; Johnson and Henderson, *Black Queer Studies*; Johnson, *No Tea, No Shade*; Michael Warner's "Queer and Then?"; Eng, Halberstam, and Muñoz, "What's Queer about Queer Studies Now?"; and Robyn Wiegman's *Object Lessons.*

6. Hartman, "The Queer Utility of Narrative Case Studies," 233.

7. See Taylor, "The 'Outness' of Queer," 70; and Krahulik, "Cape Queer?"

8. Hartman, "The Queer Utility of Narrative Case Studies," 234.

9. Dawson, interview by Matthew Jacobson, *The Education Project.*

10. Chen, "Dreams Stall as CUNY, New York City's Engine of Mobility, Sputters."

11. See Kantrowitz's "Homosexuals and Literature." Several years later, Arnie published his important early memoir, *Under the Rainbow: Growing Up Gay* (1977).

12. Kantrowitz, "Homosexuals and Literature," 324.

13. City College of San Francisco, another community college, deserves special mention as a pioneer in gay and lesbian studies. "In fall 1972, Instructor Dan Allen from City College of San Francisco's English Department developed one of the first gay literature courses in the country. . . . The high enrollment rates and the support of a gay CCSF board member paved the way for the establishment in 1989 of the first Gay and Lesbian Studies Department in the United States." This institutional history is drawn from the detailed report/manual by Gabriner, Schiorring, and Waldron, "'We Could Do That!'" One of the findings at CCSF was that "the development of a department contributes to establishing a whole academic field. It is very exciting to be part of this building process and to witness a continuing evolution that reflects the changing needs of the community." In the present chapter I both take that finding at its word—indeed, such a sentiment crystalizes my earnest hope—and I wonder whether the "whole academic field" would agree about or even recognize the contribution to Queer Studies by the LGBT Studies department at CCSF.

14. Kantrowitz, "Homosexuals and Literature," 328.

15. Stelboum, "Woman's Studies at a Community College," 46–47.

16. Roderick Ferguson charts the absorption and de-radicalization of new social movements by the academy in *The Reorder of Things.* Interestingly, when Kantrowitz tried to start a gay and lesbian club at CSI in 1973, Larry Mitchell and a colleague from women's studies—both formerly affiliated with Richmond College—insisted that the men and women students meet separately. The students did not return to the club meetings thus conceived, though Kantrowitz successfully restarted the gender-mixed group later. Mitchell reported to me separately that at Richmond College, before men were permitted ("deemed fit") to enroll in women's studies courses, they were required to take a course on the sociology of men. In those heady but volatile times, then, the democratization of higher education was contested in multiple ways and from multiple political perspectives.

17. See Bourdieu's *Distinction* and Bourdieu and Passeron's *Reproduction in Education, Society, and Culture.*

18. Hancock and Kolodner, "What It Takes to Get into New York City's Best Public Colleges." I reference the updated and corrected online version of Hancock and Kolodner's article. Hancock and Kolodner rely on 2012 and 2015 reports from the Community Service Society, "Unintended Impacts: Fewer Black and Latino Freshmen at CUNY Senior Colleges after the Recession" and "Enrollment Trends at CUNY: Changes in the Racial/Ethnic Composition of Students at the City University of New York," 2012, http://www.cssny.org/publications/entry/unintended -impactsMay2012.

19. See "Total Enrollment by Undergraduate and Graduate Level, Race/Ethnicity and College," accessed June 8, 2019, http://www.cuny.edu/irdatabook/rpts2_AY_cur rent/ENRL_0027_RACE_UGGR_PCT_HIST.rpt.pdf. See also the CSI Institutional Profile, compiled by the Office of Institutional Research, accessed June 25, 2019, https://www.csi.cuny.edu/about-csi/institutional-effectiveness/institutional -research/institutional-profile.

20. Tompkins, "We Aren't Here to Learn What We Already Know."

21. LGBTQ Faculty/Staff, CSI, accessed May 7, 2019, https://www.csi.cuny.edu /sites/default/files/pdf/currentstudents/studentlife/faculty_contact.pdf.

22. Rankin and Associates Consulting, *Climate for Learning, Working, and Living: Final Report*, November 2016, http://oae.csi.cuny.edu/climatesurvey/report.pdf.

23. Our featured speakers have been the founder and editor of RedBone Press, Lisa C. Moore; British poet Rommi Smith in conversation with sound poet Tracie Morris; and writer and activist Darnell L. Moore.

24. I have included in this interruptive bibliography only works that might be considered Queer Studies texts and only by current colleagues. My colleagues' broader publishing records are, needless to say, far lengthier than represented here.

25. Ahmed, "An Affinity of Hammers," 22.

26. Ahmed, *On Being Included*, 31–32.

27. Balay, *Steel Closets*, 6.

28. See Didier Eribon's *Insult and the Making of the Gay Self* for more on gay re-subjectification, "one's own production of oneself as a subject, the reinvention of one's subjectivity" (137). Eribon makes clear, especially in *Returning to Reims*, that re-subjectification does not accomplish a clean break from one's subjected past.

29. See the Center for an Urban Future's 2011 report, *Mobility Makers*, where Tom Hilliard writes, "Currently, too few of [CUNY's community college] students are coming away with a degree. Of the 10,185 students who started at CUNY community colleges in 2004, a staggering 63 percent dropped out within six years, 28 percent earned a CUNY degree—20 percent received an associate's degree and 8 percent a bachelor's degree—and 9 percent were still enrolled."

30. Berlant, "On the Case," 665.

Two. "You Can Write Your Way Out of Anywhere"

1. *Poor Queer Studies* was well underway when the Avital Ronell scandal broke in the summer of 2018. In one way, that case of how queer power operates, largely behind the scenes, at the highest echelons of the academy proves the urgency of this present study of class- and status-based inequities in higher education. And in another way, what is most remarkable to me now is that, despite all my hunched-over hours pursuing a sustained critique of the way elitism works in this profession, I was still shocked by the whole thing.

2. See Butler's "Imitation and Gender Insubordination," Wiegman's reading of Sedgwick's queer defenses in "Eve's Triangles," and Duberman's *Waiting to Land*. The climax of this third case of Yale drama is reported on page 24, where Duberman writes of Boswell, "I'm shocked and angry at John's behavior; isolated at the last

meeting, failing to secure control of the center for himself, he sets out to sabotage it—at Yale, anyway."

3. UC Santa Cruz hosted the 1990 conference at which queer theory began to resonate. NYU has been the institutional home to many prominent Queer Studies scholars. In 2000, UNC hosted the "Black Queer Studies at the Millennium" conference, which reenergized the intersections of Black and Queer Studies by inviting participants to be, as Vincent Woodard's review essay declared, "Just as Quare as They Want to Be." The CUNY Graduate Center became the institutional home to CLAGS (now the Center for LGBTQ Studies), "founded in 1991 as the first university-based research center in the United States dedicated to the study of historical, cultural, and political issues of vital concern to lesbian, gay, bisexual, transgender, and queer individuals and communities" (https://clags.org/about-clags/). Harvard, perhaps unfashionably late to the Queer Studies party, nevertheless arrived with a bang—a $1.5 million gift to create the F. O. Matthiessen Visiting Professorship of Gender and Sexuality, "the first endowed named chair in lesbian, gay, bisexual, and transgender studies in the country" ("Groundbreaking Professorship in LGBT Studies," *Harvard Gazette*, June 4, 2009, https://news.harvard.edu/gazette/story/2009/06/groundbreaking-professorship-in-lgbt-studies/). For more on Harvard's reluctance to make structural changes around Queer Studies, see Marine, McLoughlin, and McCarthy, "Queering Harvard Yard." Columbia University has offered visiting professorships related to Queer Studies and in 2016 ran a high-profile and successful search for a senior Queer Studies professor.

4. Butler, "Imitation and Gender Insubordination," 18.

5. See Butler's "Merely Cultural."

6. *Oxford English Dictionary*, s.v. "ordination," 1.b.

7. Abelove, "The Queering of Lesbian/Gay History," 45.

8. Abelove, "The Queering of Lesbian/Gay History," 46.

9. Abelove, "The Queering of Lesbian/Gay History," 48.

10. Abelove, "The Queering of Lesbian/Gay History," 50.

11. See James J. Gibson's theory of affordances in *The Ecological Approach to Visual Perception* (1979).

12. Abelove, "The Queering of Lesbian/Gay History," 49.

13. Abelove, "The Queering of Lesbian/Gay History," 50.

14. In fact, learning about LGBTQ history is my students' most common expectation for the course, based on the open-format survey I administer on the first day of each of my Queer Studies classes.

15. Seidman, "Class Matters . . . but How Much?," 37, 38. Seidman's commentary was published in the 2011 "Class and Sex" special issue of *Sexualities*, which attempted to make precisely the critical interventions that Seidman finds to be not robust enough. The 2005 "What's Queer about Queer Studies Now" special issue of *Social Text*, which Seidman doesn't mention, had taken political economy as its explicit starting point for rethinking "queer" and Queer Studies.

16. Seidman, "Class Matters . . . but How Much?," 38, emphasis in original.

17. I admit to being a bit unclear as to whether Seidman is actually making this case, as he seems to lament, even as he contributes to, the "thoroughly post-Marxist"

nature of most sexuality studies in the U.S. Nevertheless, he interprets the "gender-race-and-class mixed [queer] social worlds" as evidence that class is not "a central axis of difference and hierarchy" in queer life.

18. Campbell, Harris, and Brophy, "Introduction," 3.

19. See Brian Heaphy on the way queer theory has been characterized as prioritizing the cultural over the economic in "Situating Lesbian and Gay Cultures of Class Identification," 306.

20. Eribon, *Returning to Reims*, 224–25, emphasis added.

21. Eribon, *Returning to Reims*, 242.

22. See Sarah Schulman's *Ties That Bind*.

23. Duggan, "The Discipline Problem," 179.

24. Gordon, "On Community in the Midst of Hierarchy," 328.

25. Gordon, "On Community in the Midst of Hierarchy," 326–29, emphasis added.

26. Harney and Moten argue in *The Undercommons* that the "critical academic" represents the epitome of "professionalization"—the negligent, state project of "knowledge for practical advances" (34) in the American university. I return to the undercommons in my conclusion.

27. Pérez, *A Taste for Brown Bodies*, 97–98.

28. Chuh, "Pedagogies of Dissent," 159.

29. Chuh, "Pedagogies of Dissent," 159.

30. Chuh, "Pedagogies of Dissent," 161.

31. Chuh points to Tim R. Cain's *Establishing Academic Freedom* as an important study that remembers the multiple building blocks of the AAUP's construction of the academy as a site of professional elitism.

32. Chuh, "Pedagogies of Dissent," 167.

33. To take one entirely random example of a fantastically rich school crying wolf, Kimberly W. Benston, president of Haverford College—a school of 1,300 students with a half-a-billion-dollar endowment—in part justified the decision for Haverford to move from a need-blind to a need-sensitive financial aid policy by offering up as evidence the minutiae of financial stewardship: "In all fairness, the wider Haverford community has every right to ask whether we're being attentive and careful in our spending. Let me take a further moment to assure you that the College has long been stewarding its resources scrupulously. Every tray of cookies served at a tea for students is tightly accounted for in a department's budget; when the budget runs thin, faculty and staff make potluck contributions to shore up the offerings. Every photocopied page; every hour of audiovisual support services; every night of a guest lecturer's stay in the Campus Center—even every fruit bowl for the guest's room—is carefully justified." See Benston, "An Open Letter from President Kim Benston on Haverford's Finances and Need-Blind Admissions." To sum up: no penny goes unpinched at Haverford. In ostensibly unrelated news, a glance through the Campus Life section of the Haverford webpage reveals the provocative question, "Who needs football when you field the only varsity cricket team in America?" Note how persuasively the appeal to tradition and unique status

deflects or neutralizes a critique that would tally the cost of tradition. Far easier to orient one's accounting around trays of cookies and bowls of fruit than around the historical accumulations that make tradition and traditions (far beyond cricket) so valuable and so expensive.

34. Cole, "The Triumph of America's Research University."

35. I have benefited from just such efforts, as when Roderick Ferguson invited me to participate on a panel with scholars from Cornell and the University of Michigan at the American Studies Association convention several years ago.

36. Arner, "Working-Class Women at the MLA Interview."

37. Colander and Zhuo, "Where Do PhDs in English Get Jobs?," 142.

38. See Emerson, "Who Hires Whom?"

39. Finkelstein, Seal, and Schuster, *The New Academic Generation*, 37.

40. Arner, "Working-Class Women at the MLA Interview." See National Science Foundation, table 33, "Educational attainment of doctorate recipients' parents, by sex, citizenship, race, ethnicity, and broad field of study: 2012," Survey of Earned Doctorates, accessed June 13, 2019, http://www.nsf.gov/statistics/sed/2012/start.cfm.

41. Arner, "Working-Class Women at the MLA Interview." On academic prestige, see also Zelda F. Gamson's "The Stratification of the Academy" and John Guillory's "The System of Graduate Education."

42. Chinn, "Queering the Profession, or Just Professionalizing Queers?," 247. This chapter appeared in the previously mentioned *Tilting the Tower*, edited by Linda Garber.

43. Originally given as a talk to the Southern Female Rights Union in 1970, "The Tyranny of Structurelessness" was published in *The Second Wave* 2, no. 1, in 1972.

44. Benjamin Wermund writes that "a POLITICO review shows that the criteria used in the U.S. News rankings—a measure so closely followed in the academic world that some colleges have built them into strategic plans—create incentives for schools to favor wealthier students over less wealthy applicants." See Wermund, "How U.S. News College Rankings Promote Economic Inequality on Campus."

45. Mehra, Braquet, and Fielden, "A Website Evaluation," 21, emphasis added.

46. Mehra, Braquet, and Fielden, "A Website Evaluation," 40.

47. The top twenty-five public universities cited in the study are Clemson University, College of William and Mary, Georgia Institute of Technology, Ohio State University, Pennsylvania State University, Rutgers University, Texas A&M University, University of California–Berkeley, University of California–Davis, University of California–Irvine, University of California–Los Angeles, University of California–San Diego, University of California–Santa Barbara, University of Florida, University of Georgia, University of Illinois at Urbana-Champaign, University of Maryland–College Park, University of Michigan, University of Minnesota–Twin Cities, University of North Carolina–Chapel Hill, University of Pittsburgh, University of Texas–Austin, University of Virginia, University of Washington, and University of Wisconsin–Madison.

48. See "Best Colleges for LGBTQ Students," accessed June 13, 2019, https://www.bestcolleges.com/features/best-colleges-for-lgbt-students/.

49. See University of Washington Office of the Registrar, "Quick Stats Seattle Campus Spring Quarter 2019," accessed June 13, 2019, https://studentdata.washington.edu/wp-content/uploads/sites/3/2019/04/Quick_Stats_Seattle_Spr2019.pdf.

50. Davidson, *The New Education*, 50, 49.

51. Van Wyck, "Blue-Collar Ph.D."

52. Van Wyck, "Blue-Collar Ph.D.," emphasis added.

53. Rand, "After Sex?!," 272.

54. George Steinmetz argues, from a sociological perspective, both for the validity of "odious comparisons" and for the "indispensable" nature of individual case studies in sociology. See Steinmetz, "Odious Comparisons."

55. Duberman, *Has the Gay Movement Failed?*, 73.

56. Duberman, *Has the Gay Movement Failed?*, 87. In addition to SONG, Duberman praises the work of "the Sylvia Rivera Law Project, the Audre Lorde Project, FIERCE, the LGBT Poverty Collective, Women of Color against Violence, and the recently closed Queers for Economic Justice" (107).

57. Henderson, *Love and Money*, 99.

58. Henderson, *Love and Money*, 99–100.

59. Davis, "Constructing Fear in Academia."

60. Sara Ahmed provides such a materially grounded model of following people and documents around the university in *On Being Included*.

61. Greenberg, "White People Problems."

62. Davidson, *The New Education*, 271, emphasis added.

63. My school recently adopted a new strategic plan that lists the broad goals that will guide us through the next five years. The title of the strategic plan is "Opportunity to Ascend." I wonder whether in another couple decades, if we succeed in ascending, will it still be possible to write a Poor Queer Studies book from CSI?

64. Davidson, *The New Education*, 51.

65. Ricketts, *Blue, Too*, 399.

66. hooks, *Teaching Community*, 23.

67. Maynard suggests that Sedgwick's early work pointed the field of Queer Studies toward a class critique that it failed to pick up on. See Maynard, "'Respect Your Elders, Know Your Past,'" 69.

68. Video of the "Eve Kosofsky Sedgwick's *Between Men* at Thirty" conference is available at http://evekosofskysedgwick.net/conferences/BM30.html.

69. Wiegman, "Eve's Triangles," 65.

70. I rely here on the wonderful resource Eve Kosofsky Sedgwick, accessed October 30, 2018, http://evekosofskysedgwick.net/.

Three. The Queer Career

1. Bérubé, *My Desire for History*, 239.

2. Bérubé, *My Desire for History*, 269.

3. D'Emilio and Freedman, "Introduction," 16.

4. D'Emilio and Freedman, "Introduction," 16.

5. Bérubé, *My Desire for History*, 264.

6. Bérubé, *My Desire for History*, 261.

7. Medhurst, "If Anywhere," 29.

8. Russo and Linkon, "Introduction," 3.

9. For models of integrated queer-class scholarship, see Kennedy and Davis's classic *Boots of Leather, Slippers of Gold*; and, more recently, Phil Tiemeyer's *Plane Queer*.

10. Barnard, "Academic Freedom and Me."

11. Roderick Ferguson and Grace Kyungwon Hong, for example, identify "the sexual and racial contradictions of neoliberalism." They write that "social theorists such as Michel Foucault, Wendi Brown, and others have broadened [the] definition to observe that neoliberalism is marked by the extension of economic logics to every sector of culture, such that all value becomes reducible to economic value (Foucault, 2008; Brown, 2005)" (1057). For Ferguson and Hong, however, neoliberalism "produces the conditions that elaborate *and* negate contemporary processes of disenfranchisement and alienation" (1057, emphasis added). See Ferguson and Hong, "The Sexual and Racial Contradictions of Neoliberalism."

12. Volpe, *The Comprehensive College*, 175.

13. Volpe, *The Comprehensive College*, 186.

14. Volpe, *The Comprehensive College*, 175.

15. Davidson, *The New Education*, 190.

16. See, for example, Rodriguez's *Queer Latinidad* and *Sexual Futures, Queer Gestures, and Other Latina Longings*.

17. Davidson, *The New Education*, 96.

18. Davidson, *The New Education*, 14.

19. See Bousquet, *How the University Works*.

20. "SEEK stands for Search for Education, Elevation, and Knowledge. It is the higher education opportunity program at the senior (four year) CUNY colleges. It was established to provide comprehensive academic support to assist capable students who otherwise might not be able to attend college due to their educational and financial circumstances." See the CUNY "SEEK and College Discovery" web page: https://www2.cuny.edu/academics/academic-programs/seek-college-discovery/.

21. Lorde, "An Interview," 96.

22. Taylor, "Facts, Fictions, Identity Constructions," 258.

23. Taylor, "Facts, Fictions, Identity Constructions," 261.

24. Taylor, "Facts, Fictions, Identity Constructions," 264.

25. Personal notes from CLAGS Kessler Award lecture, CUNY Graduate Center, December 4, 2017.

26. Chinn, "Queer Feelings/Feeling Queer," 127.

27. Chinn, "Queer Feelings/Feeling Queer," 127.

28. Delany, *Times Square Red, Times Square Blue*, 184.

29. Delany, *Times Square Red, Times Square Blue*, 193.

30. Vaid, *Irresistible Revolution*, 87.

31. Vaid, *Irresistible Revolution*, 94.

32. Vaid, *Irresistible Revolution*, 84.

33. Lisa Duggan's *Twilight of Equality?* notably crystallizes the critique of neoliberalism.

34. Hollibaugh and Weiss, "Queer Precarity and the Myth of Gay Affluence," 23, 24.

35. Hollibaugh and Weiss, "Queer Precarity and the Myth of Gay Affluence," 24–25.

36. Bousquet, *How the University Works*, 176–77.

37. Bousquet, *How the University Works*, 93.

38. Bousquet, *How the University Works*, 13.

39. Bousquet, *How the University Works*, 13.

40. Bousquet, *How the University Works*, 28.

41. Bousquet, *How the University Works*, 154.

42. Bousquet, *How the University Works*, 15. I have personal connections to Bousquet's book. In his chapter titled "Composition as Management Science," Bousquet, whose class on American melodrama I took while a graduate student at Indiana University, strongly criticizes Joseph Harris, who directed the University Writing Program at Duke and who hired me to teach Queer Studies–based academic writing courses as a postdoctoral writing fellow. Bousquet, whose generous, open pedagogy at Indiana University sticks with me to this day as a model of collective work and agitative study, paints a portrait of Joe as a low-level manager type of boss, a characterization in which I do not recognize Joe, having worked with him for three years. Harris directed the program, true. But I would be hard pressed to name someone who devoted so much time and attention to the practice and theory of working together with colleagues in an interdisciplinary academic formation in order to do our shared work of teaching composition as well as we could. If ever I have been part of a work collective, it was with Joe and my fellow postdoctoral fellows.

43. See Robert McRuer's queer crip exploration of the possible intersections of the composition classroom and disability studies as these connect to labor organizing in *Crip Theory*, chapter 4, especially note 4 (236–37). McRuer is useful for me because he sees a way to make intersectional identity studies a vector for labor organizing, not a dissipation of the energies that might be used for labor organizing.

44. Wiegman, *Object Lessons*, 14, 15.

45. Wiegman, *Object Lessons*, 17.

46. Ferguson, *The Reorder of Things*, 230.

47. Ferguson, *The Reorder of Things*, 143.

48. Ferguson, *The Reorder of Things*, 61.

49. Ferguson, *The Reorder of Things*, 230.

50. Bousquet, *How the University Works*, 183, 183–84.

51. Bousquet, *How the University Works*, 175.

52. Timothy Reese Cain, a historian of faculty unions, points to the usefulness of social movement unionism for this purpose: "As we noted, some might join for broader social and societal reasons. We might think of social movement unionism,

through which unions focus not just on the local work issues but on bigger issues affecting society." Cain, "What Does the History of Faculty Unions Teach Us about Their Future?"

53. Frank, *Out in the Union*, 139–40.

54. Frank, *Out in the Union*, 140.

55. Frank, *Out in the Union*, 140.

56. Frank, *Out in the Union*, 4.

57. Frank, *Out in the Union*, 120.

58. Frank, *Out in the Union*, 148.

59. In addition to the possible tensions around queer-union identity politics, in "'Top-Down' or 'Bottom-Up'?," Tamara Jones finds that "union bureaucracy would pose a greater challenge to lesbian and gay workers' organizing than homophobia within the union. . . . The challenge lies in developing a strong collectivist-organizing culture with minimal bureaucratic practice" (178). In *Has the Gay Movement Failed?*, Duberman in part agrees with Jones when he writes that "back in 1970, GLF [the Gay Liberation Front, Duberman's model of radical queer left politics] as a group never sought an alliance with organized labor, in part because the trade union movement—so powerful in the 1930s—had already lost its militant edge. Once-radical unions turned bureaucratic and centrist as early as the 1950s, and racial divisions within this working class became more pronounced than the socialist vision of labor solidarity" (74).

60. Gustafson, "Welcoming Remarks," 21.

61. D'Emilio, "Introduction by John D'Emilio."

62. D'Emilio, "Introduction," 12–13.

63. D'Emilio, "Introduction by John D'Emilio."

64. Friedenberg, "Homophobia and Society," 41.

Four. Poor Queer Studies Mothers

1. I dedicate this chapter to the many student-mothers I have taught at CSI and at CUNY, to my colleague-mothers, and to the commuter students who showed me the surprisingly domestic routes Poor Queer Studies can travel.

2. Gumbs, Martens, and Williams, *Revolutionary Mothering*. I want to draw particular attention to essays within the collection by Alexis Pauline Gumbs, Victoria Law, Katie Kaput, Gabriela Sandoval, Esteli Juarez, tz karakashian tunchz, and Lindsey Campbell.

3. See the CSI Fall 2018 Student Demographic Profile, accessed June 17, 2019, https://webdocs.csi.cuny.edu/Institutional_Profile/SemesterEnroll_Profile.html.

4. Newfield, "Yes to the New Education," 688, emphasis added.

5. Villarosa, "Why America's Black Mothers and Babies Are in a Life-or-Death Crisis."

6. See Geronimus, "The Weathering Hypothesis and the Health of African-American Women and Infants."

7. Sharpe, *In the Wake*, 106.

8. Sharpe, *In the Wake*, 12.

9. Sharpe, *In the Wake*, 50.

10. For several interesting studies of student-mothers, see Beeler, "Undergraduate Single Mothers' Experiences in Postsecondary Education"; Kensinger and Minnick, "The Invisible Village"; Lashley and Ollivierre, "Exploring the Linkages of Single Black Mothers and Their College Experiences"; Mahaffey, Hungerford, and Sill, "College Student Mother Needs at Regional Campuses"; and Sullivan, "Sharing Stories of Student Mothers in Community College."

11. For many years, the Feminist Press's Clearinghouse on Women's Studies tracked women's studies or feminist course offerings nationwide. See back issues of the *Women's Studies Newsletter*, freely available through CUNY's open-access repository, CUNY Academic Works: "CUNY Academic Works is a service of the CUNY Libraries dedicated to collecting and providing access to the research, scholarship and creative work of the City University of New York. In service to CUNY's mission as a public university, content in Academic Works is freely available to all." CUNY Academic Works, https://academicworks.cuny.edu/.

12. I say "reconsider" because, like so many things queer, this work has surely been done before, though in different ways and for different reasons and, therefore, inevitably with different meanings. Still, I find few resources focused on the pedagogies enabled by mothers in and around the Queer Studies classroom, though research about working-class/working-poor students, student-mothers, queer mothers, and queer students creates a context for an examination of Poor Queer Studies Mothers.

13. See Sycamore, *Why Are Faggots So Afraid of Faggots?*; and Mitchell and Asta, *The Faggots and Their Friends between Revolutions*.

14. Torres, *We the Animals*, 24.

15. Zagar, *We the Animals*, 2018.

16. Torres, *We the Animals*, 105, 110, 119.

17. Edelman, *No Future*, 19–20.

18. Sarah Chinn and Anna Mae Duane argue that "children themselves are part of [the] terrorized collective" that Edelman associates with queers. In thinking about children, they write, "we must make visible and actively critique the discursive and actual violence that occurs in the space between 'the child' and raced, gendered, classed, and nationed children" (15). See their introduction to the "Child" special issue of *Women's Studies Quarterly* in 2015.

19. Martin, "Extraordinary Homosexuals and the Fear of Being Ordinary."

20. Martin, "Extraordinary Homosexuals and the Fear of Being Ordinary," emphasis added.

21. In a similar vein, my CSI colleague Ira Shor, who helped bring critical and dialogic pedagogies to the U.S. through his work with Paulo Freire, discusses the benefit of "a hybrid idiom through which to dialogue with the students, which integrates conceptual frameworks and vocabulary from high-status reasoning and bodies-of-knowledge [such as Queer Theory] with the non-elite colloquial knowledges, usages, lexicon and syntax [such as spelling S-E-X words] familiar to everyday life." "When," Shor reports, "I get this hybrid discourse right in actual classroom dialogues, I model to students a way of using language to examine issues

and materials which respects their own idioms while integrating analytic discourse. When a hybrid discourse does emerge, the critical classroom invents for itself a new tool for democratization, 'the third idiom,' co-constructed in dialogic practice from the contradictory linguistic habits teachers and students bring to class." See Shor et al., "Dialogic and Critical Pedagogies," s6. More generally, see Shor, *When Students Have Power*; and Shor and Freire, *A Pedagogy for Liberation*.

22. hooks, *Teaching Community*, 12.

23. hooks, "bell hooks Speaking about Paulo Freire," 145–46.

24. At Williams College, named the top liberal arts college in the nation in the 2019 *U.S. News* college rankings, students have created a Facebook page, Williams College Class Confessions. That page reads, "Class Confessions serves to illuminate the unique experiences of people from different socioeconomic backgrounds. Inspired by Columbia." The anonymous author of post #244 from March 16, 2018, reads, "I haven't been home since the beginning of the academic year because the airfare is too expensive and i never know how to answer people when they ask me why i stay on campus. #ClassConfessions." Post #255 reads, "So many people on this campus don't understand how much of a struggle it is to get home. Like no, I can't just book a flight the first flight I find. My parents spend weeks to figure out all the logistics and even then, it's still so expensive. Not even to mention storage for the summer. Trying to navigate all that plus finals makes everything so much worse.#classconfessions." Tuition plus room and board at Williams for the 2018–19 academic school year was $69,950.

25. Hamilton, *Parenting to a Degree*, 48.

26. Hamilton, *Parenting to a Degree*, 48.

27. See Moore, "Polishing the Pearl"; Bersani, "Is the Rectum a Grave?"; and Cohen, "Punks, Bulldaggers, and Welfare Queens."

28. I rely in the section that follows on student responses to an assignment that asked them to think about how they talked about, and perhaps taught, people outside our class about Queer Studies. The assignment was part of a unit, developed over years at CSI, that explicitly framed queer pedagogy as something students have been denied in almost every classroom they have ever been part of. The first thing Queer Studies must teach, consequently, is that Queer Studies is teachable and that part of the intellectual work of Queer Studies courses is discovering what kinds of pedagogical relations it opens up.

29. In the fall of 2017, 32.3 percent of CSI students resided outside of Staten Island; 352 students commuted from the Bronx, 356 from Queens, 231 from Manhattan, 2,752 from Brooklyn, and 44 from Long Island. See the CSI Fall 2018 Student Demographic Profile and Map of Enrollment by County, accessed June 17, 2019, https://webdocs.csi.cuny.edu/Institutional_Profile/SemesterEnroll_Profile .html and https://webdocs.csi.cuny.edu/Institutional_Profile/SemesterEnroll_Map .html.

30. See Michael Dorsch's work as part of the Futures Initiative at the CUNY Graduate Center. In his study, "Sociodemographics Map of New York City: Part 1—Race and Ethnicity," Dorsch finds that "across the CUNY system, enrollment characteristics tend to match the geographic communities most closely located to

their campuses." See Dorsch, "CUNY Schools Serve a Student Population as Diverse as NYC Itself."

31. See "Undocuqueer Movement," Equality Archive.

32. See Moore, *Does Your Mama Know?*

33. See Emery, "Outcomes Assessment and Standardization"; Graff, "Our Undemocratic Curriculum."

34. Graff borrows the formulation "played" from Deborah Meier, *The Power of Their Ideas*, 164.

35. Emery, "Outcomes Assessment and Standardization," 256–57.

36. Hall, "Cluelessness and the Queer Classroom," 182.

37. See Bartholomae, "Inventing the University."

Five. *Counternarratives*

1. An objection could be raised that my characterization of *Counternarratives* as a black queer primer pigeonholes the book and misrepresents Keene—a MacArthur Fellow—as somehow, only, a writer of minority literature. As I hope to make clear, Keene explodes the notion that "black queer" could possibly be a limiting formulation, just as he explodes the idea that this is the only or the best way to characterize his book.

2. I use the term "literacy" in its general sense, "the ability to read and write," though I also mean to disrupt the ease with which we imagine ourselves to be able to read and write. I also want to recognize at the outset the incredible burden shouldered by those educators who teach black queer literacies at sites across the curriculum, for they teach against the active presence of anti-black, antiqueer educational histories and student preparations.

3. Morris, *Who Do with Words*, 78.

4. Ernesto Martinez, in *On Making Sense*, suggests that queer-of-color writers have had "a recurring preoccupation with intelligibility, . . . a concern with the everyday labor of *making sense of oneself* and of *making sense to others* in contexts of intense ideological violence and interpersonal conflict" (13–14).

5. Yacovone, "Textbook Racism."

6. See Beam, "Making Ourselves from Scratch."

7. See Preston, "How Dare You Even Think These Things?"

8. Reid-Pharr, *Archives of Flesh*, 11, 189.

9. See Holland, *Raising the Dead*, chapter 4; and Brim, *James Baldwin and the Queer Imagination*, chapter 1.

10. Traub, *Thinking Sex with the Early Moderns*, 4.

11. Keene, *Counternarratives*, 98.

12. Keene, *Counternarratives*, 94.

13. For more on Degas's gaze, see Laurence, "The Modern Woman Explores the Male Gaze." For more on scientific racism and the construction of homosexuality, see Somerville, *Queering the Color Line*. For more on the objectification of female carnival performers, see Garland-Thomson, *Extraordinary Bodies*.

14. Keene, *Counternarratives*, 247.

15. Traub, *Thinking Sex with the Early Moderns*, 340.

16. Arondekar, "*Thinking Sex with* Geopolitics," 334.

17. Arondekar, "*Thinking Sex with* Geopolitics," 334.

18. The title "Gloss, or the Strange History of Our Lady of the Sorrows," it turns out, is an abbreviated—or rather, aborted—form of an even longer title that appears on the first page of the story itself: "Gloss on a History of Roman Catholics in the Early American Republic, 1790–1825; or The Strange History of Our Lady of the Sorrows." The reason for this discrepancy emerges formally on the second page of the gloss, or superficial, historical narrative that opens the story, when the reader is redirected by way of a footnote to the strange story beneath. The footnote, extending for the next seventy-two pages, becomes the main story.

19. Aida Levy-Hussen, in *How to Read African American Literature*, models the critical strategy of purposefully stepping back from well-known, normative practices for reading African American literature and, in particular, slave narratives. The core question is about how writers and critics deal, through narrative construction, with a history of pain that won't be easily dealt with. Levy-Hussen pinpoints the "historical turn" in black narrative, asking how we can write and read about slavery with neither pure (reparative) longing or pure (prohibitive) cynicism.

20. In their collection *Who Writes for Black Children?*, editors Katharine Capshaw and Anna Mae Duane pose a related set of questions about blackness, reading, and the white supremacist historical record.

21. The connection between white need and story has been most convincingly articulated by Toni Morrison in *Playing in the Dark*.

22. Keene, *Counternarratives*, 219.

23. Keene, *Counternarratives*, 235–36.

24. Jim and Huck have a longstanding critical association with nonheteronormativity, beginning with Leslie Fiedler's influential 1948 essay, "Come Back to the Raft Ag'in, Huck Honey!"

25. The counterreaders in this class, like most of my classes at CSI, were brown and black and ethnic white, mostly women and gender nonconforming, mostly working class or working poor, many first-generation and immigrant, all commuter students taking a 3.5-hour night class, often coming from work earlier in the day.

26. Reid-Pharr, *Archives of Flesh*, 9.

27. Reid-Pharr, *Archives of Flesh*, 7.

28. Reid-Pharr, *Archives of Flesh*, 11, 9.

29. Reid-Pharr, *Archives of Flesh*, 12.

30. Keene, *Counternarratives*, 10.

31. Keene, *Counternarratives*, 132.

32. Keene, *Counternarratives*, 145–46.

33. Keene, *Counternarratives*, 154.

34. In his foreword to the republication of Cedric J. Robinson's *Black Marxism*, Robin D. G. Kelley writes, "To understand the dialectic of African resistance to enslavement and exploitation, in other words, we need to look outside the orbit of capitalism—we need to look [to] West and Central African culture. Robinson

observes, 'Marx had not realized fully that the cargoes of laborers also contained African cultures, critical mixes and admixtures of language and thought, of cosmology and metaphysics, of habits, beliefs, and morality. These were the actual terms of their humanity. These cargoes, then, did not consist of intellectual isolates or deculturated Blacks—men, women, and children separated from their previous universe. African labor brought the past with it, a past that had produced it and settled on it the first elements of consciousness and comprehension' (121)" (xiv).

35. Keene, *Counternarratives*, 90.

36. Keene, *Counternarratives*, 105.

37. Lucas, "Epic Stories That Expand the Universal Family Plot."

38. Keene, *Counternarratives*, 4–5.

39. Alexis Pauline Gumbs's consideration of philosopher Sylvia Wynter's notion of "the poetic" is apt in this regard ("Nobody Mean More," 240–41).

40. Keene, *Counternarratives*, 45–46.

41. Keene, *Counternarratives*, 47.

42. Keene, *Counternarratives*, 47.

43. Keene, *Counternarratives*, 80.

44. Keene, *Counternarratives*, 83.

45. Keene, *Counternarratives*, 48, emphasis added.

46. Keene, *Counternarratives*, 83.

47. In their study of sexuality and queer studies at historically black colleges and universities (HBCUs) that formed one focal point of the Audre Lorde Project, Beverly Guy-Sheftall, Jacqui Alexander, Aaron Wells, and Taryn Crenshaw found that Queer Studies formations are largely absent at HBCUs. They suggest that Queer Studies will likely need to rely on the structure of women's studies at those institutions in order to grow. See Guy-Sheftall, "Breaking the Silence at Spelman College and Beyond"; Williams, "Women's Studies and Sexuality Studies at HBCUs"; and Alexander, "Interview with M. Jacqui Alexander."

48. Sharpe, *In the Wake*, 5.

49. Sharpe, *In the Wake*, 3.

50. See Claudia Rankine's *Citizen: An American Lyric*, for example. See also "Being a Black Academic in America," *Chronicle of Higher Education*, April 19, 2019, https://www.chronicle.com/interactives/20190418-black-academic.

51. Allen and Tinsley, "After the Love," 108.

52. Allen and Tinsley, "After the Love," 110. Allen recently moved from Yale University to the University of Miami, where he directs the Africana Studies Program.

53. Allen and Tinsley, "After the Love," 111.

54. Brody and McBride, "Introduction," 286, emphasis added.

55. Brody and McBride, "Introduction," 286.

56. Hartman, "The Territory between Us," 443.

57. Hartman, "The Territory between Us," 443.

58. Davis, "Black Women and the Academy," 426.

59. Davis, "Black Women and the Academy," 428.

60. Lorde, "The Master's Tools Will Never Dismantle the Master's House," 111.

61. See Brim, "After Queer Baldwin." Nicholas Boggs's "Queer Black Studies" bibliography, published in the "Plum Nelly" issue of *Callaloo*, documents the importance of Baldwin to seminal scholarship in Black Queer Studies.

62. Johnson, "To Be Young, Gifted, and Queer," 56.

63. Johnson, "Border Intellectual," 156. See also Johnson's "In the Merry Old Land of oz," as well as his field-redefining essay, "Quare Studies, or (Almost) Everything I Know about Queer Studies I Learned from My Grandmother," in Johnson and Henderson, *Black Queer Studies.*

64. See also Scott Herring's work, especially *Another Country: Queer Antiurbanism,* for another example of queer-class inquiry that finds queer life where the field typically has not. The opening line of *Another Country* is "I hate New York."

65. Harney and Moten, *The Undercommons,* 39.

66. Harney and Moten, *The Undercommons,* 26, emphasis added.

67. Harney and Moten, *The Undercommons,* 26.

68. Harney and Moten, *The Undercommons,* 32.

69. Harney and Moten, *The Undercommons,* 34.

70. I am thinking particularly of texts that relate church to the wild, including James Baldwin's short story "Come Out the Wilderness"; Toni Morrison's *Beloved* when Baby Suggs, holy, offers church service in the outdoor wildness of the Clearing; or even the (less wild) Congregational Christian church standard "Come to the Church in the Wildwood."

71. Gilmore, "Forgotten Places and the Seeds of Grassroots Planning," 55–56.

72. Harney and Moten write, "We aren't responsible for politics. We are the general antagonism to politics looming outside every attempt to politics" (*The Undercommons,* 20).

Epilogue

1. Sanders's 2020 presidential campaign has changed its language around college affordability from "tuition and debt free" to "tuition free" and "lower student debt." See "College for All and Cancel All Student Debt" on his campaign website, accessed June 27, 2019, https://berniesanders.com/issues/college-for-all/. The original, now-defunct 2016 campaign website quoted in this chapter was found at https://berniesanders.com/issues/its-time-to-make-college-tuition-free-and-debt-free/.

2. Davidson, "The New Education and the Old," 708.

3. Newfield, "Yes to the New Education," 689.

4. See the visualization of the data for Public Flagship Universities from the National Center for Education Statistics in Ashkenas, Park, and Pierce, "Even with Affirmative Action, Blacks and Hispanics Are More Underrepresented at Top Colleges than 35 Years Ago."

5. Krebs, "Applying to a Public Regional University?"

6. King, *Theory in Its Feminist Travels.*

7. See Gordon's original quote in "Panel Discussion 2."

bibliography

Abelove, Henry. "The Queering of Lesbian/Gay History." *Radical History Review* 62 (1995): 44–57.

Ahmed, Sara. "An Affinity of Hammers." *TSQ: Transgender Studies Quarterly* 3, nos. 1–2 (2016): 22–34.

Ahmed, Sara. *On Being Included: Racism and Diversity in Institutional Life.* Durham, NC: Duke University Press, 2012.

Ahmed, Sara. *Queer Phenomenology: Orientations, Objects, Others.* Durham, NC: Duke University Press, 2006.

Alexander, M. Jacqui. "Interview with M. Jacqui Alexander." By Alissa Trotz. Women and Gender Studies Institute, University of Toronto. Accessed September 28, 2018. http://www.wgsi.utoronto.ca/research/faculty-projects /interview-with-m-jacqui-alexander.

Alexander, M. Jacqui. *Pedagogies of Crossing: Meditations on Feminism, Sexual Politics, Memory, and the Sacred.* Durham, NC: Duke University Press, 2006.

Allen, Jafari Sinclaire, and Omise'eke Natasha Tinsley. "After the Love: Remembering *Black/Queer/Diaspora.*" *GLQ: A Journal of Lesbian and Gay Studies* 25, no. 1 (January 1, 2019): 107–12. https://doi.org/10.1215/10642684-7275586.

Amin, Kadji. *Disturbing Attachments: Genet, Modern Pederasty, and Queer History.* Durham, NC: Duke University Press, 2017.

Arner, Lynn. "Working-Class Women at the MLA Interview." *Rhizomes*, no. 27 (2014). http://www.rhizomes.net/issue27/arner.html.

Arondekar, Anjali. "*Thinking Sex with* Geopolitics." *WSQ: Women's Studies Quarterly* 44, no. 3 (October 7, 2016): 332–35. https://doi.org/10.1353/wsq.2016.0066.

Ashkenas, Jeremy, Haeyoun Park, and Adam Pierce. "Even with Affirmative Action, Blacks and Hispanics Are More Underrepresented at Top Colleges than 35 Years Ago." *New York Times*, August 24, 2017. https://www.nytimes.com /interactive/2017/08/24/us/affirmative-action.html.

Balay, Anne. *Semi Queer: Inside the World of Gay, Trans, and Black Truck Drivers.* Chapel Hill: University of North Carolina Press, 2018.

Balay, Anne. *Steel Closets: Voices of Gay, Lesbian, and Transgender Steel Workers.* Chapel Hill: University of North Carolina Press, 2014.

Baldwin, James. *Giovanni's Room*. 1956. Reprint, New York: Delta, 2000.

Baldwin, James. *The Price of the Ticket: Collected Nonfiction, 1948–1985*. New York: St. Martin's, 1985.

Bannon, Ann. *Odd Girl Out*. New York: Gold Medal, 1957.

Barnard, Ian. "Academic Freedom and Me: The Complications of Politics, Culture, and Academic Freedom in One Career." *Academe*, August 2009. https://www.aaup.org/article/academic-freedom-and-me#.Wnd4lKinHSH.

Bartholomae, David. "Inventing the University." *Journal of Basic Writing* 5, no. 1 (1986): 4–23.

Beam, Joseph. "Making Ourselves from Scratch." In *Brother to Brother: New Writings by Black Gay Men*, edited by Essex Hemphill, 335–36. Washington, DC: RedBone, 2007.

Beeler, Sydney. "Undergraduate Single Mothers' Experiences in Postsecondary Education." *New Directions for Higher Education*, no. 176 (December 1, 2016): 69–80. https://doi.org/10.1002/he.20210.

Benston, Kim. "An Open Letter from President Kim Benston on Haverford's Finances and Need-Blind Admissions." *The Clerk*, May 27, 2016. http://haverfordclerk.com/an-open-letter-from-president-kim-benston-on-haverfords-finances-and-need-blind-aid/.

Berlant, Lauren. "On the Case." *Critical Inquiry* 33, no. 4 (2007): 663–72.

Bersani, Leo. "Is the Rectum a Grave?" *October* 43 (1987): 197–222. doi:10.2307/3397574.

Bérubé, Allan. *My Desire for History: Essays in Gay, Community, and Labor History*, edited by John D'Emilio and Estelle B. Freedman. Chapel Hill: University of North Carolina Press, 2011.

Boggs, Nicholas. "Queer Black Studies: An Annotated Bibliography, 1994–1999." *Callaloo* 23, no. 1 (2000): 479–94.

Bourdieu, Pierre. *Distinction: A Social Critique of the Judgement of Taste*. 1984. Reprint, London: Routledge Classics, 2010.

Bourdieu, Pierre, and Jean Claude Passeron. *Reproduction in Education, Society, and Culture*. London: Sage, 1977.

Bousquet, Marc. *How the University Works: Higher Education and the Low-Wage Nation*. New York: New York University Press, 2008.

Brim, Matt. "After Queer Baldwin." In *After Queer Studies: Literature, Theory and Sexuality in the 21st Century*, edited by Tyler Bradway and E. L. McCallum, 87–101. New York: Cambridge University Press, 2019.

Brim, Matt. *James Baldwin and the Queer Imagination*. Ann Arbor: University of Michigan Press, 2014.

Brim, Matt. "Larry Mitchell: Novelist of New York Gay Life." Obituary. *The Gay and Lesbian Review Worldwide* 20, no. 3 (2013): 11.

Brody, Jennifer DeVere, and Dwight A. McBride. "Introduction." *Callaloo* 23, no. 1 (2000): 286–88.

Butler, Judith. "Imitation and Gender Insubordination." In *Inside/Out: Lesbian Theories, Gay Theories*, edited by Diana Fuss, 13–29. New York: Routledge, 1991.

Butler, Judith. "Merely Cultural." *Social Text* 52/53 (1997): 265–77.

Cahalan, Margaret, and Laura Perna. *Indicators of Higher Education Equity in the United States: 45 Year Trend Report*, 2015 revised edition. Pell Institute for the Study of Opportunity in Higher Education. https://eric.ed.gov/?id=ED555865.

Cain, Timothy Reese. *Establishing Academic Freedom: Politics, Principles, and the Development of Core Values.* New York: Palgrave Macmillan, 2012.

Cain, Timothy Reese. "What Does the History of Faculty Unions Teach Us about Their Future?" Interview by Andrew Hibel. Higher Ed Jobs. Accessed February 4, 2018. https://www.higheredjobs.com/HigherEdCareers/interviews.cfm?ID=315.

Campbell, James T., Leslie M. Harris, and Alfred L. Brophy. "Introduction." In *Slavery and the University: Histories and Legacies*, edited by Leslie M. Harris, James T. Campbell, and Alfred L. Brophy, 1–18. Athens: University of Georgia Press, 2019.

Capshaw, Katharine, and Anna Mae Duane. *Who Writes for Black Children? African American Children's Literature before 1900.* Minneapolis: University of Minnesota Press, 2017.

Carnevale, Anthony P., and Jeff Strohl. "White Flight Goes to College." *Poverty and Race* 22, no. 5 (2013): 1–2, 12–13.

Carnevale, Anthony P., and Martin Van Der Werf. "The 20% Solution: Selective Colleges Can Afford to Admit More Pell Grant Recipients." Center on Education and the Workforce, Georgetown University, 2017. https://cew .georgetown.edu/wp-content/uploads/The-20-Percent-Solution-web.pdf.

Chen, David W. "Dreams Stall as CUNY, New York City's Engine of Mobility, Sputters." *New York Times*, December 21, 2017, sec. New York. https://www .nytimes.com/2016/05/29/nyregion/dreams-stall-as-cuny-citys-engine-of -mobility-sputters.html.

Chetty, Raj, John N. Friedman, Emmanuel Saez, Nicholas Turner, and Danny Yagan. "Mobility Report Cards: The Role of Colleges in Intergenerational Mobility." Equality of Opportunity Project, 2017. http://www.equality-of-opportunity .org/papers/coll_mrc_paper.pdf.

Chetty, Raj, Nathaniel Hendren, Patrick Kline, and Emmanuel Saez. "Where Is the Land of Opportunity? The Geography of Intergenerational Mobility in the United States." National Bureau of Economic Research, Working Paper 19843, January 2014. http://www.nber.org/papers/w19843.pdf.

Chinn, Sarah. "Queer Feelings/Feeling Queer: A Conversation with Heather Love about Politics, Teaching, and the 'Dark, Tender Thrills' of Affect." *Transformations: The Journal of Inclusive Scholarship and Pedagogy* 22, no. 2 (2012): 124–31. http://dx.doi.org/10.17613/M6M53K.

Chinn, Sarah. "Queering the Profession, or Just Professionalizing Queers?" In *Tilting the Tower: Lesbians, Teaching, Queer Subjects*, edited by Linda Garber, 243–50. New York: Routledge, 1994.

Chinn, Sarah, and Anna Mae Duane. "Introduction." *WSQ: Women's Studies Quarterly* 43, nos. 1–2 (spring–summer 2015): 14–25.

Christopher, Renny. "New Working-Class Studies in Higher Education." In *New Working-Class Studies*, edited by John Russo and Sherry Lee Linkon, 209–20. Ithaca, NY: IRL Press, 2005.

Chuh, Kandice. "Pedagogies of Dissent." *American Quarterly* 70, no. 2 (June 2018): 159–72.

Clarke, Cheryl. *"But Some of Us Are Brave* and the Transformation of the Academy: Transformation?" *Signs: Journal of Women in Culture and Society* 35, no. 4 (2010): 779–88.

Cohen, Cathy J. "Foreword." In *No Tea, No Shade: New Writings in Black Queer Studies*, edited by E. Patrick Johnson, xi–xiv. Durham, NC: Duke University Press, 2016.

Cohen, Cathy J. "Punks, Bulldaggers, and Welfare Queens: The Radical Potential of Queer Politics?" *GLQ: A Journal of Lesbian and Gay Studies* 3, no. 4 (May 1997): 437–65. https://doi.org/10.1215/10642684-3-4-437.

Colander, David, and Daisy Zhuo. "Where Do PhDs in English Get Jobs? An Economist's View of the English PhD Market." *Pedagogy: Critical Approaches to Teaching Literature, Language, Composition, and Culture* 15, no. 1 (2014): 139–56.

Cole, Jonathan R. "The Triumph of America's Research University." *The Atlantic*, September 20, 2016. https://www.theatlantic.com/education/archive/2016/09/the-triumph-of-americas-research-university/500798/.

Cooper, Brittney. "Afterword." In *All the Women Are White, All the Blacks Are Men, but Some of Us Are Brave: Black Women's Studies*, 2nd ed., edited by Akasha (Gloria T.) Hull, Patricia Bell-Scott, and Barbara Smith, 379–85. Old Westbury, NY: Feminist Press, 2015.

Cooper, Sandi E. "Remediation's End: Can New York Educate the Children of the 'Whole People'?" *Academe* 84, no. 4 (1998): 14–20.

Crosby, C., L. Duggan, R. Ferguson, K. Floyd, M. Joseph, H. Love, R. McRuer, F. Moten, T. Nyong'o, L. Rofel, J. Rosenberg, G. Salamon, D. Spade, and A. Villarejo. "Queer Studies, Materialism, and Crisis: A Roundtable Discussion." *GLQ: A Journal of Lesbian and Gay Studies* 18, no. 1 (2012): 127–47.

Davidson, Cathy N. "The New Education and the Old." *PMLA* 133, no. 3 (2018): 707–14.

Davidson, Cathy N. *The New Education: How to Revolutionize the University to Prepare Students for a World in Flux*. New York: Basic Books, 2017.

Davis, Angela. "Black Women and the Academy." *Callaloo* 17, no. 2 (spring 1994): 422–31.

Davis, Dana-Ain. "Constructing Fear in Academia: Neoliberal Practices at a Public College." *Learning and Teaching; Oxford* 4, no. 1 (spring 2011): 42–69. http://dx.doi.org.ezproxy.gc.cuny.edu/10.3167/latiss.2011.040104.

Davis, Kai. "Ain't I a Woman?" YouTube, March 8, 2016. https://www.youtube.com/watch?v=ZoF_6GMOa-8.

Dawson, Ashley. Interview by Matthew Jacobson. *The Education Project*. Accessed August 21, 2018. http://educationproject.yale.edu/ashley-dawson/.

Delany, Samuel R. *Times Square Red, Times Square Blue*. New York: New York University Press, 1999.

D'Emilio, John. "Capitalism and Gay Identity." In *Powers of Desire: The Politics of Sexuality*, edited by Ann Snitow et al., 100–113. New York: Monthly Review Press, 1983.

D'Emilio, John. "Introduction." In *The Universities and the Gay Experience: Proceedings of the Conference Sponsored by the Women and Men of the Gay Academic Union*. New York: Gay Academic Union, 1974.

D'Emilio, John. "Introduction by John D'Emilio." *OutHistory*, April 22, 2016. http://outhistory.org/exhibits/show/gau-conference/intro.

D'Emilio, John, and Estelle B. Freedman. "Introduction: Allan Bérubé and the Power of Community History." In *My Desire for History: Essays in Gay, Community, and Labor History*, by Allan Bérubé. Chapel Hill: University of North Carolina Press, 2011.

Deresiewicz, William. "Don't Send Your Kids to the Ivy League." *New Republic*, July 21, 2014. https://newrepublic.com/article/118747/ivy-league-schools-are-overrated-send-your-kids-elsewhere.

Dews, C. L. Barney, and Carolyn Leste Law, eds. *This Fine Place So Far from Home: Voices of Academics from the Working Class*. Philadelphia: Temple University Press, 1995. http://www.jstor.org.ezproxy.gc.cuny.edu/stable/j.ctt14bswxr.

Dorsch, Michael. "CUNY Schools Serve a Student Population as Diverse as NYC Itself—and Sometimes More So." Futures Initiative, February 10, 2015. https://futuresinitiative.org/blog/2015/02/10/cuny-sociodemographics-map-of-new-york-city-part-i-race-and-ethnicity/#10/40.6014/-73.8467.

Duberman, Martin. *Has the Gay Movement Failed?* Oakland: University of California Press, 2018.

Duberman, Martin. *Waiting to Land: A (Mostly) Political Memoir, 1985–2008*. New York: New Press, 2009.

Duggan, Lisa. "The Discipline Problem: Queer Theory Meets Lesbian and Gay History." *GLQ: A Journal of Lesbian and Gay Studies* 2, no. 3 (1995): 179–91. Republished in *Sex Wars: Sexual Dissent and Political Culture*, edited by Lisa Duggan and Nan Hunter. New York: Routledge, 1995.

Duggan, Lisa. *The Twilight of Equality? Neoliberalism, Cultural Politics, and the Attack on Democracy*. Boston: Beacon, 2004.

Edelman, Lee. *No Future: Queer Theory and the Death Drive*. Durham, NC: Duke University Press, 2004.

Emerson, Michael O. "Who Hires Whom?" *Scatterplot*, January 8, 2018. https://scatter.wordpress.com/2018/01/08/who-hires-whom/.

Emery, Kim. "Outcomes Assessment and Standardization: A Queer Critique." *Profession*, 2008, 255–62.

Eng, David, Jack Halberstam, and José Muñoz, eds. "What's Queer about Queer Studies Now?" Special issue, *Social Text* 23, nos. 3–4 (2005).

Eribon, Didier. *Insult and the Making of the Gay Self*. Durham, NC: Duke University Press, 2004.

Eribon, Didier. *Returning to Reims*. Translated by Michael Lucey. South Pasadena, CA: Semiotext(e), 2013.

Escoffier, Jeffrey. "Inside the Ivory Closet: The Challenge Facing Lesbian and Gay Studies." In *American Homo: Community and Perversity*, 104–17. Berkeley: University of California Press, 1998.

"Eve Kosofsky Sedgwick's *Between Men* at Thirty: Queer Studies Then and Now." Conference, City University of New York, October 23, 2015. http://evekosofskysedgwick.net/conferences/BM30.html.

Ferguson, Roderick A. *Aberrations in Black: Toward a Queer of Color Critique.* Minneapolis: University of Minnesota Press, 2003.

Ferguson, Roderick A. *The Reorder of Things: The University and Its Pedagogies of Minority Difference.* Minneapolis: University of Minnesota Press, 2012.

Ferguson, Roderick A., and Grace Kyungwon Hong. "The Sexual and Racial Contradictions of Neoliberalism." *Journal of Homosexuality* 59, no. 7 (August 1, 2012): 1057–64. https://doi.org/10.1080/00918369.2012.699848.

Fiedler, Leslie. "Come Back to the Raft Ag'in, Huck Honey!" *Partisan Review,* 1948.

Field, Nicola. *Over the Rainbow: Money, Class, and Homophobia.* London: Dog Horn Press, 1995.

Fields, Jessica. "The Racialized Erotics of Participatory Research: A Queer Feminist Understanding." In *Imagining Queer Methods,* edited by Amin Ghaziani and Matt Brim, 63–83. New York: New York University Press, 2019.

Findeisen, Christopher. "Injuries of Class: Mass Education and the American Campus Novel." *PMLA* 130, no. 2 (2015): 284–98.

Finkelstein, Martin J., Robert K. Seal, and Jack H. Schuster. *The New Academic Generation: A Profession in Transformation.* Baltimore: Johns Hopkins University Press, 1998.

Floyd, Kevin. *The Reification of Desire: Toward a Queer Marxism.* Minneapolis: University of Minnesota Press, 2009.

Follins, Lourdes Dolores, and Jonathan Mathias Lassiter, eds. *Black LGBT Health in the United States: The Intersection of Race, Gender, and Sexual Orientation.* Lanham, MD: Lexington, 2017.

Frank, Miriam. *Out in the Union: A Labor History of Queer America.* Philadelphia: Temple University Press, 2014.

Freeman, Jo. "The Tyranny of Structurelessness." 1970–73. https://www.jofreeman.com/joreen/tyranny.htm.

Freud, Sigmund. "The Sexual Aberrations." In *The Material Queer: A LesBiGay Cultural Studies Reader,* edited by Donald E. Morton. Boulder, CO: Westview, 1996.

Friedenberg, Edgar. "Homophobia and Society." In *The Universities and the Gay Experience: Proceedings of the Conference Sponsored by the Women and Men of the Gay Academic Union,* 40–43. New York: Gay Academic Union, 1974. http://www.outhistory.org/files/original/b865f2369f78c02b4d2727b996c86c43.pdf.

Fuss, Diana, ed. *Inside/Out: Lesbian Theories, Gay Theories.* New York: Routledge, 1991. 77–94.

Gabriner, Robert, Eva Schiorring, and Gail Waldron. "'We Could Do That!' A Guide to Diversity Practices in California Community Colleges." Office of the Chancellor, California Community Colleges, 2002. https://files.eric.ed.gov/fulltext/ED476329.pdf.

Gamson, Zelda F. "The Stratification of the Academy." In *Chalk Lines: The Politics of Work in the Managed University*, edited by Randy Martin, 103–11. Durham, NC: Duke University Press, 1998.

Garber, Linda. *Identity Poetics: Race, Class, and the Lesbian Feminist Roots of Queer Theory*. New York: Columbia University Press, 2001.

Garber, Linda, ed. *Tilting the Tower: Lesbians, Teaching, Queer Subjects*. New York: Routledge, 1994.

Garland-Thomson, Rosemarie. *Extraordinary Bodies: Figuring Physical Disability in American Literature and Culture*. New York: Columbia University Press, 1997.

Gay Academic Union. *The Universities and the Gay Experience: Proceedings of the Conference Sponsored by the Women and Men of the Gay Academic Union*. New York: Gay Academic Union, 1974.

Geronimus, Arline. "The Weathering Hypothesis and the Health of African-American Women and Infants: Evidence and Speculations." *Ethnicity and Disease* 2, no. 3 (summer 1992): 207–21.

Ghaziani, Amin, and Matt Brim, eds. *Imagining Queer Methods*. New York: New York University Press, 2019.

Ghaziani, Amin, and Matt Brim. "Queer Methods: Four Provocations for an Emerging Field." In *Imagining Queer Methods*, edited by Amin Ghaziani and Matt Brim, 3–27. New York: New York University Press, 2019.

Giancola, Jennifer, and Richard D. Kahlenberg. "True Merit: Ensuring Our Brightest Students Have Access to Our Best Colleges and Universities." Jack Kent Cooke Foundation, 2016. http://web.archive.org/web/20170112020450/http:/www.jkcf.org/assets/1/7/JKCF_True_Merit_Report.pdf.

Gibson, James J. *The Ecological Approach to Visual Perception*. Boston: Houghton Mifflin Harcourt, 1979.

Gilmore, Ruth Wilson. "Forgotten Places and the Seeds of Grassroots Planning." In *Engaging Contradictions: Theory, Politics, and Methods of Activist Scholarship*, edited by Charles Hale, 31–61. Berkeley: University of California Press, 2008. http://www.jstor.org/stable/10.1525/j.ctt1pncnt.7.

Gluckman, Amy, and Betsy Reed, eds. *Homo Economics: Capitalism, Community, and Lesbian and Gay Life*. New York: Routledge, 1997.

Glynn, Jennifer. *Opening Doors: How Selective Colleges and Universities Are Expanding Access for High-Achieving, Low-Income Students*. Lansdowne, VA: Jack Cooke Kent Foundation, 2017. https://www.jkcf.org/research/opening-doors-how-selective-colleges-and-universities-are-expanding-access-for-high-achieving-low-income-students/?utm_campaign=Opening_Doors&utm_source=all&utm_medium=all.

Gordon, Deborah. "Panel Discussion 2." *Inscriptions* 3/4 (1988): 100. https://culturalstudies.ucsc.edu/inscriptions/volume-34/panel-discussion-2/.

Gordon, Ruth. "On Community in the Midst of Hierarchy (and Hierarchy in the Midst of Community)." In *Presumed Incompetent: The Intersections of Race and Class for Women in Academia*, edited by Gabriella Gutiérrez y Muhs,

Yolanda Flores Niemann, Carmen G. González, and Angela P. Harris, 313–29. Boulder, CO: Utah State University Press, 2012.

Graff, Gerald. "Our Undemocratic Curriculum." *Profession*, 2007, 128–35.

Grafton, Anthony. "Our Universities: Why Are They Failing?" *New York Review of Books*, November 24, 2011. http://www.nybooks.com/articles/2011/11/24/our -universities-why-are-they-failing/.

Gray, Herman. *Cultural Moves: African Americans and the Politics of Representation*. Berkeley: University of California Press, 2005.

Greenberg, Douglas. "White People Problems: A Critical Response to William Deresiewicz's 'Excellent Sheep.'" *Los Angeles Review of Books*, September 25, 2014. https://lareviewofbooks.org/article/white-people-problems-critical -response-william-deresiewiczs-excellent-sheep/.

Gubar, Susan. *Rooms of Our Own*. Champaign: University of Illinois Press, 2006.

Guillory, John. "The System of Graduate Education." *PMLA* 115, no. 5 (October 2000): 1154–63.

Gumbs, Alexis Pauline. "Nobody Mean More: Black Feminist Pedagogy and Solidarity." In *The Imperial University: Academic Repression and Scholarly Dissent*, edited by Piya Chatterjee and Sunaina Maira. Minneapolis: University of Minnesota Press, 2014.

Gumbs, Alexis Pauline, China Martens, and Mai'a Williams, eds. *Revolutionary Mothering: Love on the Front Lines*. Oakland, CA: PM Press, 2016.

Gustafson, Richard. "Welcoming Remarks." In *The Universities and the Gay Experience: Proceedings of the Conference Sponsored by the Women and Men of the Gay Academic Union*, 21–22. New York: Gay Academic Union, 1974. http://www.outhistory.org/files/original/b865f2369f78c02b4d2727b996c86 c43.pdf.

Guy-Sheftall, Beverly. "Breaking the Silence at Spelman College and Beyond." *Diversity and Democracy* 15, no. 1 (2012). https://www.aacu.org/publications -research/periodicals/breaking-silence-spelman-college-and-beyond.

Halberstam, Jack. "The Wild Beyond: With and For the Undercommons." In *The Undercommons: Fugitive Planning and Black Study*, by Stefano Harney and Fred Moten. Wivenhoe, UK: Minor Compositions, 2013.

Hall, Donald E. "Cluelessness and the Queer Classroom." *Pedagogy* 7, no. 2 (spring 2007): 182–91.

Halperin, David M. *How to Be Gay*. Cambridge, MA: Belknap, 2012.

Halperin, David M. "The Normalization of Queer Theory." *Journal of Homosexuality* 45, nos. 2–4 (2003): 339–43.

Hamilton, Laura T. *Parenting to a Degree: How Family Matters for College Women's Success*. Chicago: University of Chicago Press, 2016.

Hancock, Lynnell, and Meredith Kolodner. "What It Takes to Get into New York City's Best Public Colleges." *The Atlantic*, January 13, 2015. https://www .theatlantic.com/education/archive/2015/01/what-it-takes-to-get-into-new -york-citys-best-public-colleges/384451/.

Harney, Stefano, and Fred Moten. *The Undercommons: Fugitive Planning and Black Study*. Wivenhoe, UK: Minor Compositions, 2013.

Harper, Shaun R., and Kimberly A. Griffin. "Opportunity beyond Affirmative Action: How Low-Income and Working-Class Black Male Achievers Access Highly Selective, High-Cost Colleges and Universities." *Harvard Journal of African American Public Policy* 17, no. 1 (2011): 43–60.

Harris, Elizabeth A. "How CUNY Became Poetry U." *New York Times*, June 2, 2017. https://www.nytimes.com/2017/06/02/nyregion/how-cuny-became-poetry-u .html?_r=1.

Harris, Leslie M., James T. Campbell, and Alfred L. Brophy, eds. *Slavery and the University: Histories and Legacies*. Athens: University of Georgia Press, 2019.

Hartle, Terry, and Chris Nellum. "Where Have All the Low-Income Students Gone?" *Higher Education Today*, November 25, 2015. https://www.higheredtoday.org /2015/11/25/where-have-all-the-low-income-students-gone/.

Hartman, Eric. "The Queer Utility of Narrative Case Studies for Clinical Social Work Research and Practice." *Clinical Social Work Journal* 45, no. 3 (September 1, 2017): 227–37. https://doi.org/10.1007/s10615-017-0622-9.

Hartman, Saidiya. "The Territory between Us: A Report on 'Black Women in the Academy: Defending Our Name, 1894–1994.'" *Callaloo* 17, no. 2 (spring 1994): 439–49.

Hawley, John C., ed. *Expanding the Circle: Creating an Inclusive Environment in Higher Education for LGBTQ Students and Studies*. Albany: State University of New York Press, 2015.

Heaphy, Brian. "Situating Lesbian and Gay Cultures of Class Identification." *Cultural Sociology* 7, no. 3 (spring 2013): 303–19.

Hemphill, Essex, ed. *Brother to Brother: New Writings by Black Gay Men*. 1991. Reprint, Washington, DC: RedBone Press, 2007.

Henderson, Lisa. *Love and Money: Queers, Class, and Cultural Production*. New York: New York University Press, 2013.

Herring, Scott. *Another Country: Queer Anti-urbanism*. New York: New York University Press, 2010.

Hilliard, Tom. *Mobility Makers*. Center for an Urban Future, 2011. https://nycfuture .org/research/mobility-makers.

Hoad, Neville. "Queer Theory Addiction." In *After Sex? On Writing since Queer Theory*, edited by Janet Halley and Andrew Parker, 130–41. Durham, NC: Duke University Press, 2011.

Holland, Sharon Patricia. *Raising the Dead: Readings of Death and (Black) Subjectivity*. Durham, NC: Duke University Press, 2000.

Hollibaugh, Amber, and Margo Weiss. "Queer Precarity and the Myth of Gay Affluence." *New Labor Forum* 24, no. 3 (2015): 18–27.

hooks, bell. "bell hooks Speaking about Paulo Freire—the Man, His Work." In *Paulo Freire: A Critical Encounter*, edited by Peter Leonard and Peter McLaren. New York: Routledge, 2002. http://ebookcentral.proquest.com/lib/cunygc /detail.action?docID=166704.

hooks, bell. *Teaching Community: A Pedagogy of Hope*. New York: Routledge, 2003.

Hoxby, Caroline, and Christopher Avery. "The Missing 'One-Offs': The Hidden Supply of High-Achieving, Low-Income Students." *Brookings Papers on Economic*

Activity, spring 2013. https://www.brookings.edu/wp-content/uploads/2016
/07/2013a_hoxby.pdf.

Hubbard, Jim, dir. *United in Anger: A History of ACT UP*. MIX, 2012.

Hull, Akasha (Gloria T.), Patricia Bell-Scott, and Barbara Smith, eds. *All the Women
Are White, All the Blacks Are Men, but Some of Us Are Brave: Black Women's
Studies*. 2nd ed. Old Westbury, NY: Feminist Press, 2015.

Jacobsen, Joyce, and Adam Zeller, eds. *Queer Economics: A Reader*. London:
Routledge, 2008.

Jenkins, Barry. *Moonlight*. DVD. New York: A24, 2016.

Johnson, E. Patrick. "Border Intellectual: Performing Identity at the Crossroads."
In *Performance in the Borderlands*, edited by Ramón H. Rivera-Servera and
Harvey Young, 147–60. New York: Palgrave Macmillan, 2011.

Johnson, E. Patrick. "In the Merry Old Land of OZ: Rac(e)ing and Quee(r)ing the
Academy." In *The Queer Community: Continuing the Struggle for Social Justice*, edited by Richard G. Johnson III, 85–103. San Diego, CA: Birkdale, 2009.

Johnson, E. Patrick. *No Tea, No Shade: New Writings in Black Queer Studies*.
Durham, NC: Duke University Press, 2016.

Johnson, E. Patrick. "To Be Young, Gifted, and Queer: Race and Sex in the New
Black Studies." *Black Scholar* 44, no. 2 (2014): 50–58.

Johnson, E. Patrick, and Mae G. Henderson, eds. *Black Queer Studies: A Critical
Anthology*. Durham, NC: Duke University Press, 2005.

Jones, Tamara L. "'Top-Down' or 'Bottom-Up'? Sexual Identity and Workers' Rights
in a Municipal Union." In *Out at Work: Building a Gay-Labor Alliance*, edited
by Kitty Krupat and Patrick McCreery, 172–95. Minneapolis: University of
Minnesota Press, 2001. http://ebookcentral.proquest.com/lib/cunygc/detail
.action?docID=310524.

Julien, Isaac, Nadine Marsh-Edwards, Essex Hemphill, and Bruce Nugent. *Looking
for Langston: A Meditation on Langston Hughes (1902–1967) and the Harlem
Renaissance*. London: Sankofa Film and Video, 1989.

Kantrowitz, Arnie. "Homosexuals and Literature." *College English* 36, no. 3
(November 1974): 324–30.

Kantrowitz, Arnie. *Under the Rainbow: Growing Up Gay*. New York: William Mor-
row, 1977. 2nd ed., Pocketbooks, 1978. 3rd ed., St. Martin's, 1996.

Kantrowitz, Arnie, and Judith Stelboum. "A Date with Judith." In *Sister and Brother:
Lesbians and Gay Men Write about Their Lives Together*, edited by Joan Nestle
and John Preston, 273–86. San Francisco: HarperSanFrancisco, 1994.

Keene, John. *Counternarratives*. New York: New Directions, 2015.

Kelley, Robin D. G. "Foreword." In *Black Marxism: The Making of the Black Radical
Tradition*, 2nd ed., by Cedric J. Robinson. Chapel Hill: University of North
Carolina Press, 2000.

Kennedy, Elizabeth Lapovsky, and Madeline D. Davis. *Boots of Leather, Slippers of
Gold: The History of a Lesbian Community*. New York: Taylor and Francis, 1993.

Kensinger, Courtney, and Dorlisa J. Minnick. "The Invisible Village: An Exploration
of Undergraduate Student Mothers' Experiences." *Journal of Family and*

Economic Issues 39, no. 1 (March 1, 2018): 132–44. https://doi.org/10.1007
/s10834-017-9535-6.

King, Katie. *Theory in Its Feminist Travels: Conversations in U.S. Women's Movements*. Bloomington: Indiana University Press, 1994.

Krahulik, Karen Christel. "Cape Queer? A Case Study of Provincetown, Massachusetts." *Journal of Homosexuality* 52, nos. 1–2 (2006): 185–212.

Kramer, Daniel C., and Richard M. Flanigan. *Staten Island: Conservative Bastion in
a Liberal City*. Lanham, MD: University Press of America, 2012.

Krebs, Paula. "Applying to a Public Regional University?" Chronicle Vitae, January 26, 2016. https://chroniclevitae.com/news/1266-applying-to-a-public
-regional-university.

Lashley, Maudry-Beverley, and Linda Ollivierre. "Exploring the Linkages of Single
Black Mothers and Their College Experiences." *Global Education Journal*,
no. 3 (July 2014): 138–55.

Laurence, Robin. "The Modern Woman Explores the Male Gaze." *Georgia Straight*,
June 7, 2010. http://www.straight.com/article-327462/vancouver/modern
-woman-explores-male-gaze.

Laymon, Kiese. *Heavy: An American Memoir*. New York: Scribner, 2018.

Levy-Hussen, Aida. *How to Read African American Literature: Post–Civil Rights
Fiction and the Task of Interpretation*. New York: New York University Press,
2016.

Looney, Adam. "A Comparison between the College Scorecard and Mobility Report
Cards." *Treasury Notes*, January 19, 2017. https://www.treasury.gov/connect
/blog/Pages/A-Comparison-between-the-College-Scorecard-and-Mobility
-Report-Cards.aspx.

Lorde, Audre. "An Interview: Audre Lorde and Adrienne Rich." In *Sister Outsider:
Essays and Speeches*, rev. ed., 81–109. Berkeley, CA: Crossing Press, 2007.

Lorde, Audre. "The Master's Tools Will Never Dismantle the Master's House." In
Sister Outsider: Essays and Speeches, rev. ed. Berkeley, CA: Crossing Press,
2007.

Love, Heather. "Doing Being Deviant: Deviance Studies, Description, and the
Queer Ordinary." *differences: A Journal of Feminist Cultural Studies* 26, no. 1
(2007): 74–95.

Love, Heather. "Feminist Criticism and Queer Theory." In *A History of Feminist
Literary Criticism*, edited by Gill Plain and Susan Sellers, 301–21. Cambridge:
Cambridge University Press, 2007.

Love, Heather. "How the Other Half Thinks: An Introduction to the Volume." In
Imagining Queer Methods, edited by Amin Ghaziani and Matt Brim, 28–42.
New York: New York University Press, 2019.

Lucas, Julian. "Epic Stories That Expand the Universal Family Plot." *New York Times*,
September 1, 2017.

Magness, Phillip W. "For-Profit Universities and the Roots of Adjunctification in
U.S. Higher Education." *Liberal Education* 102, no. 2 (2016): 50–59. https://
www.aacu.org/liberaleducation/2016/spring/magness.

Mahaffey, Barbara A., Gregg Hungerford, and Sage Sill. "College Student Mother Needs at Regional Campuses: An Exploratory Study." *AURCO Journal* 21 (spring 2015): 105–15.

Manalansan, Martin F., Chantal Nadeau, Richard T. Rodríguez, and Siobhan B. Somerville. "Queering the Middle: Race, Region, and a Queer Midwest." *GLQ: A Journal of Lesbian and Gay Studies* 20, nos. 1–2 (April 1, 2014): 1–12. https://doi.org/10.1215/10642684-2370270.

Marine, Susan B., Paul J. McLoughlin II, and Timothy Patrick McCarthy. "Queering Harvard Yard: Four Decades of Progress for BGLTQ Equality." In *Expanding the Circle: Creating an Inclusive Environment in Higher Education for LGBTQ Students and Studies*, edited by John C. Hawley, 163–84. SUNY Series in Queer Politics and Cultures. Albany: State University of New York Press, 2015.

Martin, Biddy. "Extraordinary Homosexuals and the Fear of Being Ordinary." *differences: A Journal of Feminist Cultural Studies* 6, nos. 2–3 (1994): 100. http://link.galegroup.com.ezproxy.gc.cuny.edu/apps/doc/A17250596/LitRC?u=cuny_gradctr&sid=LitRC&xid=e883128f.

Martinez, Ernesto. *On Making Sense: Queer Race Narratives of Intelligibility.* Stanford, CA: Stanford University Press, 2012.

Maynard, Steven. "'Respect Your Elders, Know Your Past': History and the Queer Theorists." *Radical History Review*, no. 75 (October 1, 1999): 56–78. https://doi.org/10.1215/01636545-1999-75-56.

McRuer, Robert. *Crip Theory: Cultural Signs of Queerness and Disability.* New York: New York University Press, 2006.

Medhurst, Andy. "If Anywhere: Class Identifications and Cultural Studies Academics." In *Cultural Studies and the Working Class*, edited by Sally R. Munt, 19–35. New York: Bloomsbury Academic, 2000.

Mehra, Bharat, Donna Braquet, and Calle M. Fielden. "A Website Evaluation of the Top Twenty-Five Public Universities in the United States to Assess Their Support of Lesbian, Gay, Bisexual, and Transgender People." In *Expanding the Circle: Creating an Inclusive Environment in Higher Education for LGBTQ Students and Studies*, edited by John C. Hawley, 19–48. SUNY Series in Queer Politics and Cultures. Albany: State University of New York Press, 2015.

Meier, Deborah. *The Power of Their Ideas: Lessons for America from a Small School in Harlem.* Boston: Beacon, 1995.

Mitchell, Larry. *Acid Snow: A Novel.* New York: Calamus Books, 1993.

Mitchell, Larry. *In Heat: A Romance.* New York: Gay Presses of New York, 1985.

Mitchell, Larry. *The Terminal Bar.* New York: Calamus Books, 1982.

Mitchell, Larry, and Ned Asta. *The Faggots and Their Friends between Revolutions.* New York: Calamus Books, 1977. Republished, New York: Nightboat, 2019.

Moore, Lisa C., ed. *Does Your Mama Know? An Anthology of Black Lesbian Coming Out Stories.* 1997. Reprint, Washington, DC: RedBone Press, 2009.

Moore, Lisa Jean. "Polishing the Pearl: Discoveries of the Clitoris." In *Introducing the New Sexuality Studies*, 2nd ed., edited by Steven Seidman, Nancy Fischer, and Chet Meeks, 95–99. New York: Routledge, 2011.

Morris, Tracie. *Who Do with Words: (A Blerd Love Tone Manifesto)*. Victoria, TX: Chax Press, 2018.

Morrison, Toni. *Playing in the Dark: Whiteness and the Literary Imagination*. Cambridge, MA: Harvard University Press, 1992.

Morton, Donald. "The Class Politics of Queer Theory." *College English* 58, no. 4 (1996): 471–82. https://doi.org/10.2307/378860.472.

Mullen, Ann L. *Degrees of Inequality: Culture, Class, and Gender in American Higher Education*. Baltimore: Johns Hopkins University Press, 2010.

Newfield, Christopher. "Yes to the New Education, but What Kind?" *PMLA* 133, no. 3 (2018): 686–93.

Oldfield, Kenneth, and Richard Greggory Johnson III, eds. *Resilience: Queer Professors from the Working Class*. Albany: State University of New York Press, 2008.

Pérez, Hiram. *A Taste for Brown Bodies: Gay Modernity and Cosmopolitan Desire*. New York: New York University Press, 2015.

Porter, Lavelle. *The Blackademic Life: Academic Fiction, Higher Education, and the Black Intellectual*. Evanston, IL: Northwestern University Press, 2019.

Preston, John. "How Dare You Even Think These Things?" In *High Risk: An Anthology of Forbidden Writings*, edited by Amy Scholder and Ira Silverberg, 1–15. New York: Dutton, 1991.

Rand, Erica. "After Sex?!" In *After Sex? On Writing since Queer Theory*, edited by Janet Halley and Andrew Parker, 270–79. Durham, NC: Duke University Press, 2011.

Rankine, Claudia. *Citizen: An American Lyric*. Minneapolis, MN: Graywolf, 2014.

Reid-Pharr, Robert. *Archives of Flesh: African America, Spain, and Post-Humanist Critique*. New York: New York University Press, 2016.

Renn, Kristen A. "LGBT and Queer Research in Higher Education: The State and the Status of the Field." *Educational Researcher* 39, no. 2 (2010): 132–41.

Ricketts, Wendell. *Blue, Too: More Writing by (for or about) Working-Class Queers*. N.p.: FourCats Press, 2014.

Riggs, Marlon, dir. *Tongues Untied*. San Francisco: Frameline, 1989.

Robinson, Cedric J. *Black Marxism: The Making of the Black Radical Tradition*. 1983. Reprint, Chapel Hill: University of North Carolina Press, 2000.

Rodriguez, Juana María. *Queer Latinidad: Identity Practices, Discursive Spaces*. New York: New York University Press, 2003.

Rodriguez, Juana María. *Sexual Futures, Queer Gestures, and Other Latina Longings*. New York: New York University Press, 2014.

Rothwell, Jonathan. "The Stubborn Race and Class Gaps in College Quality." Brookings Institution, Social Mobility Papers, December 18, 2015. https://www.brookings.edu/research/the-stubborn-race-and-class-gaps-in-college-quality/.

Russo, John, and Sherry Lee Linkon. "Introduction: What's New about New Working-Class Studies?" In *New Working-Class Studies*, edited by John Russo and Sherry Lee Linkon, 1–16. Ithaca, NY: ILR Press, 2005.

Saul, Stephanie. "A Push to Make Harvard Free Also Questions the Role of Race in Admissions." *New York Times*, November 8, 2017.

Schulman, Sarah. *Ties That Bind: Familial Homophobia and Its Consequences*. New York: New Press, 2009.

Seidman, Steven. "Class Matters ... but How Much? Class, Nation, and Queer Life." *Sexualities* 14, no. 1 (2011): 36–41. https://doi.org/10.1177/1363460710390571.

Sharpe, Christina. *In the Wake: On Blackness and Being*. Durham, NC: Duke University Press, 2016.

Sherlock, Molly F., Jane G. Gravelle, Margot L. Crandall-Hollick, and Joseph S. Hughes. "College and University Endowments: Overview and Tax Policy Options." Congressional Research Service, May 4, 2018. https://fas.org/sgp/crs/misc/R44293.pdf.

Shor, Ira. *When Students Have Power: Negotiating Authority in a Critical Pedagogy*. Chicago: University of Chicago Press, 2014.

Shor, Ira, and Paulo Freire. *A Pedagogy for Liberation: Dialogues on Transforming Education*. Westport, CT: Greenwood, 1987.

Shor, Ira, Eugene Matusov, Ana Marjanovic-Shane, and James Cresswell. "Dialogic and Critical Pedagogies: An Interview with Ira Shor." *Dialogic Pedagogy: An International Online Journal* 5 (July 3, 2017). https://doi.org/10.5195/DPJ.2017.208.

Somerville, Siobhan. "Locating Queer Culture in the Big Ten." *Learning and Teaching* 6, no. 3 (winter 2013): 9–23.

Somerville, Siobhan. *Queering the Color Line: Race and the Invention of Homosexuality in American Culture*. Durham, NC: Duke University Press, 2000.

Sowinska, Susanne. "Yer Own Motha Wouldna Reckanized Ya: Surviving an Apprenticeship in the 'Knowledge Factory.'" In *Working-Class Women in the Academy: Laborers in the Knowledge Factory*, edited by Michelle M. Tokarczyk and Elizabeth A. Fay, 148–61. Boston: University of Massachusetts Press, 1993.

Staley, Willy. "When 'Gentrification' Isn't about Housing." *New York Times Magazine*, January 23, 2018. https://www.nytimes.com/2018/01/23/magazine/when-gentrification-isnt-about-housing.html.

Stein, Arlene, and Ken Plummer. "'I Can't Even Think Straight': 'Queer' Theory and the Missing Sexual Revolution in Sociology." *Sociological Theory* 12, no. 2 (1994): 178–87.

Steinberg, Stephen. "Revisiting Open Admissions at CUNY." *Clarion*, February 2018. http://www.psc-cuny.org/clarion/february-2018/revisiting-open-admissions-cuny.

Steinmetz, George. "Odious Comparisons: Incommensurability, the Case Study, and 'Small N's' in Sociology." *Sociological Theory* 22, no. 3 (2004): 371–400.

Stelboum, Judith P. "Woman's Studies at a Community College: A Personal View." In *Female Studies V: Proceedings of the Conference, Women and Education: A Feminist Perspective*, edited by Rae Lee Siporin, 43–48. Pittsburgh: Women and Education: A Feminist Perspective; Pittsburgh: Know, Inc., 1972.

Stryker, Susan, and Stephen Whittle. *The Transgender Studies Reader*. New York: Routledge, 2006.

Sullivan, Kamisha A. "Sharing Stories of Student Mothers in Community College." PhD thesis, California State University, Long Beach, 2018. http://search.proquest.com/docview/2076440367/abstract/A89AAFDD2AF141DAPQ/1.

Sycamore, Mattilda Bernstein. *Why Are Faggots So Afraid of Faggots? Flaming Challenges to Masculinity, Objectification, and the Desire to Conform.* Chico, CA: AK Press, 2012.

Taylor, Yvette. "Facts, Fictions, Identity Constructions: Sexuality, Gender and Class in Higher Education." In *Educational Diversity: The Subject of Difference and Different Subjects*, edited by Yvette Taylor, 257–67. New York: Palgrave Macmillan, 2012.

Taylor, Yvette. "The 'Outness' of Queer: Class and Sexual Intersections." In *Queer Methods and Methodologies: Intersecting Queer Theories and Social Science Research*, edited by Kath Browne and Catherine J. Nash, 69–83. Abingdon, UK: Routledge, 2016. http://www.oapen.org/record/645090.

Tiemeyer, Phil. *Plane Queer: Labor, Sexuality, and AIDS in the History of Male Flight Attendants.* Berkeley: University of California Press, 2013.

Tokarczyk, Michelle M., and Elizabeth A. Fay. *Working-Class Women in the Academy: Laborers in the Knowledge Factory.* Boston: University of Massachusetts Press, 1993.

Tompkins, Kyla Wazana. "We Aren't Here to Learn What We Already Know." *Avidly*, September 13, 2016. http://avidly.lareviewofbooks.org/2016/09/13/we-arent-here-to-learn-what-we-know-we-already-know/.

Torres, Justin. *We the Animals.* New York: Houghton Mifflin Harcourt, 2011.

Traub, Valerie. *Thinking Sex with the Early Moderns.* Philadelphia: University of Pennsylvania Press, 2016.

Tuhkanen, Mikko. Review of *Archives of Flesh: African America, Spain, and Post-Humanist Critique*, by Robert Reid-Pharr. In *American Literary History Online Review Series XI*, June 13, 2017. https://academic.oup.com/DocumentLibrary/ALH/Online%20Review%20Series%2011/Mikko%20Tuhkanen%20Online%20Review%20XI.pdf.

tunchz, tz karakashian. "Telling Our Truths to Live: A Manifesta." In *Revolutionary Mothering: Love on the Front Lines*, edited by Alexis Pauline Gumbs, China Martens, and Mai'a Williams. Oakland, CA: PM Press, 2016.

"UndocuQueer Movement." Equality Archive, November 2, 2015. http://equalityarchive.com/issues/undocuqueer-movement/.

Vaid, Urvashi. *Irresistible Revolution: Confronting Race, Class and the Assumptions of LGBT Politics.* New York: Magnus, 2012.

Valente, Ken G., Molly Merryman, and Warren J. Blumenfeld, eds. "25 Years On: The State and Continuing Development of LGBTQ Studies Programs." Special issue, *Journal of Homosexuality* (2018). https://doi.org/10.1080/00918369.2018.1528073.

Van Wyck, James M. "Blue-Collar Ph.D." Interview with Lynn Arner. *Inside Higher Ed*, August 10, 2017. https://www.insidehighered.com/advice/2017/08/10/conversation-about-class-and-professoriate-essay.

Villarosa, Linda. "Why America's Black Mothers and Babies Are in a Life-or-Death Crisis." *New York Times*, April 11, 2018, sec. Magazine. https://www.nytimes.com/2018/04/11/magazine/black-mothers-babies-death-maternal-mortality.html.

Volpe, Edmond L. *The Comprehensive College: Heading toward a New Direction in Higher Education.* San Jose: Writers Club, 2001.

Ward, Jane. *Not Gay: Sex between Straight White Men*. New York: New York University Press, 2015.

Warner, Michael. "Queer and Then?" *Chronicle of Higher Education*, January 1, 2012. https://www.chronicle.com/article/QueerThen-/130161.

Weeks, Kathi. "Down with Love." *WSQ: Women's Studies Quarterly* 45, nos. 3–4 (fall–winter 2017): 37–58.

Wermund, Benjamin. "How U.S. News College Rankings Promote Economic Inequality on Campus." *Politico*, September 10, 2017. https://www.politico.com/interactives/2017/top-college-rankings-list-2017-us-news-investigation/.

White, Byron P. "Beyond a Deficit View." *Chronicle of Higher Education Online*, April 19, 2016. https://www.insidehighered.com/views/2016/04/19/importance-viewing-minority-low-income-and-first-generation-students-assets-essay?utm_content=buffer5f245&utm_medium=social&utm_source=facebook&utm_campaign=IHEbuffer.

Wiegman, Robyn. "Eve's Triangles, or Queer Studies Beside Itself." *differences: A Journal of Feminist Cultural Studies* 26, no. 1 (January 1, 2015): 48–73. https://doi.org/10.1215/10407391-2880600.

Wiegman, Robyn. *Object Lessons*. Durham, NC: Duke University Press, 2012.

Williams, Erica Lorraine. "Women's Studies and Sexuality Studies at HBCUs: The Audre Lorde Project at Spelman College." *Feminist Studies* 39, no. 2 (2013): 520–25. http://www.jstor.org.ezproxy.gc.cuny.edu/stable/23719065.

Wolf, Sherry. *Sexuality and Socialism: History, Politics, and Theory of LGBT Liberation*. Chicago: Haymarket, 2009.

Woodard, Vincent. "Just as Quare as They Want to Be." *Callaloo* 23, no. 4 (fall 2000): 1278–84.

Woolf, Virginia. *A Room of One's Own*. 1929. Orlando, FL: Harcourt, 2005.

Yacovone, Donald. "Textbook Racism: How Scholars Sustained White Supremacy." *Chronicle of Higher Education*, April 8, 2018. https://www.chronicle.com/article/How-Scholars-Sustained-White/243053.

Zagar, Jeremiah, dir. *We the Animals*. The Orchard, 2018.

index

as expression of, 82; as local phenom-
enon, 91; rhetorics of, 79. *See also* auster-
ity; student-workers, as central to Poor
Queer Studies
New Education, The (Davidson), 86, 92,
105–6, 195–96
Newfield, Christopher, 137, 196
New York University, 10, 57, 59, 65, 211n3
*No Tea, No Shade: New Writings in Black
Queer Studies* (Johnson), 15, 187–88

Ohio State University, 205n35
*Out in the Union: A Labor History of Queer
America* (Frank), 129–31

*Pedagogies of Crossing: Meditations on
Feminism, Sexual Politics, Memory, and
the Sacred* (Alexander), 200
pedigree, academic, 9, 80–83, 87; Black
Queer Studies and, 182–83, 185–89;
faculty offspring and, 82; professional
mobility and, 97–98. *See also* prestige
pipeline
Pérez, Hiram, 77–78
Plummer, Ken, 14–15, 206n50
police, 111–13, 133–34
Poor Black Queer Studies: black queer
literacies and illiteracy feelings, 159–63,
172, 176; black queer publishing and,
166–67; class-based contradictions and,
184–87; as general education, 159–60;
as knowledge project, 6; material
conditions of, 2–3; quare studies and,
187–89; relationship to Rich Black Queer
Studies, 181–84; the undercommons
and, 189–93. See also *Counternarratives*
(Keene); Johnson, E. Patrick; Lorde,
Audre; Poor Queer Studies
Poor Queer Studies: anti-elitism of, 36–38;
graduation and, 43, 61, 139, 140; as
praxis, 146; rationale for using "poor,"
18–19, 25–26; relationship to Rich Queer
Studies, 17–19, 66–73, 88–89, 144–46;
as reorientation of the field of Queer
Studies, 3–4, 15–16; student-teachers
of, 147–52; student-workers as central
to, 102–5, 111–13, 133–34; unrecogniz-
ability/inscrutability of, 20–22, 31–36,

41–42, 57, 92–94; as working-class
studies, 101–3. *See also* College of Staten
Island; methods and methodologies of
Poor Queer Studies; Poor Black Queer
Studies; Poor Queer Studies mothers;
vocational Queer Studies
Poor Queer Studies mothers: knowledge
creation and, 141–46; as pedagogic
atmosphere, 137–41; as unheard-of
analytic, 135–37
prestige pipeline, 81–84. *See also* pedigree,
academic
Preston, John, 162
public education: free, 195–97; vs. private
education, 196–98. *See also* City University of New York

quare studies, 187–89
Queens College, CUNY, 35, 40
queer career studies. *See* vocational Queer
Studies
queer commuting, 152–55; immigration
and, 154; inordinate measurements of,
153–54
queer dinners, 2–3
queer ferrying, 197–202
queer home schooling, 147–52
"Queering the Middle: Race, Region, and
a Queer Midwest" (Manalansan et al.),
24–26
queer pedagogies: in cross-class graduate
training, 199–202. *See also* methods and
methodologies of Poor Queer Studies
queer publics, 155–58, 197
queer status agent, 74–75; as complex
figure, 95–96; vs. low-status professional
zombie, 74–75; whiteness and, 80–81.
See also specific scholars
Queer Studies: academic elitism and,
9–11, 13–17, 78, 195; aspirational mood
of, 85–89, 92, 97–98; as divided field,
3, 88–90, 92–94, 147; hierarchy within,
75–81; as interdiscipline, 126; material conditions of, 2, 17, 88–95, 100; as
maturing discipline, 94–95; opposition
to job training, 102, 114–15; professionalization of, 82–83; radicality, claims to,
9, 14, 17, 38, 78, 89–90, 95, 126, 132,